THE CHANGING FAMILY AND CHILD DEVELOPMENT

The Changing Family and Child Development

Edited by
CLAUDIO VIOLATO
ELIZABETH ODDONE-PAOLUCCI
MARK GENUIS
National Foundation for Family Research and Education

Ashgate

Aldershot • Burlington USA • Singapore • Sydney

Published by
Ashgate Publishing Ltd
Gower House
Croft Road
Aldershot
Hants GU11 3HR
England

Ashgate Publishing Company
131 Main Street
Burlington
Vermont 05401
USA

Ashgate website: http://www.ashgate.com

British Library Cataloguing in Publication Data
The changing family and child development
    1. Family - Congresses 2. Child development - Congresses
    I. Violato, Claudio II. Oddone-Paolucci, Elizabeth
    III. Genuis, Mark
    306.8'5

Library of Congress Catalog Card Number: 99-85919

ISBN 0 7546 1025 X

Printed and bound by Athenaeum Press, Ltd.,
Gateshead, Tyne & Wear.

Contents

SECTION II: FAMILY ADJUSTMENT AND TRANSITIONS

SECTION III: CHILD AND ADOLESCENT DEVELOPMENT

SECTION IV: ATTACHMENT

List of Figures

List of Tables

x

xi

List of Contributors

Gerald R. Adams, Ph.D., University of Guelph, Canada.

Christopher Bagley, Ph.D., Professor, Southampton University, U.K.

Madeleine Beaudry, Ph.D., Professor, Université Laval, Canada.

Laura Belsito, Ph.D., University of Guelph, Canada.

Diane Benoit, M.D., Psychiatrist, University of Toronto, Canada.

Wilma Binda, Ph.D., Researcher, Center for Family Studies and Research, Catholic University of Milan, Italy.

Cécile Charbonneau, Ph.D., Professor Université Laval, Canada.

Franca Crippa, Ph.D., Professor, University of Pavia, Italy.

Sylvie Drapeau, Ph.D., Professor, Université Laval, Canada.

James S. Frideres, Ph.D., Professor, University of Calgary, Canada.

Mark Genuis, Ph.D., Executive Director, National Foundation for Research and Education, Canada.

Yen Hsueh, Ph.D., Graduate School of Education, Harvard University, USA.

Thomas P. Keenan, Ph.D., Professor, Canterbury University, U.K.

Margherita Lanz, Ph.D., Researcher, Center for Family Studies and Research, Catholic University, Milan, Italy.

Darla J. Maclean, Ph.D., Researcher, Brock University, Canada.

Kanka Mallick, Ph.D., Associate Professor, Manchester Metropolitan University, U.K.

Dawn McBride, M.Sc., Research Assistant, National Foundation for Family Research and Education, Canada.

Jonathan Midgett, Ph.D., University of Guelph, Canada.

Carol Miles, Ph.D., Assistant Professor, University of Ottawa, Canada.

Leigh A. Moore, Ph.D., Researcher, Brock University, Canada.

Elizabeth Oddone-Paolucci, Ph.D., Researcher, National Foundation for Research and Education, Canada.

Stephane Robitaille, M.A., Research Assistant, National Foundation for Family Research and Education, Canada.

Clare Russell, Ph.D., Researcher, University of Calgary, Canada.

Bruce A. Ryan, Ph.D., University of Guelph, Canada.

Eugenia Scabini, Ph.D., Professor, Center for Family Studies and Research, Catholic University of Milan.

Marie Simard, Ph.D., Professor, Université Laval, Canada.

LeRoy D. Travis, Ph.D., Professor, University of British Columbia, Canada.

Claudio Violato, Ph.D., Professor, University of Calgary and National Foundation for Family Research and Education, Canada.

Qi Wang, Ph.D., Department of Psychology, Harvard University, USA.

Chris Wilkes, M.D., Psychiatrist, University of Calgary, Canada.

Aldo Zanon, M.D., Pediatrician, Ospedale Civile-Cittadella, Padova, Italy.

Acknowledgements

A number of people contributed in several ways in completing this book. LiAnna Appelt dedicated innumerable hours in a variety of activities in preparing the manuscript. She was always cheerful and a pleasure to work with. Annette Hendrix prepared the final camera ready copy of the manuscript with her usual efficiency and competence. Lori Henriksson assisted in proof reading and Angela Violato helped in preparing the figures and tables. We thank all of these people for their dedication and efforts in helping us complete this book.

Introduction

CLAUDIO VIOLATO, ELIZABETH ODDONE-PAOLUCCI, AND MARK GENUIS

Worldwide the family continues to undergo transformations. Changing economic, social, political, democratic and other forces are creating stressors on both family dynamics and individual development. During this century we have seen dramatic increases in family dissolution throughout most of the western world. We have also seen changing definitions of the family in various family configurations such as the extended, nuclear, reconstituted, blended and single parent families. As increasing numbers of families have both parents working outside the home, there has been a rise of institutionalized child care.

How do various family configurations affect children's development and well-being? Who should care for the children in modern society? Paid caregivers in day-cares? Parents? Which if any arrangements are conducive to societal, parental and children's well-being? What is the future likely to bring for families in modern society? What are the implications of this for society as a whole? What political, health, economic, legal and demographic issues bear on these questions?

In 1997, the National Foundation for Family Research and Education sponsored the first *International Congress on the Changing Family and Child Development* to address some of these questions. The main objective of this congress was to provide an interdisciplinary forum for scholars from around the world on issues that pertain to the family. This congress was held at University of Calgary in July of 1997. There were submissions and presentations by psychologists, physicians, social workers, sociologists, educators, economists, social policy analysts and other scholars from more than a dozen countries. A sometimes controversial, but always spirited and worthwhile dialogue ensued from this conference. Subsequent to the conference we solicited the best of the presentations to assemble as a printed document. The present book, *The Changing Family and Child Development*, is the result of this work.

A large number of papers were submitted for this volume. All papers were subjected to peer review and careful editing. The nineteen papers included in this book are the ones that met the standards and criteria of peer review and were thus selected from the submissions to be included in this volume. They have been organized into four thematic sections: 1) The Context of Families, 2) Family Adjustment and Transitions, 3) Child and Adolescent Development, and 4) Attachment.

Section I: The Context of Families

Section 1, *The Context of Families*, consists of six papers that focus on the social, economic, historical and political contexts in which the family exists. The first paper by Eugenia Scabini, "New Aspects of Family Relations" focuses on some of the psychological features of families with two adult generations (parents and adult children) using the findings of quantitative and qualitative research. In both cases a relational/intergenerational approach based on analysis of exchanges between generations is adopted. The focus is on the extension of the life stage spanning the transition from childhood to adulthood -- an increasing phenomenon. In Europe in general, and in some Mediterranean countries in particular, the transition to adulthood either occurs within the family of origin, or depends on the family of origin for its successful outcome.

These families are both a new resource and a new source of risk. The ongoing family may offer excellent opportunities for dialogue, exchange and emotional warmth, as well as an opportunity for young people to fulfill themselves personally. It can also become closed and inward-looking, however, if it breaks generational continuity by discouraging young people from leaving the nest and accepting parenthood. This is the result of increasingly ambiguous relationship between the family and society.

The second paper, "Dual Images: The Family in Perspective" by James S. Frideres explores factors in the family which influences the structure society. The family is considered one of the most important institutions of our society. In its various manifestations, the family is thought to play an important role in determining the nature of society in the future. Policy makers and social scientists wish to know if this is true and if so, how this happens and what is it about the family that is important. Why is there a disjuncture between what is publicly proclaimed by leaders and the overt actions taken by them and their organizations with regard to the family and its functions. Such policies and changes to political action is likely to have implications for the role of the family in the future. These dual images are explored by Frideres in this paper.

LeRoy D. Travis in his paper, "Adolescentology: Youth, Their Needs, and the Professions at the Turn of the Century", reviews central features of our world as it is experienced by youth at the end of the 20th century. Such analyses has lead him to the following conclusions: (1) that the prospects for the great mass of contemporary adolescents are grim; (2) that the professions that serve the well-being of youth face challenges that are beyond their capacity to deal with in isolation from one another. Thus Travis proposes that the emergent multi-profession endeavor called adolescentology is one promising adaptation to this situation.

The fourth paper in this section, "A Meta-Analysis of the Published Research on the Effects of Pornography" is by Elizabeth Oddone-Paolucci, Mark Genuis and Claudio Violato. It is a meta-analysis of 46 published studies which was undertaken to determine the effects of pornography on sexual deviancy, sexual perpetration, attitudes regarding intimate relationships, and attitudes regarding the rape myth. A total sample size of 12,323 people comprised this meta-analysis. Effect sizes ($\underline{d}$) were computed on each of the dependent variables for studies which were published in an academic journal, had a total sample size of 12 or greater, and included a contrast or comparison group. Average unweighted and weighted $\underline{d}$'s for sexual deviancy (.68 and .65), sexual perpetration (.67 and .46), intimate relationships (.83 and .40), and the rape myth (.74 and .64) provide clear evidence confirming the link between increased risk for negative development when exposed to pornography. These results suggest that the research in this area can move beyond the question of whether pornography has an influence on violence and family functioning.

Qui Wang and Yen Hsueh in their paper, "Parent-Child Interdependence in Chinese Families: Change and Continuity" report on parent-child relationships in Chinese families. With rapid economic growth, the parent-child relations in Chinese families have shifted from an emphasis on material reciprocity to an emphasis on psychological interdependence. Western academia and media tend to believe that interdependence is associated with economic hardship and to view individualism as the end of family transformation. Based on cross-cultural and indigenous studies, however, Wang and Hsueh argue that the transformation of Chinese intrafamilial relationships preserves the essence of the Confucian doctrine of filial piety and the philosophical view of a relational self. The transformed parent-child interdependence facilitates the child's adaptation to the present and future Chinese society.

In the sixth and final paper in this section, "Psychosocial Factors Influencing Breastfeeding: A Stepwise Discriminant Analysis Employing a Sample of Italian Women", Aldo Zanon and Claudio Violato studied breastfeeding in Italian women. Their major purpose was to investigate empirical factors that influence breastfeeding behavior in women with infant children. There are at least four classes of factors that influence decision-making about breastfeeding (1) attitudes of mother towards breastfeeding, (2) sociocultural variables (e.g., income, employment), (3) family factors (e.g., support from family members, and (4) physiologic factors (e.g., lactation status). In the present study we focused on all four classes of variables employing multivariate procedures in order to better understand breastfeeding behavior.

A total of 358 post-partum women with neonates, some who breastfed (77.9%) and some who didn't (21.5%), participated in the Zanon and Violato study. While the majority (77.9%) of women breastfed their infant at birth, 48.6% had stopped at 6 months and 70.0% stopped by 10 months. The number of months sisters breastfed, the interval of breastfeeding immediately post-partum, and the number of visits to the pediatrician in the first year of the infant's life all were significantly different between the groups. Zanon and Violato discuss the significance of their findings for children's development generally and child-mother relations specifically.

Section II: Family Adjustment and Transitions

Four papers which are thematically related around transitions and adjustment comprise the second section, *Family Adjustment and Transitions*. In the first paper, "Spiraling Up and Spiraling Down: A Longitudinal Study of Adjustment", Christopher Bagley and Kanka Mallick report the results of a longitudinal study of 565 children from birth to age 9. Their results support the proposition that later adjustment reflects the complex interaction of early temperament profiles, Central Nervous System (CNS) disability, parental interactions with the child, family disruption, and external stressors (particularly, economic poverty). A regression model predicted 28% of variance in conduct disorder measured at age 9. Variables in this model are difficult temperament at age 2, CNS disability at age 6, maternal stress when child aged 6, and child's parental separation > 6 months, at ages 2 to 9. While statistical models rarely demonstrate causal pathways beyond reasonable doubt, Bagley and Mallick provide intuitive insights gained from these statistical analyses as a basis for understanding causal pathways to adjustment.

    Madeleine Beaudry, Marie Simard, Sylvie Drapeau and Cécile Charbonneau address post-divorce sibling relationships in their paper, "What Happens to the Sibling Subsystem Following Parental Divorce?" Divorce can lead to two patterns of organization in the sibling subsystem: it may remain intact (all siblings live together under the same roof) or it may be split (siblings don't all live together). Moreover, physical custody can take different forms: to the mother, to the father, or to both parents. Beaudry et al have three objectives in this paper. First, they explore the two patterns of organization in the sibling subsystem (intact/split) in relation to the custody form (mother/father/both) and to characteristics of the child and of his sibling relationship(s). Second, for each custody form, they verify if these characteristics vary with the patterns of organization in the sibling subsystem. Third, they examine how the previously-analyzed characteristics may vary within a model where the status of the sibling group (intact/split) and the custody form (mother/father/both) are considered simultaneously. Their discussion highlights the impact modifications in the sibling subsystem after parental divorce has on child development.

Wilma Binda and Franca Crippa in their paper, "Parental Self-Efficacy and Characteristics of Mother and Father in the Transition to Parenthood", report data from a longitudinal study that examines how normal couples cope with the transition to parenthood. They focus on parental self efficacy during this family life phase. Self-efficacy - which in this research was conceived as a level of beliefs which concern judgments of one's ability to perform competently and effectively during pregnancy and afterwards with the new child - is the mediating link between beliefs, knowledge and behavior. Perceived ability to be able to deal with the complex needs associated with the new role means to feel able to respond to the necessity of a baby, one's own needs and those of the partner. Employing 60 couples (60 mothers and 60 fathers, in total 120 subjects) expecting their first child, data were to be collected twice (6-8 month of pregnancy and 3-4 months postpartum). Data from both husband and wife were collected and analyzed.

The last paper in this section, "From Adolescence to Young Adulthood: A Family Transition", by Margherita Lanz concentrates on adolescence as a "joint developmental enterprise" between parents and offspring. This involves all family members and is characterized by transformation and continuity. The aim of Lanz's study was to investigate how the parent-child dyad and the whole family modify their relationships from adolescence to young adulthood. Using a sample of 325 intact families with a child aged between 11 and 24, congruence scores between parents and their adolescents were calculated. Young adulthood appears to be characterized by a realignment in the relationships between parents and their adolescence.

Section III: Child and Adolescent Development

Six papers comprise this third section, *Child and Adolescent Development*. The first paper by Diane Benoit, "Regulation and Its Disorders", deals with the development of self-regulation. A brief review of self-regulation is presented, in addition to current knowledge about the prevalence, classification, etiology, phenomenology, outcome and treatment of regulatory disorders. The role of the environment as external regulator or dysregulator is also described by Benoit, in addition to the importance of assessing both internal (within the infant) and external (within the environment) aspects of regulation in infants who have clinical problems. The case of an 11-month-old infant with regulatory disorder is used to illustrate the role of the family environment on the perpetuation of regulatory disorders and the impact of regulatory disorders on the family.

Jonathan Midgett, Laura Belsito, Bruce A. Ryan and Gerald R. Adams in the next paper in this section, "Children's and Parent's Perceptions of Parental Attitudes and Behaviors Pertaining to Academic Achievement", invoke ecological theories of social development which describe a hierarchy of influence for the multiple layers or contexts of factors affecting a child's progress through school. Accordingly, they studied grades 4, 7 and 11 children together with their parents. Both the children and their parents completed the Inventory of Parental Influence. This instrument assessed children's and parent's perceptions of school-focused, parental behaviors from the child's view of each parent, as well as mothers and fathers views of their own behaviors. Factor analyses produced five factors for children's viewpoint (Help, Support, Pressure, Press for Intellectual Development, and Monitoring) and five factors for parents (Help, Support, Expectations to Excel, Concern for Child's Motivation, and Management/Promotion of Learning). Midgett et al's evidence indicates that children and parents share a similar view of help and support. They diverge in their perceptions of the remaining parenting behaviors and attitudes pertaining to education, however. The findings suggest that children and parents' perspectives are similar on some perceived parenting behaviors yet different on others.

Delinquency continues to be a major social and mental health problem. Elizabeth Oddone-Paolucci, Claudio Violato and Chris Wilkes tackle the problem of delinquency in the next paper, "A Stepwise Discriminant Analysis of Delinquent and Nondelinquent Youth". The purpose of this research was to determine the similarities and differences between nondelinquent and delinquent youth, and to investigate the impact of family variables on delinquency. Based on a review of 285 records of institutionalized youth, patient demographic and developmental life history variables were examined. A stepwise discriminant analysis revealed that several variables distinguish between delinquent and nondelinquent adolescents. In comparison to nondelinquents, more delinquent youth were diagnosed as conduct disordered, had histories of prenatal complications, reached developmental milestones at unpredictable rates, performed poorly in school, experienced physical abuse, reported maternal psychopathologies, and were insecurely attached to both parents. Oddone-Paolucci et al interpret their results within the context of attachment theory and developmental psychopathology.

Claudio Violato and Mark Genuis address developmental psychopathology directly in their paper, "Origins of Psychopathology: A Developmental Model". The main purpose of this study was to test a latent variable path model of the

xxi

influence of childhood attachment on psychological adaptation in adolescence. A total of 138 adolescents along with their mothers and fathers formed Violato's and Genuis' sample. Approximately 40% of the adolescents were drawn from a clinical sample and the remainder were from the community. Data were collected on the adolescents and their mothers and fathers on affective, cognitive, life history and demographic variables. The latent variable path model which specified that childhood attachment is central to the development of psychological adaptation in adolescence was fit to the data. Using an Arbitrary Distribution Least Squares (ALS) method, the model resulted in a good fit to the data (Comparative Fit Index = .984). A single path from Childhood Attachment to psychological adaptation was confirmed by a significant path coefficient (.48, $p < .01$). The significance of these findings for a general theory of developmental psychopathology are discussed by Violato and Genuis.

"Parallels Between Dyadic Interactions: Parent-Child and Child-Peer", is a paper contributed by Leigh A. Moore, Darla J. Maclean and Thomas P. Keenan. In this study they set out to draw parallels between two dyadic interactions. The first, a parent and child interaction and the second, interactions between the child and a peer of their choice. From coded video each interaction, three variables were obtained: (1) a sensitivity measure, (2) a global scaffolding measure, and (3) a measure of positive verbal reinforcement. Measures of warmth and control were also obtained. Results showed a strong parallel between the two dyads through the reinforcement measure. A higher frequency of positive verbal reinforcement in the parent-child dyad was related to higher frequencies of reinforcement in the child-peer dyad. Verbally reinforcing parents were good scaffolders and very sensitive teachers. Verbally reinforcing children were also good scaffolders. Measures of warmth and control were weakly correlated with the three main measures from the video tapes. It appears that parents are undoubtedly highly influential in the lives of their children.

Carol Miles in "Modern Approaches to Children's Cognitive Development" reviews theories of human intelligence, perhaps the most highly disputed general concept in the field of psychology. This problem stems, in part, from intelligence's role as both a scientific, and a lay concept. Popular public opinion holds that intelligence refers to the capacity of an individual, and carries the interpretation that intelligence is an inherited, unchangeable characteristic. These ideas have lead to the expectation that a test of "real intelligence" should measure this unalterable capacity. None of the tests designed, to date, have been able to meet this ultimate ideal. In contrast to this idealistic view of intelligence as a finite, measurable, unified quantity, intelligence has alternatively been defined as a family resemblance concept, meaning that it is a concept with no defining attributes but with prototypical instances, a hierarchical organization, and a stable correlational structure. This implies that intelligence at different points in life may be conceptualized by different prototypes, hierarchical organization, and correlational structures. Miles reviews the theories and data relevant to how children develop in areas of cognition commonly associated with intelligence.

Section IV: Attachment

Attachment theory and research has become very widespread in the last several decades. Several papers relevant to attachment and children's development are included in this final section, *Attachment*. The first paper by Mark Genuis and Claudio Violato, "Attachment Security to Mother, Father, and the Parental Unit", is about patterns of attachment to mother, father and the parental unit. The purpose of this study was to test for a relationship between security of childhood attachment (secure/insecure) to parents individually and parents as a unit. A total of 138 adolescent subjects participated in a retrospective-longitudinal study in which their childhood attachments (prior to 10 years of age) to each parent and the parental unit were assessed. Subjects reported the same attachment type (secure/insecure) to each parent individually as well as to the parental unit. That is, children who were insecurely attached to one parent were significantly more likely to be insecurely attached to the other parent as well as the parental unit. These findings are consistent with other empirical findings in this area of study.

In the second paper in this section, "Pilot Study of the Psychometric Properties of the Adolescent Attachment Survey," Mark Genuis, Claudio Violato, Elizabeth Oddone-Paolucci, Stephane Robitaille and Dawn McBride present the results of a pilot study investigating the psychometrics properties of an instrument, the Adolescent Attachment Survey (AAS) and the Adolescent Attachment Survey - Parent Version (AAS-P). Four measures were used in order to assess childhood attachment and current level and type of psychopathology. These measures included the AAS and AAS-P, the Parental Bonding Instrument, the Youth Self-Report Instrument, and the Child Behavior Checklist. Data were collected from a total of 53 male and female adolescents between the ages of 12 and 17 years, and each of their parents wherever possible. Adequate internal consistency, using Cronbach's Alpha was found for all of the variables used in the AAS. Criterion-related validity coefficients for the attachment scale in the AAS were also consistent and significant. Genuis et al conclude that the psychometric properties established for the AAS provide evidence for validity and reliability thus it can be used in the assessment of adolescent attachment patterns.

In the final paper, "Effects of Nonmaternal Care on Child Development: A Meta-Analysis of Published Research", Claudio Violato and Clare Russell report the results of a meta-analysis of published research on the effects of nonmaternal care on child development. One hundred and one studies published between 1957 and 1995 involving 32,271 children met the inclusion criteria. Dependent variables in four domains (attachment, social-emotional, behavioral, and cognitive) were coded and effect sizes ($\underline{d}$) between maternal and nonmaternal care (independent variable) were computed for both unweighted and weighted effects size. Results of unweighted effect size analysis indicated that there was a small effect and negative effects of nonmaternal care in the cognitive ($\underline{d} = .14$) and social-emotional ($\underline{d} = .26$) domains, and larger negative consequences for nonmaternal care for behavioral outcomes ($\underline{d} = .38$), and attachment to mother ($\underline{d} = .39$). Weighted effects size analysis decreased the magnitude of effect sizes in the social-emotional ($\underline{d} = .16$) and behavioral domains but not in the cognitive and attachment domains. Moreover, males tended to fare more poorly with nonmaternal care than did females in all domains. A number of potentially mediating family, quality of care, and study characteristic variables were assessed and analyzed. Violato and Russell discuss the results within the context of attachment theory and they raise the possible implications for public policy.

Summary

The nineteen papers that have been collected in the present volume represent a wide variety of perspectives and divergent research approaches to the problem of changing families and child development. This is the collected work of psychologists, social workers, physicians, psychiatrists, educators and sociologists as well as others. Both social science research and public policy is likely to be challenged in the next decade and beyond in the type of families we may wish in society and the effects these may have on the children growing within these families. The papers in this book may elucidate some of these questions and open further discussions on the changing family and child development.

Section I:

The Context of Families

1 New Aspects of Family Relations

EUGENIA SCABINI

Abstract

The extension of the life stage spanning the transition from childhood to adulthood is an increasing phenomenon. In Europe in general, and in some Mediterranean countries in particular, the transition to adulthood either occurs within the family of origin, or depends on the family of origin for its successful outcome.

In this paper some of the psychological features of the families with two adult generations is outlined using the findings of quantitative and qualitative research. In both cases a relational/intergenerational approach based on analysis of exchanges between generations is adopted.

These families are both a new resource and a new source of risk. The ongoing family may offer excellent opportunities for dialogue, exchange and emotional warmth, as well as an opportunity for young people to fulfill themselves personally. It can also become closed and inward-looking, however, if it breaks generational continuity by discouraging young people from leaving the nest and accepting parenthood. This is the result of increasingly ambiguous relationship between the family and society.

Introduction

The extension of the life stage spanning the transition from childhood to adulthood is an increasingly common phenomenon in European countries (Cavalli & Galland, 1993). This temporal extension is causing a prolongation of adolescence, and is giving rise to a new phase in the life-cycle called post-adolescence, or young adulthood (Sherrod, Haggerty & Featherman, 1993). The transition to adulthood is therefore taking on new features. It's no longer a short span of time made up of precise steps, but a long transition characterized by numerous microtransitions (Breunlin, 1988) beginning in late adolescence.

This lengthy transition is in opposition to primitive societies where the process is to a rapid, highly ritualized "leap" featuring rites of passage which unambiguously define both the transition to adulthood and the impossibility of reverting to the previous situation.

We are also in a different situation from that of our own recent past, when the transition was clearly mapped out by well defined markers which occurred in a clear sequence: finishing school, entering the labor market, and getting married. Depending on social timing, there was a certain time span in which these tasks could be carried out, particularly for women whose time range for getting married was quite restricted. The ordering of these markers has now been altered by a modern life cycle which increasingly allows previously-made choices to be 'revised and reversed, with the result that the most widespread model is now one of experimentation and reversibility (Sciolla, 1993). In short, the transition to adulthood is progressively breaking down into a sequence of individual (Hurrelman & Engel, 1989) transition states based on a variety of social and temporal models. Young people, especially those from upper and middle class backgrounds, can now choose when to make the transition.

The prolongation of the transition to adulthood has given more value and more influence to the family of origin during a period of the life-cycle which, in past decades, has tended to play only a minor role. In modern European society, beginning from late adolescence, we are now witnessing an essentially smooth transformation in family relations. The adolescent and young adult constructs his or her adult identity not outside the family, but within the family. The passage to adulthood is a "joint enterprise" of both children and parents. Indeed, parents are in some ways actively engaged in this developmental task (Scabini, 1995; Sroufe, 1991; Youniss & Smollar, 1985).

In contrast to past decades, late adolescents are given a great deal of freedom in decision-making within the home by being able to negotiate processes in a familial context which is both supportive and without serious conflict. This is probably because adolescents and their families are well aware that they face a long period of time before leaving the family. Conversely, late adolescents have difficulty in finding a place for themselves in society. Only a small percentage of them achieve a stable position in the labor market. The main and practically only extrafamilial agency available to them is the school. Adolescents therefore have little bargaining power and little real influence on society: they are in a marginal social situation and experience status inconsistency as a result (Hurrelmann, 1989).

The passage from late adolescence to young adulthood is a slow and gradual adjustment of the familial and social situation I have just described. If, in late adolescence, freedom is somewhat limited within the family by gender or social class (males have more freedom than females, as do adolescents from upper and middle class compared to those from working class backgrounds) during young adulthood these differences become less evident. The entry of the young adult into society is a gradual extension of the late adolescent's condition: it is marked by profound insecurity in the labor market, and indecision over whether to start a family.

Due to an economic recession in Europe, which has affected the younger generation particularly, job opportunities have become increasingly scarce. This situation is further compounded by the fact that young people have high academic and professional aspirations, and are looking for the best opportunities to realize them. Moreover, the decision to get married and have children is increasingly more difficult to make and less compelling than in previous times. It is therefore postponed. Young people desire room for exploration and don't want to make important, far-reaching decisions early on in their lives. But this is possible only because they can rely on their families. This willingness of families to support their younger members in the long transition to adulthood is a new phenomenon.

In appears that in Europe in general, and in some Mediterranean countries in particular, the transition to adulthood either occurs within the family of origin, or depends on the family of origin for its successful outcome (Nave-Hertz, 1997). A greater percentage of young people in Europe (and to a lesser extent the USA and Canada) tend to live with their parents, or at least rely on them for economic and emotional support.

The Mediterranean model of the transition to adulthood

Galland (1993) has identified three kinds of transition to adulthood in young Europeans. Each model implies a different relationship between the family of origin and the new family which is formed. The first kind of transition is the Mediterranean model which is typical of Italy, Spain and Greece, and is characterized by prolonged co-residence with parents. Marriage tends to occur later, though soon after detachment from the parental home. The second is more prevalent in Northern Europe and France, and is marked by a long interim period between detachment from the family of origin and the setting up of a new family. During this period, cohabitation or life as a single person is common, the latter especially in France. In the third, which is typical of Great Britain, both detachment from the family of origin and marriage occur earlier, while the decision to have children is delayed and life as a childless couple is more prolonged.

The common outcome of these three models is delay in the appearance of a next generation: there is now a "generational vacuum", largely unknown in the past, and family relationships develop between different adult generations living together or apart as the case may be. Our current focus is on the first model, which is giving rise to a genuinely new type of "ongoing" or "prolonged" family with its own advantages and drawbacks. As has recently been shown (Cherlin, Scabini & Rossi, 1997), the phenomenon of young adults living in the parental home is on the increase in Europe, and especially in Southern European countries like Italy, Spain and Greece.

As Cordon (1997) has shown, in these countries the percentage of young people aged 20-24 years living with their parents is very high (91% in 1994) and is almost the same as the percentage of similarly placed adolescents aged 15-19 (96% in 1994). Living at home also extends beyond the 24-year threshold. In 1994 about 65% of males and 44% of females aged 25-29 were living with their families of origin, even when they were economically independent, while in 1986 the proportion was about 51% males and 29% females (see Tables 1.1 and 1.2).

It is worthwhile noting that "generational cohabitation" (Righi & Sabbadini, 1994) is more common in countries with lower birth rates like Italy and Spain. Italy, for example, has the lowest birth rate in Europe (1.23 in 1996). Obviously, remaining with the family of origin is not always a choice, and can sometimes be imposed by external circumstances. Young people from working class backgrounds are more affected by the precariousness of the labor market and are less happy about living at home than their upper and middle class contemporaries.

The ongoing family is rooted in important cultural and structural factors roles, values and attachments to the family by its members . On the other hand, it underlies protracted education, and high rates of unemployment. The family is at the root of a high standard of living in adult and older generations which have benefited from the welfare state.

Psychologically, these families of two adult (or quasi-adult) generations are both a new resource and a new source of risk. Some of the psychological features of these families using the findings of quantitative and qualitative research carried out by the researchers of the Center for Family Studies and Research at the Catholic University of Milan over the past decade (for a summary, see Tables 1.3 and 1.4), are outlined below.

A relational/intergenerational approach based on analysis of exchanges between generations has been adopted. An intergenerational approach enables us to see that, as in a social relationship, familial relationships are not simply interactive and horizontal, but also vertical (Scabini & Cigoli, in press). Both children's and parent's points of view are compared and contrasted, as is usual in "authentic" family research.

Analysis of critical areas in intergenerational relationships: The children's point of view

First of all, let us examine sons' and daughters' views about family climate, beginning with two central variables for understanding family functioning: cohesion and adaptability. To investigate these variables, we have conducted numerous studies in recent years (Farina & Galimberti, 1993; Scabini & Galimberti, 1995) using Olson's FACES III which explores representations of the perceived and the ideal family.

These studies reveal that children perceive the real family as characterized by intermediate levels of cohesion and high levels of adaptability. In the ideal family, young people desire an increase in adaptability. Consequently, children in this phase of the life-cycle demand greater flexibility and social openness from their parents.

In other studies (Lanz, 1997; Lanz & Rosnati, 1995; Scabini, in press; Scabini & Marta, 1995. For further details of each, see Table 1.3) we investigated other variables which are crucial to the study of the family: parent-child communication and parent-child support[1].

For communication and support, our research findings consistently show that:

a) on the whole, late adolescents and young adults perceive communication with their parents to be good, very open and largely problem free. They consider that their relationships to their parents are highly supportive.

b) late adolescents and young adults perceive a better, more open and supportive relationship with their mothers than with their fathers (Lanz & Rosnati, 1995; Scabini, in press; Scabini & Marta, 1995);

c) late adolescent males perceive better communication with their fathers than do females (Scabini, in press; Scabini & Marta, 1995);

d) young adults (both male and female) perceive fewer problems in communication with their fathers than do late adolescents (Lanz, 1997).

What does positive communication between parents and children depend on? The most common topic of conversation between parents and children (in which the mother is the preferred interlocutor of both sons and daughters) is extra-familiar achievement (school or work) and future plans (Di Nicola, 1998; Scabini, in press; Scabini & Marta, 1995). "Future choice" is frequently discussed by more than 80% of the adolescents with their mother, and by more than 70% with their father, with obvious differences between males and females which confirm the pattern previously described.

We can conclude this overview of children's perceptions of family functioning with a "synthetic" variable, namely satisfaction with the family. Our studies indicate that:

a) on the whole, there is a good level of satisfaction with the family during this phase in the family life cycle,

b) a relationship between satisfaction and social class: satisfaction is greatest in families with more economic and cultural resources,

c) males are more satisfied than females, i.e., fathers (who usually score highest) and sons (late adolescents and young adults) score higher than mothers and daughters.

These trends appear to be stable. A recent study by Lanz (1997) shows that indicators of communication, support and family climate (the last measured by certain subscales in Moos' Family Environment Scale) do not change in the transition from late adolescence to young adulthood, while, as girls grow older, their satisfaction increases noticeably.

Taken together, these findings reveal new features in the transition to adulthood. Late adolescence is no longer the end of adolescence, but the beginning of a transitional phase which takes place progressively and slowly during young adulthood. The most problematic indicators tend to improve with the passing of time. Thus, the young adult arrives at the end of the transition period completely reconciled with his/her parents.

Family functioning and offspring adjustment

What is the relationship between the processes described here, and some outcomes regarding offspring? We have conducted several studies which examine the relationship between family functioning and psychosocial risk in late-adolescents, and the function of fathers and mothers in cases of child maladjustment.

Our studies - which are in line with the literature on European and American data (Hess, 1995; Gecas & Seff, 1990; Jackson & Bosma, 1992) - show that family satisfaction, support and adequate communication are positively correlated with the individual and social adjustment of adolescents, and negatively correlated with deviant or delinquent attitudes. One study carried out at our center for Family Study and Research (Scabini & Marta, 1996; Scabini, Marta & Rosnati, 1995) with a sample of 595 late adolescents (16-19 years) shows that late adolescents' perceptions of support and openness in communication (with both mothers and fathers) are inversely related to risk for the adolescent ($p < .001$). The presence of problems in communication with mothers and fathers is directly related to the risk for the adolescent ($p < .001$). Moreover, the adolescents' perception of family satisfaction are also inversely correlated with the risk[2] for themselves.

The mean scores for openness in communication and support decrease from the low risk group to the medium risk group, and from this to the high risk group, while the mean scores of problems in communication increase. Also, the mean scores for family satisfaction decrease from the low risk group to the medium risk group, and from this to the high risk group. No differences emerged between boys and girls in their perceptions of the relationship with their parents. Accordingly, satisfaction, support and adequate communication appear to be important protective factors in preventing psychosocial risk in late adolescents and young adults.

For today's adolescents it is more important to have good family relationships than it was for their parents at the same age. This is the principal result of an intergenerational study in which we compared parents and children to discover who are the significant others for present-day Italian late adolescents, and who were the significant others for their parents during their adolescence (Lanz et al., 1998; Scabini & Marta, 1995).

In particular, we asked parents to imagine themselves as children and to indicate, in order of importance, who were the most significant persons for them when they were the same age as their own offspring, whereas we asked their adolescent children to indicate who are the most significant figures in their lives right now. Our findings indicated that parents are the most significant others for both the present and past generation of adolescents: father and mother are put in first or second place in the list of significant others by both generations. A more detailed analysis revealed the central position of the mother for both generations: now as in the past, the mother is the principal reference figure from whom children can seek advice, help and support.

Discrepancies emerged in the relative importance of other significant adults, however. Contemporary adolescents seem to rely exclusively on their parents, or, in their absence, on their peers, while the adolescents of the past (i.e. the adolescents' parents) could also count on the support of adults outside the family, such as a teacher or a youth counselor.

The parent's point of view

The perceptions of mothers and fathers convey even more emphatically than their children's, the image of a harmonious, conflict-free family characterized by good parent-children relationships and middle to high satisfaction with the family.

Our findings can be summarized as follows:

a) Fathers and mothers perceive their own real families as characterized by high cohesion and flexibility. It is interesting to note that, unlike their children, parents desire an even more cohesive family. This is particularly true of mothers, who thus assume a central role within the family system (Scabini & Galimberti, 1995).

b) The fathers and mothers of late adolescents and young adults do not perceive differences in their relationship with their children (measured here in terms of communication, support and family climate) caused by age or gender. What seems to be most important for the parents is the gender roles of children. Parents thus show difficulty both in perceiving changes in their offspring over time, and in clearly perceiving differences connected with their children's gender.

There are several differences between fathers and mothers:

a) Mothers perceive better communication which is more open and less problematic with their offspring than do fathers (Lanz 1997; Scabini, in press; Scabini & Marta, 1995). From these results, we might construct a scale of intergenerational relationships that takes account of the communication and parent/child gender variables of parents and children. It could be used to show that the most open and least problematic relationship is the one between mother and daughter, followed by those between mother and son, father and son, and finally, father and daughter.

b) Mothers influence the academic and work choices of their children (both male and female) and also convey the father's expectations regarding his children (Rosnati, 1996).

In order to examine the family influence on adolescents' academic and work choices, a recursive structural model was tested by LISREL analyses. If we consider the first model concerning the family's influence on children's cultural plans, the most surprising feature of all is the mother's role, in the sense that she exerts a predominant influence on male aspirations (Figure 1.1).

The father serves as a model for his son in terms of his professional achievement, but not directly in terms of parental expectation, though the strong correlation between father's and mother's expectations should also be noted. By contrast, daughters take both parents into account (Figure 1.2), though the mother's direct influence is greater than the father's because the mother influences her daughter's educational plans by her own expectations and by her own educational level.

Thus, even tasks traditionally assigned to the father, such as guidance in the choice of work or career, are being performed by mothers in Italian families with late adolescents. In this respect, one of our preliminary findings in a study-in-progress which compares "satisfied" and "dissatisfied" families is also significant. In satisfied families, the father is an important point of reference in planning the son's or daughter's future, and plays a decisive role in their striving for self-fulfillment in individual and social spheres. This finding suggests that the relational imbalance in favor of the mother, who seems to take most of the child-rearing burden upon herself, can be rectified in adequate families by the significant presence and participation of the father.

The role of fathers and mothers and comparisons with children

The role of fathers and mothers emerges even more clearly when we compare parents' and children's perceptions of the extent to which the son or daughter is at risk. It is precisely this comparison of findings for parents and children which has enabled us to identify new features in family relationships.

First, our studies over the past few years have consistently shown that certain variables - communication, support, cohesion and adaptability - point to greater agreement between fathers and children than between mothers and children. Secondly, our studies have shown that fathers are able to perceive different levels of communication and support in relation to the level of risk which children attribute to themselves, while the level of communication and support perceived by mothers does not vary according to their children's level of risk[3] (see for example, Marta, 1997 – Table 1.5).

If, as we have seen, the mother is the crucial point of reference in family relationships, our research shows that, within the couple, the father is the most reliable source of information on family relationships and on the real condition of the children. His perspective on reality, like that of his children, is an objective one. Indeed, the mother is less likely to notice problematic aspects of her relationship with her children, or to perceive distress signals (Marta, 1997). We could almost say, then, that mothers are "blind" to the psychosocial state of their adolescent children. This is probably because mothers identify strongly with their children, and therefore have greater difficulty in describing their family situation in an objective way.

These "new" findings about the father are very important from the practical point of view of preventing situations of distress from developing. They show that, though less socially visible and less easily detectable than that of the mother, the father's role is just as important, precisely because fathers perceive more accurately the true situation of their children.

Summary

1) When functioning adequately, the family does effectively protect its younger members against risk. In their struggle to achieve identity, late adolescents and young adults look for help in their relationships from both the mother and father, so that each plays either an enabling or a constraining role in the adolescent's development. For families experiencing the transition from adolescence to adulthood in one of their members, adequate communication and the possibility of freely expressing opinions and feelings becomes an important protective factor against psychosocial risk in adolescents and young adults. Similarly, the active effort that is put into the relationship, which manifests itself in the perception of feeling encouraged and supported, of being able to "count on" someone (the perception of reliable bonds between family members) helps the entire family to renegotiate rules and roles. Because of their isolation, today's adolescents and young adults have more need of good family relationships than their parents did, first and foremost as protection against psychosocial risk.

2) Daughters find themselves in a less stable and more complex situation than do sons. This is important if we take into account the evolving role of young women in the Italian social and cultural context. Over the past two decades, women have moved quickly to close the economic and political gap that separates them from men. At present, females are attaining higher educational levels than males, show greater self-esteem and relational skill, and a greater desire for professional self-fulfillment. In Italy, this is the first generation that has realized on a large scale that it faces the difficult task of combining the "double role" of family and work (Leccardi, 1993). Girls therefore experience more stress than boys during the transition to adulthood.

3) The roles of mothers and fathers are being redefined in ways that could mislead us if we focus only on small areas of family life rather than the total situation. As we have seen, mothers play a central role in family life. They have the task of spinning the webs of family relationships, of making known the mutual expectations of each family member to the others, but, overburdened by these delicate and important tasks, they may lose their ability to make objective

assessments. Fathers do have this ability, however. Their perceptions correlate well with those of their offspring. Even if he is less central to the family, and exerts his influence in only a few specific areas - the adolescent's "concrete" choices regarding his-her academic/professional future - the father nevertheless plays a decisive role in the family because he is better able to grasp both the positive and negative aspects of the family situation.

The reciprocal advantages of living at home for children and parents

The preceding provides a fairly precise picture of the relational features of the ongoing family. Other findings of studies based on semi-structured or in-depth interviews administered jointly to males and females aged 20-30 and their parents help supplement these results. This will give us greater insight into the kind of psychological pact that sustains this long-term child/parent cohabitation which both find so satisfactory. Table 1.6 is a summary of the main areas that we investigated.

Several major findings have emerged. Which psychological needs does this type of family form fulfill?

The young person's point of view is clear: within the parental home they construct an autonomous area from which to acquire "controlled" experience of the adult world. They are worried about finding a good job. Starting a family is not a clearly defined goal. They also want to delay making final decisions. Adolescents want more time to think things over and test themselves in both private relationships and work before taking on the responsibilities that a final choice entails.

Adult life is feared: it seems to offer fewer possibilities for freedom, self-fulfillment and expression than those enjoyed by young people during adolescence. They hesitate to enter adult life because they don't want to lower their expectations of unrestricted self-fulfillment. Their present family represents stability for the precarious future. The stability of being able to rely on their family, its support, affective warmth, and help in case of need, enables young people to put off final assumption of adult responsibilities.

"Forever young" is the dream of young people, but what is the parent's dream? It is to be forever a parent, forever a resource, forever an unfailing caregiver. Time passes, but the in-between generation doesn't want to stand back and make room for the younger one. It still wants to occupy center stage.

This attitude is typical of Italy's postwar generations, which are financially secure and not heavily burdened with children. They feel no urge to drive their children out; on the contrary, they are afraid of finding themselves the sole occupants of an empty nest. Most Italian families have one or, at most, two children. The child is, in a sense, an "emotional distillate". It is easy for parents to identify with and mirror themselves in their children. From our interviews, it is clear that parents are happy to be able to give their children what they themselves could not possibly have had in their youth: the ideal parent-child relationship they always wanted but never experienced because they grew up in stricter families. This is why they are so understanding and supportive of their children.

As De Nicola (1998) has shown, it is mothers especially who employ a participative/egalitarian style based on dialogue, affection and understanding. Children are regarded as friends. Mothers tends to eliminate intergenerational distance and assume they are living in a peer family. While to an extent sharing this style, fathers prefer to remain more aloof, maintain intergenerational distance, and place more importance on the transmission of family values and traditions. But both parents accept that they have to make room within the family for their children to fulfill themselves, and lend their support to their children's efforts to do this. Therefore, from both sides, there are motives for encouraging the prolongation of youth within the family, and there are reciprocal advantages for both generations in creating an ongoing family. Parents and children have a shared representation of adult life as a difficult transition which is best postponed in order to keep as many opportunities open as possible for self-fulfillment in the social world.

Contemporary families have thus risen to the challenges of a post-modern society, which makes it increasingly difficult for young people to acquire adult status. They have done this by providing help and support over many years to the young generations which willingly accept this situation. In this sense, the family is a major source of protection and solidarity.

The self-fulfillment of young people which parents willingly lend their support to, however, doesn't clearly include the creation of a new family and the responsibility for giving birth to and caring for a new generation. This goal is rather less explicit and seems dependent on hazily-defined future events. Thus, the family of origin makes no real effort to make the generational leap. In this respect, the family is both a source of risk and a critical context for development.

The ongoing family may offer excellent opportunities for dialogue, exchange and emotional warmth, as well as an opportunity for young people to fulfill themselves in the personal sphere. It can also become closed and inward-looking, however, a source of relational encystment, if it breaks generational continuity by discouraging young people from leaving the nest and accepting parenthood. This is the situation which some European countries now face.

This raises an important question. Why is it that the European family, and especially the Italian one which has traditionally had such a strong sense of family, now runs this risk more than any other? The answer lies in the ambiguous relationship between the family and society, and in the opposing behaviors of generations within the family and society.

In today's gerontocratic society, the generations are growing further apart and increasingly remote from each other, and the adult generation is failing to make room for younger ones. This is the outcome of a strongly individualistic and competitive social mentality (Bellah et al., 1985; Doherty, 1995; Taylor, 1982). Market logic now pervades everything, including human relationships (Godbout, 1992). Cultivating and investing in relationships is no longer considered of interest or value.

By contrast, different generations display solidarity with each other within the family, and the adult generation supports the younger one. The individualistic mentality is also present in the family to a certain extent however. The result is that the family lacks the force to direct the self-fulfillment of young people. Wherein both parents and children collaborate, for the creation of the next generation. The family alone is unable to assert the relevance of its symbolic relational code based on reciprocity and generativity. Generativity is not simply reproduction and replication but also loving care based on trust in the dynamic force of the next generation, whether of one's own or someone else's making. As Erickson (1982) indicated, the generational task is "cultivating strength in the next generation. For this indeed is the 'store' of life" (p.67). Self-fulfillment is achieved through commitment to strengthening the next generation. As a result, the loop is closed and the source of new generations is provided for the family. An adult generation that has staked everything on the next generation thus achieves its own identity.

This symbolic generative code has been weakened because it is confined to the private sphere alone. Society has increasingly refused to have anything to do with this symbolic generative, as if it were a private concern of the family, or even just of women.

The generative task concerns all men and women. It is a universal task. Society must again place at its center both the family, and reciprocal solidarity and care-giving between generations. Both family and society have to invest in future generations, and commit themselves to ensuring that they are able to carry forward and strengthen our unique family histories and shared social histories. Thus we can confidently rise to the challenge of the new millennium.

Table 1.1 **Proportion of men still living with parents by age group, in two groups of E.U. countries (in % of age group total)**

Age Countries	15-19 Years 1986	15-19 Years 1994	20-24 Years 1986	20-24 Years 1994	25-29 Years 1986	25-29 Years 1994
Central countries	94.4	94.6	59.9	61.2	23.1	24.7
France	94.8	94.8	56.9	61.8	19.3	22.5
Germany	94.8	95.4	64.8	64.6	27.4	28.8
United Kingdom	93.6	93.2	57.2	56.8	21.9	20.8
Southern countries	96.5	96.4	87.1	90.9	51.3	65.3
Spain	95.6	95.6	88.1	91.5	63.2	64.8
Greece	94.6	95.2	76.5	79.3	53.8	62.6
Italy	97.4	97.3	87.8	92.2	49.6	66.0

Table 1.2 Proportion of women still living with parents by age group, in two groups of E.U. countries (in % of age group total)

Age	15-19 years 1986	15-19 years 1994	20-24 years 1986	20-24 years 1994	25-29 years 1986	25-29 years 1994
Countries						
Central countries	89.9	90.9	37.9	41.3	9.4	11.4
France	89.8	90.9	36.4	41.6	8.4	10.3
Germany	92.0	93.2	42.8	44.6	11.0	12.7
United Kingdom	87.8	88.2	33.8	37.0	8.6	10.8
Southern countries	94.4	94.7	71.1	81.3	28.8	44.3
Spain	93.9	94.6	76.1	84.3	35.3	47.6
Greece	89.2	92.5	52.3	62.3	23.8	32.1
Italy	95.7	95.3	70.4	82.4	25.5	44.1

Table 1.3　Quantitative research (questionnaire)

Study	Sample: Age #	Research goal	Instruments
FRAP-Family Relationships and Adolescents Project a.Scabini & Marta (1995, 1996) b.Scabini, Marta & Rosnati(1995) Rosnati (1996) Marta (1997)	595-Late adolescents (16-19 ys old) (269 girls, 326 boys) 419 Mothers (36-52 ys old) 403 Fathers (37-66 ys old)	- Family functioning and psychosocial risk for the adolescent - Mothers' and fathers' influence on the adolescents' - school and occupational expectations	❖ Parent-Adolescent Communication Scale by Olson ❖ Family Satisfaction Scale by Olson ❖ Family Environment Scale by Moos ❖ Parent-Adolescent Support Scale by Scabini & Cigoli ❖ Marital Relationship Quality Scale by Scabini ❖ Self-esteem scale by Rosemberg ❖ Items on future expectations ❖ Items on significantothers and friends ❖ Socio-demographic items
Farina (1997)	230 Families with a young-adult child (20-30 ys old)	- Family relationships and their influence on children future life planning	❖ Parent-Adolescent Communication Scale by Olson ❖ Family Satisfaction Scale by Olson ❖ Family Environment Scale by Moos ❖ Parent-Adolescent Support Scale by Scabini & Cigoli ❖ Sense of Coherence Scale by Antonovsky
Lanz (1997)	75 Families with a late adolescent child (17-19 ys old)110 Families with a young-adult child (20-26 ys old)	- Continuity and discontinuity in the family relationships between the two phases of the life cycle	❖ Parent-Adolescent Communication Scale by Olson ❖ Family Satisfaction Scale by Olson ❖ Family Environment Scale by Moos ❖ Parent-Adolescent Support Scale by Scabini & Cigoli

Table 1.4   Qualitative research (interview)

Study	Sample: Age,#	Research goal	Instruments
Cigoli (1988)	40 Young-adults (19-24 ys old) (20 boys, 20 girls), 40 sets of parents	- Intergenerational relationships - Past assessment and future prefiguration - Occupational and emotional changes	In depth interview
Galimberti (1994)	14 Young-adults (23-30 ys old) 12 sets of Parents (50-70 ys old)	- Past assessment and future prefiguration - Meaning of being adult	Semi-structured interview
Di Nicola (1998)	53 Families (grandparents, parents, child- 14- 28 ys old)	- Young and parents orientation toward the society,	Semi-structured interview
Scabini & Cigoli (1997)	25 Young-adults (20-30 ys old) 25 sets of parents	- The perception of the present and the future - The intergenerational transmission of values	Semi-structured interview

Table 1.5   Risk-effect on openness and problems in communication and support (parents' scores)

Dependent variable	Effect (independent variable)	Pillais	p	F	p
	Father				
openness in communication	Risk	3.53	.002	6.05	.005
problem in communication				6.23	.002
support				3.51	.05
	Mother				
openness in communication	Risk	1.49	.178	.88	.415
problem in communication				3.06	.048
support				1.85	.159

1= low level of risk; 2=medium level of risk; 3=high level of risk

Table 1.6   Main areas investigated in the interviews

	Interviews with young adults	Interview with parents
	Relationship with parents	Relationship with children
	Representation of the "ideal" relationship with parents	Comparison between the present situation and the past generations
Areas	Plans for future	
	Meaning of being adult	Meaning of being adult
	Values received from family	Values received from family
		Values transmitted to children
	Representation of leaving the parental house	Representation of leaving the parental house

References

Bellah., R.N., Madsen, R., Sullivan, W., Swidler, A., & Tipton, M. (1985). Habits of the heart: *Individualism and commitment in American life*. Berkeley: University of California Press.

Breunlin, D.C. (1988).Oscillation theory and the family development. In C. Falicov (Ed.), *Family transition* (pp. 133-155). New York: Guilford Press.

Caprara, G.V., Scabini, E., Barbaranelli, C., Pastorelli, C., Regalia, R., & Bandura, A. (1997). *Impact of adolescents' perceived self regulatory efficacy on familial communication and antisocial behavior.* Manuscript submitted for publication.

Cavalli, A. & Galland, O. (1993). *L'allongement de la jeunesse*. Arles: Hubert Nissen Editeur.

Cherlin, A.J., Scabini, E. & Rossi, G. (Eds.) (1997). Delayed home leaving in Europe and United States [Special issue]. *Journal of Family Issues, 18.*

Cigoli, V. (1988). Giovani adulti e loro genitori. In E. Scabini and P. Donati (Eds.), *La famiglia lunga del giovane adulto [The ongoing family of the young-adult]* (pp. 156-170). Milano: Vita e Pensiero.

Cordon, J.A. (1997). Youth residential independence and autonomy: A comparative study. In A.J Cherlin, E. Scabini and G. Rossi, G. (Eds.) Delayed home leaving in Europe and United States. *Journal of Family Issues, 18*, 576-607.

Di Nicola, P. (Ed.) (1998). *Onde del tempo* [Waves of time]. Milano: Angeli.

Doherty W. (1995). *Soul searching*. New York: Basic Books.

Edwards, W. & Newman, R. (1982). *Multiattribute evaluation.* Sage University Paper series on Quantitative Application in the Social Sciences, 26. Beverly Hills: Sage.

Erickson, E. (1982). *The life cycle completed. A review*. New York: Norton.

Farina, M. & Galimberti C. (1993). Relazioni intergenerazionali ed ipotesi di autonomizzazione nella famiglia del giovane adulto. *Età Evolutiva, 45*, 35-46.

Farina, M. (1997). Restare in famiglia: percezioni del clima familiare, dell'ambiente sociale e progeti di autonomizzazione. In E. Scabini and G. Rossi (Eds.), *Giovani in famiglia tra autonomia e nuove dipendenze [Young people in their family between autonomy and new addictions]* (pp.69-93). Milano: Vita e Pensiero.

Galimberti, C. (1994). Voci e forme della transizione: produzioni discorsive e meccanismi spazio-temporali nelle transizioni familiari. In E. Scabini and P. Donati (Eds.), *Tempo e transizioni familiari [Time and family transition]* (pp. 251-286). Milano: Vita e Pensiero.

Galland, O. (1993). Qu'est-ce que le jeunesse?. In A. Cavalli and O.Galland (1993). *L'allongement de la jeunesse,* (pp.25-48) Arles: Hubert Nissen Editeur.

Gecas, V. & Seff, M.A. (1990). Families and adolescents: A review of the 1980s. *Journal of Marriage and the Family, 52*, 941-958.

Godbout, J.T. (1992). *L'esprit du don*. Paris: la Découverte.

Hess, L. (1995). Changing family patterns in Western Europe: Opportunity and risk factors for adolescent development. In M. Rutter and D. Smith (Eds.). *Psychosocial disorder in young people*, (pp.104-119) Chichester: Wiley.

Hurrelmann, K. (1989). The social world of adolescence: A sociological perspective. In K. Hurrelmann and U. Engel (Eds.) *The social world of adolescence* (pp.3-26). Berlin: de Gruyter.

Hurrelmann, K. & Engel, U. (Eds.) (1989). *The social world of adolescence.* Berlin: de Gruyter.

Jackson, S. & Bosma, H. (1992). Developmental research on adolescence: European perspectives for 1990s and beyond. *British Journal of Developmental Psychology, 10,* 319-337.

Lanz, M. (1997). *Dall'adolescenza alla giovinezza: analisi di un percorso familiare.* Unpublished Doctoral Dissertation – Catholic University , Milan, Italy.

Lanz, M., Iafrate, R., Marta, E., & Rosnati, R. (1997). Significant others in Italian families with late adolescents. Manuscript submitted for publication.

Lanz, M. & Rosnati, R. (1995). La comunicazione nella famiglia con adolescenti. *Ricerche di Psicologia, 19,* 81-98.

Leccardi, C. (1993). Adolescenti, gruppo dei pari e orientamenti di valore. Alcune considerazioni problematiche. In S. Ansaloni and M. Borsari (Eds.), *Adolescenti in gruppo [Adolescents in the group]* (pp. 95-112). Milano: Angeli.

Marta, E. (1997). Parent-adolescent interaction and psycho-social risk in adolescent: An analysis of communication, support and gender. *Journal of Adolescence, 20,* 473-487.

Nave-Hertz, R. (1997). The family and young-adults in Germany. *Journal of Family Issues, 18,* 671-689.

Righi, A. & Sabbadini, L.L. (1994). *La permanenza dei giovani adulti nella famiglia di origine degli anni '80.* Paper presented at the International Congress "Mutamenti della famiglia nei Paesi Occidentali" [Family changes in the Western Countries], Bologna 6-8 Ottobre 1994.

Rosnati, R. (1996). Adolescents' life plans: A family point of view. In M. Cusinato (Ed.), *Research on Family Resources and Needs Across the World* (pp. 375-394). Padova: Led.

Scabini, E. (1995). *Psicologia sociale della famiglia [The social psychology of the family].* Torino: Bollati Boringhieri.

Scabini, E. (in press). Adolescenza e relazioni familiari. In A. Cavalli (Eds.), *La famiglia di fronte alle scelte di studio e di lavoro dei giovani. Indagine Iard [The family in front of the youngs'study and work choice. Iard survey]* Bologna: Il Mulino.

Scabini, E. & Cigoli, V. (1997). An evolutionary slowdown or a breakdown in the generational transition? *Journal of Family Issues, 18,* 608-626.

Scabini, E. & Cigoli, V. (in press). The role of theory in the study of family psychopathology. In L. L'Abate (Ed.), *Handbook of family psychopathology.* New York: Guilford.

Scabini, E. & Galimberti, C. (1995). Adolescents and young adults: a transition in the family. *Journal of Adolescence, 18,* 593-606.

Scabini, E. & Marta, E. (1996). Family with late adolescents: social and family topics. In M. Cusinato (Ed.), *Research on Family Resources and Needs Across the World* (pp. 177-197). Padova: Led.

Scabini, E. & Marta, E. (1995). La famiglia con adolescenti: uno snodo critico intergenerazionale. In P. Donati (Ed.), *IV Rapporto sulla Famiglia in Italia [Fourth report on the family in Italy]* (pp.221-257). Milano: Edizioni Paoline.

Scabini E., Marta E., Rosnati R. (1995). Rischio familiare e rischio sociale: una ricerca sulle famiglie con tardo adolescenti. In M. D'Alessio, P. Ricci Bitti, anf G. Villone Betocchi (Eds.), *Gli indicatori psicologici e sociali del rischio [Marks of psychological and social risk]*(pp. 285-299). Napoli: Idelson Liviana.

Sciolla, L.(1993). Identità e trasmissione dei valori. Un problema di generazioni. In: S. Ansaloni and M. Borsari (Eds.), *Adolescenti in gruppo [Adolescents in the group]* (pp. 63-78). Milano: Angeli.

Sherrod, L., Haggerty, R., & Featherman, D. (1993). Introduction: Late adolescence and the transition to adulthood. *Journal of Research on Adolescence, 3,* 217-226.

Sroufe, J.W. (1991). Assessment of parent-adolescent relationships: Implications for adolescent development. *Journal of Family Psychology*, 5, 21-45.

Taylor, C. (1982). *The ethics of authentics*. Cambridge: Harvard Press.

Youniss, J., & Smollar, J. (1985). *Adolescent relations with mothers, fathers, and friends*. Chicago: University of Chicago Press.

Notes

1   Support is defined as the reliability of the parent-child bond, the perception of being able to "count on" one another when in need.

2   For this study, the risk index was constructed using MAUT (Multiattribute Utility Technology, Edwards and Newman, 1982). It was constructed using variables which the literature has shown to address principal aspects of the life and development of adolescents (identity construction, socialization, upbringing) and to be correlated with the adjustment of the adolescent (self-esteem, socialization, educational success). The group of adolescents was then divided into three subgroups (low, medium, high risk) using the +/- one criterion (sigma) on the means of the index of risk scores.

3   It is worth mentioning that a recent study of middle adolescents reached the same conclusion (Caprara et al., 1997).

2 Dual Images: The Family in Perspective

JAMES S. FRIDERES

Each Generation imagines itself to be more intelligent than the one that went before it, and wiser than the one that comes after it (George Orwell, Animal Farm, 1945).

The family is considered one of the most important institutions of our society. We think it plays an important role in determining the nature of our society in the future (Veevers, 1991). Yet the data we have on hand does not allow us to answer the question! As policy makers and social scientists, we want to know if this is true and if so, how this happens and what is it about the family that is important. We also want to know why there seems to be a disjuncture between what is publicly proclaimed by leaders of our society and the overt actions taken by these same individuals and their organizations with regard to the family and its functions.

Before we address these issues, we must first provide you with the context in which the family now operates. We begin with the identification of several major trends in Canadian society which have influenced the nature, structure and size of the family.[1] We begin by noting the dramatic shift in the age-sex structure of our society. Beginning with a typical pyramid at the beginning of this century, the structure, as we head into the 21st century, has now changed to an inverted pyramid (Figure 2.1).[2] In addition, the ethnic composition of Canadian society has undergone substantial changes over the past century so that multiculturalism is the most accurate description of the makeup of our society. These changes will have profound implications for the role of the family as we head into the 21st century.

There are other changes that have taken place as this population shift has occurred. First, there has been a modification of gender roles. Second, a marked increase in sexual freedom with a concurrent decrease in the application of the "double standard". Third, there is an increase in the number and visibility of unmarried individuals. Fourth, there has been a dramatic increase in divorce and remarriage. Fifth, the number of women in the work force (for both single and married) has increased. And finally, there has been a decline in the fertility rate below replacement level.

The central question we now face is how have these changes impacted the role of the family in providing children the necessary skills to succeed in society, the necessary values about work, community, marriage, family (kin), education, children, and perhaps equally important, values about tolerance and understanding (Glick & Parke, 1977). It is certain that the family has influenced values about other issues and objects but for the present, I will limit my discussion to issues involving the family.

Today's "family values" debate is driven by the concern about the moral fiber of this country. Unfortunately, "family values" as a term, has become a politically charged phrase. Some conservatives have appropriated the term and use it to bash anyone who disagrees with them. By doing so, they have done a disservice to the legitimate concern over the role of the family in today's society. As Betsy Rubiner (1996) points out, people begin to see those people using the buzzword as a mean-spirited, self righteous bunch, armed with an ironclad list of old-fashioned family values that don't include individual freedom, compassion and tolerance" (p. 15).

Our task is to reintroduce such a concern into the research and theoretical literature in such a way that we can divest ourselves from the ideological dimension and assess and test the assumptions, the hypotheses and ideas that lie behind such a concern. We need to take the political and ideological dimension away from the concept and place it into its proper theoretical and practical context. For example, we need to examine the concept and its implications as to how it contributes to, as well as fits into a civil society. More importantly, we need to ask what are these values? How are these values to be transmitted? And finally, why have these values? In addition, we must always be mindful that a conflict in the priorities assigned to values can bring about considerable bitterness in feelings and behaviors when these concepts are operationalized. For example, we can all agree to the value of "beauty", but when it comes to defining it, there may be considerable disagreement.

We turn then, to a discussion of values. Values are the overriding themes that identify important goals and provide the individual with standards for evaluating her/his behavior. Values are not usually explicit but they provide motives for action, shaping people's choices and help them justify their behavior. In short, values are the general ideas of what is good or bad (Warme, Malus, & Lundy, 1994). Values guide and determine actions, ideology, presentation of self to others, judgments, justifications and attempts to influence others. Hence, the study of values are important because they have extensive consequences for individuals and others cognition's and behaviors. Values help individuals to make choices, resolve dilemmas and accept resolutions as valid and binding. These rules and guidelines are developed from values which in turn provide standard information to members on such issues as how to achieve goals, administer rewards and punishment, as well as a host of other behaviors. Values provide a legitimacy as to how individuals govern their own behavior as well as their behavior toward others. As Wilson (1992) points out,

> ....they (values) are also guideposts that describe an individual's place in society, justify allegiance, and spell out the goals and means of group activity. Additionally, they are part of specific rules that compel particular forms of loyalty (p. 13).

The entire constellation of values within a society can be viewed as a "compliance ideology". This compliance ideology provides a blueprint for each of us as we carry out our behavior. As such, a compliance ideology is constructed and shared with the members of society over time (Figure 2.2).

In an academic sense, the question then turns to how this compliance ideology (values) is transmitted from one generation to the next. Stability in society is a function of how consistent values and attitudes are transmitted from one generation to the next or how commensurate changes in other institutional structures meet those impinging upon the family. Yet it is clear that children's expression of some values are not the same as exhibited by their parents. The issue is then, why have parents been unable to take on the role of socializing agent for conveying values to children? And which values have they been unable to transmit? We now turn to this issue.

Socialization is nothing more than development and it involves the dialectic of interaction--exposure to accessible roles in contextualized situations. Group members filter gestures and symbols according to the context and the time. The range of cultural elements made available in practice and the kinds of situations in which people take part depend on their social positions. The family regulates enculturation through selecting elements judged appropriate for socialization. In the main, this process seems to be successful and there is a general trend in standardization over the past century. For example, the median age of marriage for women has not changed significantly over the past century (23.3 in 1901 and 22.5 in 1991). The percent ever married has remained constant over this period--88.7% and 93.7%.[3] The percentage of people married has not changed substantially over the past 100 years. Available data suggests that parents of today, like their parents of yesterday, cherish similar kinds of values. In my own research focusing on political values, government and politics, I have shown that generational differences are remarkably small. As Bibby and Posterski (1992) point out, families still have traditional values of freedom, friendship, being loved, which were espoused by our parents and grandparents. Success in what you do, honesty, cleanliness and being respected are still values held by family members, young and old. Rodgers and Witney (1981) also compared cohorts of families over time and found striking similarities.

Despite economic, legal and social changes affecting the structure of family life, people still value intimacy and lifestyle stability. All these suggest that some compliance ideology is being transmitted and social control processes are working in our society. On the other hand, we have seen other statistics change over time which suggests that socialization efforts and social control mechanisms have not met the structural conditions of the post industrial society. For example, while social controls operated through the extended family and ties to the local community in the past, these are not the appropriate structures today.

There are reasons why deliberate socialization is not always successful. How the child is instructed is diverse and interrupted by many external factors. Meanings of symbols are not always learned by children. In short, there are many external agents and institutions which intervene between the socialization efforts of the family and the child. Hence, it is important that the actions and reactions of these external agents (institutions) need to be studied.

For too long people have viewed the family as the "cause" of the problem. Ills in our society are characterized as emanating from the family and the lack of family values promulgated. Today I wish to argue that the root cause of our problem is not the family (although it will become involved in the chain of events) but rather the major institutional structures that impinge upon the family. The values embedded in these external institutions have changed over time and their influence on the family has been considerable. Instead of blaming the "victim", lets look at how some of today's institutional structures have influenced the family as we know it today.

Economic Todays income distribution shows that it is becoming more and more skewed (See Figure 3.3).   Additional data show that a greater concentration of wealth is increasing each year. As a result, greater wealth and power is being wielded by fewer and fewer people. Generational income disparities are also widening. Older people now have considerable wealth and continue to extract wealth from the poor, while young people and other working people do not have adequate incomes to maintain a quality of life beyond that of poverty. Yet we over tax the young and working and not the aged. Statistics Canada shows that one in three families (headed by someone under 25) has an income that can be defined as below the poverty level.[4] In contrast, for those aged 70+, only three percent are below the poverty level (about $18K). Twenty-three percent of working age singles are below poverty level. How are we to expect these individuals to operationalize "family and civic values" when parents and children are faced with a life of poverty and inability to expect or achieve social mobility.[5] While social mobility may have been an expectation of past generations, given hard work, education and dedication, it is clear that these values are no longer applicable in today's high technology, user pay, downsizing economy. Finally, my own research shows that young people do not see business leaders representing positive role models. A new "greed" ethic is perceived by young people as the *modus operandi* for many business leaders today.

Voluntary associations are now being asked to contribute to the tax base of our municipal government. They are being viewed as economic entities even though they have no extrinsic production process. Instead of promoting voluntary associations (as supporting the family and our civic society), we are punishing them (and the people who volunteer) for engaging in activities which would support the family and contribute to the development of a civil society. In the end, we are far more likely to support the production of technological gadgets than we are to support the social and psychological needs of families and their children.

Bureaucracy We are enveloped and constrained by the numerous bureaucracies that touch our lives every day. These structures have lost touch with everyday working people. Bureaucrats' concern is solely with enforcing the rules, whatever they may be. They are no longer concerned with helping individuals but rather in minimizing conflict in their working lives. They receive a paycheck every month, no matter what they do to the people they serve and who pay their salary. Their ability to solve problems (or even want to) is at an all time low. Taking responsibility is lacking, and placing blame is a major activity which draws focus away from them.

Political structure Support for families and structures which are in immediate contact with families are not strengthened by the actions of government policy or programs. In an era in which all agree that the youth are the strength of tomorrow, one should ask how well we are treating our future leaders. Have social, economic, health and educational programs, all vital ingredients to a vibrant and innovative youth, been supported in the past decade? What programs have been put in place which support the family's socialization role? How have our political leaders contributed to the role parents play in promoting healthy values?

Justice/law enforcement The role of law enforcement used to be the establishment of justice and the rehabilitation of the offender. Today the major goal of law seems to be the extraction of money from the offender and revenge. There is little consideration to rehabilitate or otherwise deal with norm breakers in our society. Moreover, the number of police, lawyers and judges who are leaving their profession because of both legal and ethical violations are indicative of the lack of commitment these individuals have to bringing justice and rehabilitation to a community. The fact that Canada has one of the highest arrest rates and the highest rate of incarceration in the developed world suggests that law enforcement officials are following the model of their bureaucratic brethren. For example, the fact that the total dollar intake by the city of Calgary for speeding offenses continues to increase suggests that the use of the multa-nova as a norm enforcer or educational force is a failure. However, faced with loosing a cash cow and not wishing to engage in long term, difficult issues of education and rehabilitation, law enforcement agencies are moving to more intrusive measures utilizing more complex technology.

We are exchanging our *rights* for *security* and this is a dangerous trend as Jean Elshtain (1996) has noted in her seminal presentation on "Marriage in Civil Society". We are still a nation looking for a quick fix and unable or unwilling to fix the underlying structures upon which a just and moral society are based and in which the family is a pivotal actor!

External institutional consequences

As a result of the influence of these external structures, and the values they espouse, the family has changed in both structure and ideology. There is a weakening of the normative consensus that marriage and childcaring are integral parts of the adult role. Children are viewed as a means through which adults can receive affective gratification and blossom as individuals. Many have concluded that children can interfere with this affective individualism. Children are viewed as liabilities, not assets. The achievement of economic consumerism is interfered with by the existence of children. Mass media, through advertising promotes this value unrelenting.

People no longer see marriage in traditional terms, based on established roles, expectations and mutual obligations, where the continuation of the relationship is not dependent on the maintenance of the love that was initially experienced. The majority feel that a continuation of strong emotional exchanges is essential to the marriage. Continued personal fulfillment is essential and therefore they do not make a definite commitment to a given partner.

People have become less interested in living up to external norms and more interested in living up to what they themselves want (Beaujot, 1990). There is a rising importance of self gratification in relationships. As Beaujot (1990) points out, people are more likely to be committed to their relationships only to the extent that these remain gratifying.

Older individuals are of the "dutiful" generation, committed to sacrificing themselves for groups beyond themselves while their children are a "me" generation with high expectations of success and personal gratification. For example, marriage is no longer based upon commitment but on contractual arrangements which have clearly defined boundaries which allow the disputants to claim contractual violations. An example of this is taken from a popular magazine directed at young women 13-18 years of age called *Self Confidence*. One of the recent feature articles focused on "prenuptial agreements". It stated,

> At its heart, marriage is a partnership. As with any partnership, it is important to work out in advance your rights and responsibilities. If you can't, you should think twice about tying the knot.

One major, all encompassing consequence of unsupportive institutional structures has been the development of an alienated family.[6] Alienation is a state of being which reflects an individual-environment relationship.[7] Alienation has emerged not from a lack of freedom but an overdose of "freedom" or rather unmanageable environmental complexity but from a lack of institutional organizations supporting the activities of the family. Families are confronted, on a daily basis, with a bewildering and complex environment with little external support, which promotes attitudes of apathy and withdrawal from a wider social involvement.[8]

Conclusion

There seems to be broad agreement that what a child experiences in his or her environment is important, yet there is much that we don't know about the specifics or pathways of how environment affect child development. Isn't this something of importance that we need to research? Finally, it should be noted that research on social issues are small compared to the support afforded technological issues. In more concrete terms, for every $100,000 invested in technology research, $1 is invested in social research.

For example, let me correct a myth that is being perpetuated today. Single parent families are not the major source of "problem" children. A majority of at-risk children come from two parent families. Most children with difficulties did not come from single mother families. Thus, programs aimed at helping children with emotional and behavioral problems and social and academic difficulties must be aimed at children from all types of families.

Another example reveals that seventeen percent of children in two parent and 68% of children in one parent families are living in poverty. We also know that household income and parents' educational levels have a significant impact on school readiness and school performance which in turn will effect the life chances and quality of live of these children as they grow up. The long term consequences of such conditions should concern all of us. Isn't it important that policy makers have accurate, current information about the family, its role and impact in society? Wouldn't we want to have enough information to ensure that the next generation will have the opportunity to succeed?

Children sit at the center of overlapping social, economic, cultural and spiritual environments. The task facing families, communities and society at large is to create environments that assist children in confronting their difficulties and in fostering their strengths and capabilities. All of us can play a role in creating the nurturing childhood environment that is critical to an individual's future health and well being. At the societal level, governments set the context within which families raise children. The distribution of income, taxation, and the allocation of community resources are obviously three of the most important influences on the healthy development of children. It is within this environment that families must make choices. Parents make choices about how they care for and nurture their children. All these factors set children on their life courses, at some point during which they begin to make life decisions on their own behalf.

A single pronged approach, focused solely on the family, is doomed to failure. We need to take a multifaceted approach and establish an early warning, rapid response and action plan to support the family. The link between information and action needs to be formalized and strategies to build a more supportive environment for the family within a civil society must begin today. These are only possible if we have a solid social research base upon which to make both policy and program decisions. We need to agree that young people are the guardians of our society as we get old. We need to provide them with the best skills possible if they are to effectively and efficiently continue to work in our society. It is in the best interest of society, and in our best interests to have a young population which is educated, liberated and humanitarian.

Figure 2.1   Population distribution of Canada, 1900-2000, by age

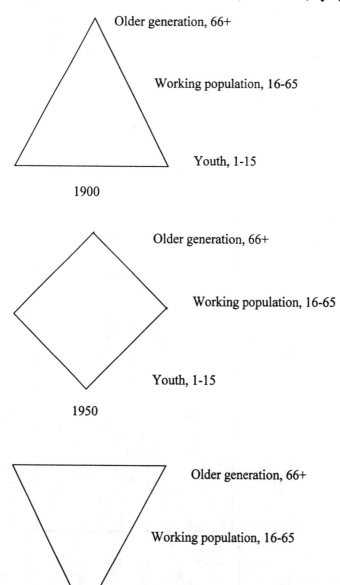

Figure 2.2   Socialization process

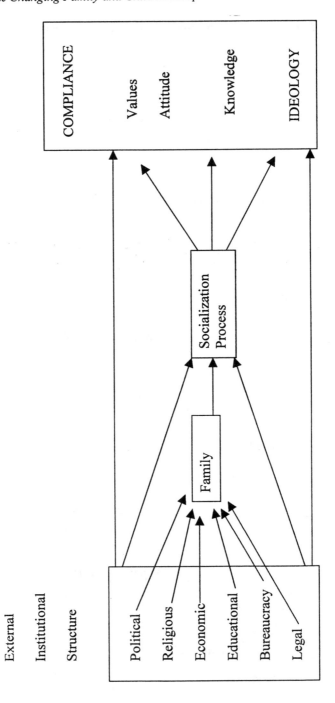

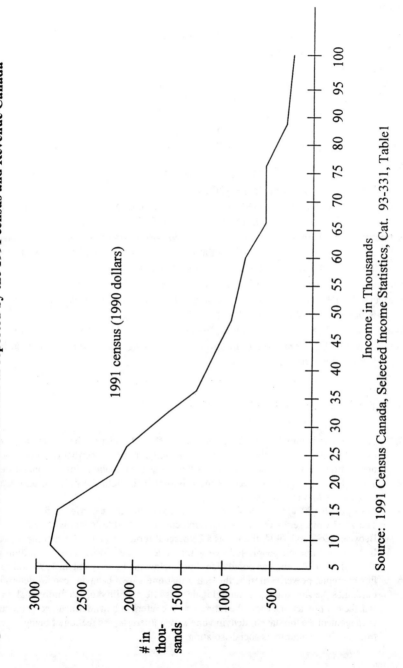

Figure 2.3 **Total 1990 individual income as reported by the 1991 census and Revenue Canada**

1991 census (1990 dollars)

in thou-sands

Income in Thousands

Source: 1991 Census Canada, Selected Income Statistics, Cat. 93-331, Table1

References

Beaujot, R. (1990). The Family and Demographic Change in Canada: Economic and Cultural Interpretations and Solutions. *Journal of Comparative Family Studies*, *21*, 87-112.

Bibby, R. and D. Posterski (1992). *Teen Trends: A Nation in Motion*. Toronto, Stoddart. Canada, Government of (1997). *Applied Research Bulletin*. Ottawa: Human Resources Development Canada, 3, 1.

Elshtain, J. (1996). Marriage in Civil Society. *Family Affairs*, 7, 1-5.

Geyer, F. (Ed) (1996). *Alienation, Ethnicity, and Postmodernism*. London: Greenwood Press.

Glick, P. and R. Parke (1977). New Approaches in Studying the Life Cycle of the Family. *Demography*, 2, 187-202.

Rodgers, R. and G. Witney (1981). The Family Cycle in Twentieth Century Canada. *Journal of Marriage and the Family*, 43,727-740.

Romaniuc, A. (1994). *Fertility in Canada: Retrospective and Prospective.* In Perspectives on Canada's Population, by F. Travato and C. Grindstaff (Eds), Toronto, Oxford University Press, pp. 214-230.

Rubiner, B. (1996). The Family Beat, 1987-1996. *Family Affairs*, 7, 15-17.

Veevers, J. (1991). *Continuity and Change in Marriage and Family*. Toronto: Holt, Rinehart and Winston of Canada, ltd.

Warme, B., E. Malus and K. Lundy (1994). *Sociology*. Toronto: Nelson Canada.

Wilson, R. (1992). *Compliance Ideologies: Rethinking Political Culture*. Cambridge: Cambridge University Press.

Notes

1   This is not to ignore that the family may have affected society. The relationship between the institution of the family and other societal structures is somewhat reciprocal although one institution will not have as much influence as the remaining institutional order.

2   The role of the aged has become more important in both the political and economic dimensions of our society.

3   Most people (70%) who get divorced, on the average, get remarried in four years.

4   The 1997 value set by the federal government is $31,000 for a family of four.

5   Between 1993 and 1994, there was a 25 percent turnover in the low income population. In 1994, 1.2 million people fell below the poverty line. More than 4.4 million people (16% of the total Canadian population) lived below the poverty line in 1993 and/or 1994.

6   For example, powerlessness is the belief that one's own behavior cannot determine the outcomes he/she wants; meaninglessness is the inability of an individual to make satisfactory predictions about the future; anomie refers to bewilderment; self and cultural-estrangement are the state of denying one's own interests; the feeling of being segregated from one's community is social-isolation.

7 Alienation is an umbrella concept, pulling together several different, but related dimensions such as powerlessness, meaninglessness, normlessness (anomie), social isolation, self estrangement and cultural estrangement (Geyer, 1996).

8 To be adapted to a modern complex society, we need to engage in metalearning: learn to unlearn under conditions of environmental change. Thus far families have had no support in developing this capacity.

3 Adolescentology: Youth, Their Needs, and the Professions at the Turn of the Century

LEROY D. TRAVIS

Abstract

A review of central features of our world as it is experienced by youth at the end of the 20th century leads to three conclusions: (1) that the prospects for the great mass of contemporary adolescents are grim; (2) that the professions that serve the well-being of youth face challenges that are beyond their capacity to deal with in isolation from one another; and (3) that the emergent multi-profession endeavor called adolescentology is one promising adaptation to the situation.

Introduction

This paper focuses on the experience and needs of youth in the conditions that exist as the twentieth century comes to an end. It also addresses the problems of the professions that have responsibilities to serve youth in a context that has been radically changed by the emergence of the so-called global economy. An argument is developed which begins with the premise that the prospects for most of today's youth are grim. They are grim because the conditions which have emerged entail a serious diminution of the security of family life and the economic conditions which affect the same; a diminution of career and employment opportunities which affect the making of choices, plans and commitments for developing a viable adult identity; and an increase in cultural confusion about the purposes and character of the schooling, education, and knowledge which adolescents need to understand themselves, the world, and their possibilities within the world (Travis, 1995; 1994).

Implicit to the argument is the idea that, to thrive, humans in general, and adolescents in particular, need to have the sense that life can be made to seem meaningful. Such meaning depends on the experience of adequate love, rewarding work, and non-trivial or significant knowledge.

In the conditions that have emerged during the final quarter of the twentieth century, love, work, and knowledge, as these are experienced by adolescents, have taken a severe drubbing as families, employment and schools have been battered by forces that care little for such things. These forces were let loose and unfettered when those hostile to government gained direct control of governments in the major liberal states. These developments constitute a new reality for the professions which serve youth. We need to consider how we can adapt to meet the new reality of changed economic life, schooling and experience of home and family.

Family attachments and the roots of care

The cohesion and interpersonal relations of families have been affected adversely by forces that have reduced the time a great many parents devote to tending home affairs and to interacting with their children. This diversion of parental energies and attention can have important consequences (Hacker, 1997). Consider the following realms that suffer.

The protracted experience of loving care (over much time and widely varying situations) seems to be important in the development of a child's ideals, standards, conscience and capacity for self-control and self-direction. In addition, a child's chances of gaining maximum benefits from schooling are also affected adversely when parents don't make a habit of reading to their young children. Moreover, our youngsters' preparations for and interest in exploring the wealth of human experience that posterity has bequeathed us, are diminished when parents don't engage them regularly in conversations about ideas, feelings and possibilities that arise from human experience.

Add to these considerations, the development of children's capacity to feel affection and empathy for others; when parents are not a reliable and vivid presence in the lives of their children, the emotional and social development of such children is adversely affected. Experience with past attachments, or lack thereof, affects our orientations to and expectations of future attachments. Many works (Ainsworth, 1982; Bowlby, 1987; van den Haag, 1963) indicate that the etiology of the affectionless character, abusive personalities and psychopaths point to these matters. The common background to certain profiles drift among those with severe identity problems, also underscores the importance of protracted, secure provision of parental love in cohesive family life. Yet family fractures of both the daily and the permanent varieties multiply as, more and more, economic and other forces separate family members from one another or reduce the quality and span of contacts to a level that jeopardizes personal and social prospects (Rutter, 1996).

Work, money, identity and the ways of the world

As with love, work too has come upon hard times. For many, work is more and more difficult to secure and retain. Moreover, work is not only more difficult to find now, it is also less well-paid, less likely to be satisfying, and less reliable as a source of economic security (Jordan, 1989; Mintzberg, 1996; Soros, 1997; *World Economic Affairs*, 1996). This makes the adolescents' task of making choices, plans, and commitments to prepare for a vocation or career much more difficult (Steinberg, 1993; Travis, 1994; 1997).

Since this task of sorting out one's orientation to work and vocation is a central task in the reformation of identity during adolescence, the problem of identity has been made more difficult in the past two decades (Steinberg, 1993).

Knowledge and schooling

The acquisition and contemplation of non-trivial knowledge, another major source of meaning in life, has also been affected adversely by developments in the latter decades of the 20th century. For many, schooling has come to reflect a concern with many projects other than that of helping youngsters make themselves less ignorant, or more informed and caring about the world and all in it (Bloom 1987; Lasch 1995).

Where once schools provided encouragement of the outward gaze as the principal beacon for curiosity, and where once knowledge content formed the grounds upon which it was supposed claims to understanding had to be made, we now see more and more interest being directed to the subjective or psychological state of those kept in the custody of "facilitators" (people some of us still call teachers). Since processes are widely assumed to have more importance than content much of the time, the importance of knowledge and the disciplined pursuit of it has been discounted more and more (Travis, 1994).

Amusement values too, have come to be preferred by many over the values of work and understanding. This also undermines the third source of meaning: for now knowledge, has been reduced in its standing at school; and so it joins love and work as casualties of the developments of the late twentieth century. Nowadays, the ethos of the entertainment world dominates what students of communications call the information environment (Denby, 1996; Postman, 1986). Both pupils and teachers (as well as parents - and all others) live in that environment. Like the atmosphere we breathe, the information environment surrounds us and invades us wherever we go. So it is not surprising that as public discourse of all kinds is transformed by the prominence and dominance of amusement or entertainment argot, images, values, and priorities, educational exercises and discourse become increasingly, manifestations of commitments to amusement (Postman, 1986).

If this development on its own, was not sufficiently subversive to genuine education to raise serious concern, its conjunction with forces that amplify the custodial impulse in schooling must surely give us cause for alarm. Few doubt that popular schooling was ever an exercise in the service of one and only one purpose. State-funded schools have always been custodial as well as educational instruments. The practices and values and commitments that best serve to retain youngsters (in custody) are frequently, and perhaps inherently, in conflict with or run at cross purposes with, those that best serve the education of youngsters (Cote and Alahar, 1994; Denby, 1996; Douglas, 1993).

So when parents are spending more time chasing income (and other goals), their need for proxies or child-tenders increases; and when paid work becomes more difficult to find, the apparatus of the state has more reason to press schools to retain youth in schools (that is, minimize drop-outs) so unemployment and public disorder are not inflated by youth at-large. Since youth taxed by work is harder to retain than youth entertained, school people are supplied with a plethora of fine sounding projects, objectives and curricular fiddles to play away the days (Hughes, 1993; Postman, 1986).

The costs of replacing the pursuit of disciplined knowledge and refinement with exercises in consumer satisfaction and ego boosting are evident in the lamentable state of literacy; in the inexorable spread of tastelessness; in the coarsening of public speech and behavior; and in civic decay, political incompetence, and the epidemic of economic superstition that signals a deep and widespread incomprehension of what constitutes a civilized way of life (Denby, 1996; Lasch, 1995; Mintzberg, 1996; Saul, 1995; Schmidt, 1995; Selbourne, 1994; Soros, 1997).

In sum, the convergence of these (and some other) forces has downgraded the place of knowledge and its pursuit in schooling during the last years of the twentieth century. So the list of casualties of our time include three major sources of meaning: love, work, and knowledge. We who understand the significance of this state of affairs need to realize how this situation affects our capacity to serve the well-being of our youth (Cable, 1995; Cole & Cole, 1993).

The professions, specialization and the new reality

The effects of these developments are profound for not only adolescents, but for those whose professional commitments are to serve the well-being, education, and prospects of youth.

The conventional practices of professionals as they evolved in the passing century, have tended to focus on one or another aspect of an individual's life. Specialism has been an assumed highway to advantage for both the server and the served (Cassidy, 1995; Collins, 1979).

Few would dispute that specialists did confer advantages on individuals and society at large - even if the increasing enthusiasm for the credentials that licensed and institutionalized specialists as experts was not a singular or unmixed blessing (e.g., Collins 1979). The burgeoning of professional services was part of the pursuit of "progress" (Lasch, 1991). But progress of this sort was bought at the price of breadth and fullness of understanding. For the specialist's depth can only be gained by a sacrifice of breadth. And breadth is required to grasp the fullness and complexity of a person's life and situation. No technical specialty can grasp all that counts in the ledgers of pain or suffering and anguish (Collins, 1979; Howard, 1994; Vacca, 1974; van den Haag, 1963). No single profession takes in all that accounts for all deficits of meaning and love and security.

A body's chemistry is embedded in a particular social reality; physiology carries on in public. Anatomy has both cultural and personal, as well as biological or medical meanings. Pimples erupt in real civic circumstances. Economic threats speak to a biological substate that may or may not be of a tolerant temperament. So while the practitioner of adolescent medicine bases the foundation of his understanding on the sciences of genes, biochemical substances and so forth, he must also notice what such sciences don't address or consider because there is more to a life than biology and chemistry. Even so, given his educational and professional preparation and involvement the picture that is seen always puts the bio-chemical reality in the foreground. Thus, each case is dealt with as it is met.

Psychologists also have a place of privilege reserved for the matters they take to be most interesting. The subjective realm is rarely in the background of their picture of reality. While they too cannot help but acknowledge the existence and importance of the civic, economic, familial and biological forces, the subjective life is placed in the foreground by their involvement and professional concerns.

Educators, like psychologists and physicians, also have their professional preoccupation and fundamental epistemological presuppositions. They don't see the same realities as do other professionals and specialists even as they look upon the same human beings who occupy a common information environment.

Perhaps all of the major professions that take the well-being of the young as their principal professional concern have important observations and ideas to share with one another. How each profession discerns what the common environment and the emergent global order portend for the well-being of contemporary adolescents and its capacity to serve such well-being may be of great significance to the other professions in the circumstances we now face. Consider the case of the information environment.

Nowadays, billions of dollars are invested in the farming of adolescent anxieties: teenagers' fears that their real or imagined flaws and blemishes will, on discovery, bring on the menaces of rejection, failure, humiliation, or disgrace are presently cultivated with great and unprecedented efficiency by the commercial culture. For in the standard fare of commercial culture, the parables of deliverance (from the Menaces) promote the harvest of such cash as youngsters will invest in maneuvers to prevent the detection of real or imagined departures from unattainable standards of physical allure, social acceptance, economic success and so forth (e.g., see Denby, 1996; Poulton, 1996).

Since such cash crops grow best in the acidic soils of secret fears, and the magic coin that buys deliverance is for most, dependent on the securing of work, youngsters are frequently distracted from educational and social pursuits by the chasing of money from part-time employment. The results of this conventional pattern are not pretty (Steinberg, 1993; Travis, 1997).

Now one's ignorance or sense of incomprehension, and one's loneliness or sense of rejection or disconnection, are as personal and individual as one's face or one's health. Each of these departments of experience affects the others. But the educator, psychologist, physician or social worker focuses on the variables favored by the specialties they represent. So each profession's reality differs with regard to the same human object.

In the past, this state of affairs may not have had many unfortunate consequences - although professional blinders no doubt have been the source of too many unnecessary tales of woe. However, given the simultaneous appearance of an unprecedented scale of family fractures and personal bankruptcies; and given the chronic high unemployment that has accompanied de-industrialization, deregulation, downsizing, dislocations, cultural confusion and debasement of national sovereignty and power, the professions in the modern liberal states face a serious crisis (Jordon, 1989; Selbourne, 1994).

In effect, the economic decline and emasculation of the state has engendered widespread anxiety and pessimism about economic security and future prospects (Cable, 1995; Cassidy, 1995; *The Economist*, 1995). Such economic insecurity and the scale of troubles faced by a massive proportion of the population may produce far more than we can handle given our customary professional habits. Moreover, there are few signs that these matters will soon improve (Reid, 1996; Soros, 1997). It seems likely that the prevalence of difficulties will tax the professions with such high incidences of troubles, we will not meet the challenge unless we collaborate and forge joint endeavors.

Adolescentology: Rational response to globalization effects

Adolescentology, is such a joint endeavor. The new global economy has created new national and local life situations. Just as national and local economic entities have been forced to reorient themselves, so too do the professions. They too will have to learn how to "think globally and act locally". While adolescentology is a relatively new and emergent multi-profession response to the impact of the contemporary world on the well-being of adolescents, it expresses a recognition of the importance of both the general or common and the particular or individual.

As members of the liberal professions we recognize the dignity and liberty of individuals is realized in or restricted by the particulars of national, cultural, and local contexts wherein they live. As students of the human condition and observers of the contemporary world we recognize that humans share a common lot and that impersonal and distal forces can be indifferent to the particulars of national, cultural or local preferences.

So both national and local particulars have to be recognized and reflected in national societies and local chapters of adolescentology, just as is so in the international organization. However, the recognition of common purposes, shared plight, and an informed vision of the contemporary world that calls for the multi-discipline and international collaborative forums and work, must not downgrade the sense of life at the local and national levels.

While particular cultural, socio-economic, and historical givens are recognized, so too is the common fact of trans-national instruments of economic and political power that, more and more, shape local horizons. So professionals who share in the adolescentology project take account of both; and they collaborate and cooperate in the interest of the well-being of both local youth and the world's young people.   Adolescentology recognizes that local particulars are nowadays, variants of a shared global reality.

References

Ainsworth, M. (1982). Attachment: Retrospect & Prospect. In C. Parkes & J. Stevenson- Hinde (Eds.) *The Place of Attachment in Human Behavior.* New York: Basic Books.

Arendt, H. (1958). *The Human Condition.* Chicago: The University of Chicago Press.

Belsky, J., Fisk M., & Isabella, R. (1991). Continuity and discontinuity in infant negative and positive emotionality: Family antecedents and attachment consequences. *Developmental Psychology, 27,* 421-31.

Bloom, A. (1987). *The Closing of the American Mind.* New York: Simon & Schuster.

Bowlby, J. (1987). Attachment. In R. Gregory (Ed.). *The Oxford Companion to the Mind.* Oxford University Press, pp. 57-58.

Cable, V. (1995). The diminished nation-state: A study in the loss of economic power. *Daedalus, 124,* 23-54.

Cassidy, J. (1995). Who killed the middle class? *The New Yorker, 71,* 113-124.

Chasseguet-Smirgel, J. (1985). *The Ego Ideal: A Psychoanalytic Essay on the Malady of the Ideal.* New York: Norton.

Cole, M. & Cole, S. (1993). *The Development of Children* (2nd Ed). New York: Scientific American Books/W.H. Freeman.

Collins, R. (1979). *The Credential Society.* New York: Academic Press.

Cote, J. & Alahar, A. (1994). *Generation on Hold: Coming of Age in the Late Twentieth Century.* Toronto: Stoddart.

CSSE News. (1987). Illiteracy (May), p. 7.

de Grazia, S. (1964). *Of Time, Work, and Leisure.* Garden City, N.Y: Doubleday Anchor.

Denby, C. (1996). Annals of Popular Culture: Buried alive - our children and the avalanche of crud. *The New Yorker, 72,* 48-58.

Doi, T. (1981). *The Anatomy of Dependence.* Tokyo: Kodansha International/Harper & Row (Translated by J. Bester).

Douglas, K. (1993). Playtime for postgrads. *New Scientist, 140,* 36-40.

The Economist. (1995). The disappearing family, *336,* 19-20.

The Economist. (1995). The family: Home sweet home, *336,* 25-29.

Freud, S. (1963). *General Psychological Theory.* New York: Collier Macmillan.

Freud, S. (1962/1923). *The Ego and the Id* (Translated by Joan Riviere). New York: Norton.

Freud, S. (1961/1930). *Civilization and its Discontents* (Translated by J. Strachey). New York: Norton.

Freud, S. (1959/1922). *Group Psychology and the Analysis of the Ego* (Translated by J. Strachey). New York: Norton.

Frye, N. (1963). *The Educated Imagination*. Toronto: CBC.

Gregory, R. (Ed.)(1987). *The Oxford Companion to the Mind*. Oxford: Oxford University Press.

Hacker, A. (1997). The war over the family. *The New York Review of Books, 44*, 34-38.

Hare, R. (1993). *Without Conscience*. New York: Simon & Schuster.

Heilbroner, R. (1992). *Twenty-first Century Capitalism* (The 1992 Massey Lectures). Concord, ON: Anansi.

Henighan, T. (1996). *The Presumption of Culture: Structure, Strategy & Survival in the Canadian Cultural Landscape*. Raincoast.

Howard, P. (1994). *The Death of Common Sense*. New York: Random House.

Hughes, R. (1993). *Culture of Complaint*. Oxford: Oxford University Press.

Jones, B. (1982). *Sleepers Wake! Technology & the Future of Work.* Brighton, UK: Wheatsheaf Books.

Jordan, B. (1989). *The Common Good: Citizenship, Morality and Self-Interest*. Oxford: Basil Blackwell.

Lasch, C. (1995). *The Revolt of the Elites and the Betrayal of Democracy.* New York: Norton.

Lasch, C. (1991). *The True and Only Heaven: Progress and its Critics*. New York: W.W. Norton.

Mintzberg, H. (1996). The myth of "Society Inc." *Report on Business Magazine, 11*, 3 -117.

Palladino, G. (1996). *Teenagers*. New York: Basic Books.

Postman, N. (1993). *Technopoly: The Surrender of Culture to Technology*. New York: Vintage.

Postman, N. (1986). *Amusing Ourselves to Death: Public Discourse in the Age of Show Business*. New York: Penguin.

Poulton, T. (1996). *No Fat Chicks: How Women are Brainwashed to Hate Their Bodies and Spend Their Money.* Toronto: Key Porter.

Reid, A. (1996). *Shakedown: How the New Economy is Changing Our Lives*. Toronto: Doubleday.

Rieff, P. (1968). *The Triumph of the Therapeutic*. New York: Harper Torchbooks.

Rieff, P. (1963). "Introduction" . In S. Freud, *General Psychological Theory*. New York: Collier Macmillan, pp. 7-20.

Rutter, M. (1996). Psychosocial Adversity: Risk, Resiliance & Recovery. In L. Verhofstadt-Deneve, et al (Eds.). *Conflict and Development in Adolescence*. Leiden, NL: DSWO Press: Leiden University, pp. 21-33.

Sampson, R. & Lamb, J. (1994). Urban poverty and the family context of delinquency: A new look at structure and process in a classic study. *Child Development, 65*, 523-540.

Saul, J. (1995). *The Unconscious Civilization* (The 1995 Massey Lectures). Concord, ON: Anansi.

Schmidt, V. (1995). The new world order incorporated: The rise of business and the decline of the nation state. *Daedalus, 124*, 75-106.

Selbourne, D. (1994). *The Principle of Duty: An Essay on the Foundations of the Civic Order*. London: Sinclair-Stevenson.

Soros, G. (1997). The capitalist threat. *The Atlantic Monthly, 279*, 45-48, 50-55, 58.

Steinberg, L. (1993). *Adolescence* (3rd Ed.). New York: McGraw-Hill.

Travis, L. (1997). *Youth, Work & Identity* (Lecture Series). Vancouver: University of British Columbia. adolescence. *Medicine and Mind, 9*, 5-38.

Travis, L. (1995). Adolescent psyches in contexts and contexts in psyches. *Medicine and Mind, 10*, 17-33.

Travis, L. (1994). Adolescent experience reconceptualized: Lacunae, imagination and the mental provinces. *Lecture Series*, Abrosiana University, Milan.

Vacca, R. (1974). *The Coming Dark Age*. New York: Doubleday Anchor.

van den Haag, E. (1963). *Passion and Social Constraint*. New York: Delta/Dell.

Verhofstdt-Deneve, L., Kienhorst, I., & Braet, C. (Eds.) (1996). *Conflict and Development in Adolescence*. Leiden NL: DSWO Press/Leiden University.

Winter, J. (1996). Democracy's Oxygen: How Corporations Control the News. Black Rose. *World Economic Affairs, 1*.

4   A Meta-Analysis of the Published Research on the Effects of Pornography

ELIZABETH ODDONE-PAOLUCCI, MARK GENUIS, AND CLAUDIO VIOLATO

Abstract

A meta-analysis of 46 published studies was undertaken to determine the effects of pornography on sexual deviancy, sexual perpetration, attitudes regarding intimate relationships, and attitudes regarding the rape myth. Most of the studies were done in the United States (39; 85%) and ranged in date from 1962 to 1995, with 35% (n=16) published between 1990 and 1995, and 33% (n=15) between 1978 and 1983. A total sample size of 12,323 people comprised the present meta-analysis. Effect sizes ($\underline{d}$) were computed on each of the dependent variables for studies which were published in an academic journal, had a total sample size of 12 or greater, and included a contrast or comparison group. Average unweighted and weighted $\underline{d}$'s for sexual deviancy (.68 and .65), sexual perpetration (.67 and .46), intimate relationships (.83 and .40), and the rape myth (.74 and .64) provide clear evidence confirming the link between increased risk for negative development when exposed to pornography. These results suggest that the research in this area can move beyond the question of whether pornography has an influence on violence and family functioning.

Various potentially moderating variables such as gender, socioeconomic status (SES), number of incidents of exposure, relationship of person who introduced pornography to the participant, degree of explicitness, subject of pornography, pornographic medium, and definition of pornography were assessed for each of the studies. The results are discussed in terms of the quality of the pornography research available and the subsequent limitations inherent in the present meta-analysis.

A meta-analysis of the published research on the effects of pornography

The issue of exposure to pornography has received a great deal of attention over the years. An overwhelming majority of adults in our society, both men and women, report having been exposed to very explicit sexual materials. In fact, Wilson and Abelson (1973) found that 84% of men and 69% of women reported exposure to one or more of pictorial or textual modes of pornography, with the majority of the group first being exposed to explicit materials before the age of 21 years. Coupled with more opportunities for people to access materials via a greater variety of media (e.g., magazines, television, video, world wide web), it is becoming increasingly important to investigate whether exposure to pornography has an effect on human behaviour. While the list of psychological sequelae that researchers have shown to be statistically common in persons exposed to pornography is immense, controversy and doubt are prevalent. Though the ongoing academic debate has relevant and significant socio-political implications, it is apparent that the issue of pornography has frequently been approached from a philosophical and moral stance rather than an empirical position.

The present meta-analytic investigation attempts to redirect the focus of the question of pornography's potential effects to an empirical platform. The aim is to determine whether exposure to pornographic stimuli over the lifespan has any effect on sexual deviancy, sexual offending, intimate relationships, and attitudes regarding the rape myth. The results are expected to provide information which may assist families, educators, mental health professionals, and social policy directors in making decisions consistent with promoting human health and social growth.

Method

Operational definitions

Pornography is defined as any commercial product in the form of fictional drama designed to elicit or enhance sexual arousal (Mosher, 1988). Three specific forms of pornography were examined. Mild pornography consists of stimuli of nudes, persons engaging in petting, and nonviolent acts of sexual intercourse without genitalia visible; erotica or explicit pornography involves stimuli portraying consensual nonviolent sexual acts with genitalia visible; and violent pornography includes depictions of rape, degradation, sexual aggression, or sadism. Four outcome variables of *sexual deviancy* (i.e., non-normative sexual behaviours such as early age of first intercourse, excessive or ritualistic masturbation), *sexual perpetration* (i.e., aggressive, sexually hostile, and violent behaviours), attitudes regarding *intimate relationships* (i.e., perceptions of dominance, submission, courtship, sex role stereotyping, or viewing persons as sexual objects), and belief in the *rape myth* (i.e., women cause rape, should resist or prevent it, and rapists are normal) were coded for effect sizes. An effect size refers to the strength of a relationship or an estimate of the degree to which a phenomenon is present in a population (Vogt, 1993).

Sample of studies

A total of 46 empirical investigations were included. The studies selected consisted of published literature ranging from 1962 to 1995. A computer-based literature search of PsychLIT, Educational Resources Information Center (ERIC) documents, and SOCIOFILE was conducted using *pornog**, *data*, and *empirical* as the keywords.

Variables examined and planned analyses

Cohen's $\underline{d}$ was utilized for all of the effect size calculations. Nine potential moderators (i.e., age of exposure, gender of user, SES of user, number of exposure incidents, relation of person who introduced pornography to subject, degree of explicitness, subject, medium, and definition of pornography) were examined.

Results

The 46 research studies included a total of 12,323 persons (sample sizes ranged from 29 to 1,393), and 85% (n=39) were conducted in the United States versus 11% (n=5) conducted in Canada. Though studies from Denmark tend to be cited to support the contention that availability of pornography is related to lower rates of sexual offending, those located by the researchers did not meet the criteria for inclusion for the present meta-analysis. For example, in Kutchinsky's (1973) study, a comparison or contrast group was not included. Table 4.1 presents the average unweighted, weighted, and weighted corrected $\underline{d}$'s which were computed for each of the dependent variables, along with their corresponding 95% confidence intervals. A positive $\underline{d}$ indicates exposure to pornography had negative outcomes, while a negative $\underline{d}$ indicates positive consequences in relation to sexual deviancy, sexual perpetration, intimate relationships, and rape myth outcomes. As can be noted, no negative $\underline{d}$'s emerged in the current meta-analysis, thereby indicating the consistent negative effect of exposure to pornography in each of these four areas.

Corresponding raw counts and percentages in the form of a Binomial Effect Size Display (BESD) are also shown. This display demonstrates the practical importance of any effect indexed by a correlation coefficient (Rosenthal, 1994, 1995). The correlation ($\underline{r}$) refers to the difference in outcome rates between the experimental and control groups, whereby the column and row totals always sum to 100. In the analysis of sexual deviancy, correlations were computed for the average $\underline{d}$ ($\underline{r}$ =.32), average weighted $\underline{d}$ ($\underline{r}$ =.31), and average weighted corrected $\underline{d}$ ($\underline{r}$ =.37). The results indicate that there is a 32, 31, and 37 percent respective increase over the baseline in sexual deviancy outcome for persons reporting exposure to pornography. Similarly, in the analysis of sexual perpetration, correlations were computed for the average $\underline{d}$ ($\underline{r}$ =.32) and average weighted $\underline{d}$ ($\underline{r}$ =.22), indicating a 32 and 22 percent respective increase in sexual perpetration. For negative intimate relationships, correlations were computed for the average $\underline{d}$ ($\underline{r}$ =.39), average weighted $\underline{d}$ ($\underline{r}$ =.20), and average weighted corrected $\underline{d}$ ($\underline{r}$=.24), revealing a 39, 20, and 24 percent respective increase in negative intimate relationships. Finally, in the analysis of attitudes toward the rape myth, correlations were computed for the average $\underline{d}$ ($\underline{r}$ =.35) and average weighted $\underline{d}$ ($\underline{r}$ =.31), indicating a 35 and 31 percent respective increase in believing in the rape myth for persons exposed to pornographic materials. Thus, it appears that the magnitude of the effect of pornography on each of the four outcomes examined is large.

An estimate of the Fail Safe N was computed to determine the number of studies required to refute the present findings. Forty-six studies would be required to refute the results for sexual deviancy, 142 for sexual perpetration, 49 for intimate relationships, and 47 to contradict the rape myth findings. Overall, 284 unreported studies averaging a null result would be required before the present meta-analytic findings could be reasonably ascribed to sampling bias. Accordingly, the results of the meta-analysis are stable and generalizable.

Analysis of mediating variables

A number of mediating variables were analyzed individually using univariate analyses, in order to examine the possibility of mediating influences of specific variables on pornography outcome or effect size. Of the total 108 analyses conducted, two moderators were found to be statistically significant: unweighted $\underline{d}$ of sexual deviancy and gender ($\underline{F}_{(1,3)}$ = 68.26, $\underline{p}$ = .004) and average weighted $\underline{d}$ of rape myth endorsement and definition of pornography ($\underline{F}$

$_{(1,3)}$ = 18.45, $\underline{p}$ = .023). Although there may be a gender difference on sexual deviancy outcome as a result of exposure to pornography, and people may be more likely to ascribe to the rape myth when exposed to one type of pornography over another (i.e., mild, erotica, violent), these results may well be a statistical artifact. As the total number of ANOVA's executed were large, the risk of Type I errors is increased substantially (i.e., the Bonferroni Inequality, .05 H 108 = 5.4; Violato & Russell, 1994). In 108 statistical tests when alpha is set at .05, then, it is probable that six of the tests will emerge significant by chance alone. It is, therefore, prudent to regard these two "significant" results as spurious. The most salient feature of the results summarized in Table 4.2, is that there are no generally significant effects of the variables on $\underline{d}$ across all four domains. Still, although none of these identified variables appear to mediate the effect of exposure to pornography on sexual deviancy, sexual perpetration, intimate relationships, and rape myth outcome, it is recommended that these findings be interpreted with caution. The nonsignificant results may be due more to the lack of information documented in the original studies than to the fact that the variables do not really moderate the relationship between pornography and the specific outcomes examined.

Discussion

Consistent with previous meta-analyses (Allen, D'Alessio, & Brezgel, 1995) and single studies (Baron & Straus, 1987; Fisher & Barak, 1991; Garcia, 1986; Gray, 1982; Gunther, 1995; Hui, 1986; Lottes, Weinberg, & Weller, 1993), the results of the present meta-analysis suggest that exposure to pornography produces a variety of substantial negative outcomes. Using the social learning theory and imitation model, it may be argued that themes of aggression, impulse gratification, sexual flexibility and gymnastics, and objectification in pornography may reinforce and/or justify similar attitudes and behaviours in everyday human-life contacts. Persons viewing pornographic materials may believe that the way the characters perform sexually is a "normal" and appropriate portrayal of reality. Armed with these expectations, they may engage in activities which are not socially acceptable or even desirable at the individual level. While likely not a solitary influence, it appears that exposure to pornography is one important factor which contributes directly to the development of sexually dysfunctional attitudes and behaviours.

The results are clear and consistent; exposure to pornographic material puts one at increased risk for developing sexually deviant tendencies, committing sexual offenses, experiencing difficulties in one's intimate relationships, and accepting the rape myth. In order to promote a healthy and stable society, it is time that we attend to the culmination of sound empirical research.

Table 4.1   Pornography outcome measures and effect sizes

Outcome	# of Studies	Total N	Average Unweighted d	S.D.	C.I. (95%)	Average Weighted d	S.D.	C.I. (95%)	Average Weighted Corrected d	S.D.	C.I. (95%)
Sexual Deviancy	11	4,450	.68	.27	.41 to .95	.65	.03	.62 to .68	.80	.04	.72 to .87
Sexual Perpetration	34	3,760	.67	.56	.11 to 1.23	.46	.03	.42 to .49	N/A	N/A	N/A
Intimate Relations	9	2,170	.83	.76	.07 to 1.60	.40	.05	.36 to .45	.50	.05	.40 to .61
Rape Myth	10	1,943	.74	.87	-.13 to 1.62	.64	.05	.59 to .69	N/A	N/A	N/A

Outcome	File Drawer Analysis		BESD	Percent Increase
Sexual Deviancy	46.21	Average d = .32	66.01 / 33.98	32
		Av. Wghtd. d = .31	65.47 / 34.52	31
		Av.Wghtd.Corr. d = .37	68.47 / 31.52	37
Sexual Perpetration	141.o9	Average d = .32	65.91 / 34.08	32
		Av. Wghtd. d = .22	61.14 / 38.85	22
Intimate Relationships	48.81	Average d = .39	69.26 / 30.73	39
		Av. Wghtd. d = .20	59.85 / 40.14	20
		Av.Wghtd.Corr. d = .24	62.15 / 37.84	24
Rape Myth	47.14	Average d = .35	67.40 / 32.59	35
		Av. Wghtd. d = .31	65.27 / 34.72	31

*N/A results were obtained since it was not possible to correct for attenuation because reliabilities were not reported in the original studies.

Table 4.2   Potential effect of moderating variables on average unweighted d outcomes

Part A: Unweighted d

Outcome Variable	df	Sexual Deviancy F	p	Sexual Perpetration df	F	p	Intimate Relationships df	F	p	Rape Myth df	F	p
Age of Exposure	2, 8	.71	.52	1, 31	.63	.43	---	---	---	2, 7	.42	.68
Gender of Porno. User	2, 8	1.31	.32	2, 30	.31	.74	2, 6	1.46	.30	2, 7	.38	.70
# Exposures	1, 9	1.59	.24	2, 30	.33	.72	1, 7	.43	.53	1, 8	.51	.49
Degree of Explicitness	2, 8	.05	.95	2, 29	1.07	.36	---	---	---	1, 8	.04	.84
Pornographic Medium	2, 8	.05	.95	1, 31	.04	.85	---	---	---	---	---	---
Definition of Pornography	1, 8	.94	.36	2, 29	.13	.88	2, 5	.31	.75	2, 5	.20	.83

Part B: Weighted d

Outcome Variable	df	Sexual Deviancy F	p	Sexual Perpetration df	F	p	Intimate Relationships df	F	p	Rape Myth df	F	p
Age of Exposure	2, 8	.45	.65	1, 31	.75	.40	---	---	---	2, 7	.45	.65
Gender of Porno. User	2, 8	.13	.88	2, 30	.37	.70	2, 6	.22	.81	2, 7	.44	.66
# Exposures	1, 9	.98	.35	2, 30	3.12	.06	1, 7	.14	.72	1, 8	.66	.44
Degree of Explicitness	2, 8	.34	.72	2, 29	.94	.40	---	---	---	1, 8	1.05	.33
Pornographic Medium	2, 8	.47	.64	1, 31	.64	.43	---	---	---	---	---	---
Definition of Pornography	1, 8	5.01	.06	2, 29	.15	.86	2, 5	.40	.69	2, 5	1.05	.42

*Note: 108 ANOVA's were conducted on unweighted, av. weighted, & av. weighted corrected d's (not reported here) with a range of 1 to 3 & range of 2 to 3 (not reported here).

Dashes indicate results of fewer than two non-empty groups when analysed.

References

Allen, M., D'Alessio, D., Brezgel, K. (1995). A meta-analysis investigating the effects of pornography II: Aggression after exposure. *Human Communication Research, 22*, 258-283.

Baron, L. (1990). Pornography and gender equality: An empirical analysis. Special Issue: II. Feminist perspectives on sexuality. *Journal of Sex Research, 27*, 363-380.

Baron, L. & Straus, M.A. (1987). Four theories of rape: A macrosociological analysis. *Social Problems, 34*, 467-489.

Baron, R.A. (1979). Heightened sexual arousal and physical aggression: An extension to females. *Journal of Research in Personality*, 13, 91-102.

Baron, R.A. & Bell, P.A. (1977). Sexual arousal and aggression by males: Effects of type of erotic stimuli and prior provocation. *Journal of Personality and Social Psychology, 35*, 79-87.

Baron, R.A. (1974). The aggression-inhibiting influence of heightened sexual arousal. *Journal of Personality and Social Psychology, 30*, 318-322.

Boeringer, S.B. (1994). Pornography and sexual aggression: Associations of violent and nonviolent depictions with rape and rape proclivity. *Deviant Behaviour, 15*, 289-304.

Briere, J., Henschel, D., & Smiljanich, K. (1992). Attitudes toward sexual abuse: Sex differences and construct validity. *Journal of Research in Personality, 26*, 398-406.

Briere, J., Malamuth, N., & Check, J.V.P. (1985). Sexuality and rape-supportive beliefs. *International Journal of Women's Studies, 8*, 398-403.

Burgess, A.W., Hartman, C.R., McCausland, M.P., & Powers, P. (1984). Response patterns in children and adolescents exploited through sex rings and pornography. *American Journal of Psychiatry, 141*, 656-662.

Cantor, J.R., Zillmann, D., & Einsiedel, E.F. (1978). Female responses to provocation after exposure to aggressive and erotic films. *Communication Research, 5*, 395-411.

Corne, S., Briere, J., & Esses, L.M. (1992). Women's attitudes and fantasies about rape as a function of early exposure to pornography. *Journal of Interpersonal Violence, 7*, 454-461.

Davis, K.E. & Braucht, G.N. (1973). Exposure to pornography, character, and sexual deviance: A retrospective survey. *Journal of Social Issues, 29*, 183-196.

Demare, D., Lips, H.M., & Briere, J. (1993). Sexually violent pornography, anti-women attitudes, and sexual aggression: A structural equation model. *Journal of Research in Personality, 27*, 285-300.

Demare, D., Briere, J., Lips, H.M. (1988). Violent pornography and self-reported likelihood of sexual aggression. *Journal of Research in Personality, 22*, 140-153.

Donnerstein, E. & Berkowitz, L. (1981). Victim reactions in aggressive erotic films as a factor in violence against women. *Journal of Personality and Social Psychology, 41*, 710-724.

Donnerstein, E. (1980). Aggressive erotica and violence against women. *Journal of Personality and Social Psychology, 39,* 269-277.

Donnerstein, E. & Barrett, G. (1978). Effects of erotic stimuli on male aggression toward females. *Journal of Personality and Social Psychology, 36,* 180-188.

Donnerstein, E. & Hallam, J. (1978). Facilitating effects of erotica on aggression against women. *Journal of Personality and Social Psychology, 36,* 1270-1277.

Emerick, R.L. & Dutton, W.A. (1993). The effect of polygraphy on the self report of adolescent sex offenders: Implications for risk assessment. *Annals of Sex Research, 6,* 83-103.

Fisher, R.D., Cook, I.J., & Shirkey, E.C. (1994). Correlates of support for censorship of sexual, sexually violent, and violent media. *Journal of Sex Research, 31,* 229-240.

Fisher, W.A. & Barak, A. (1991). Pornography, erotical, and behaviour: More questions than answers. Special Issue: Socio-legal studies of obscenity. *International Journal of Law and Psychiatry, 14,* 65-83.

Fisher, W.A. & Byrne, D. (1978). Individual differences in affective, evaluative, and behavioral responses to an erotic film. *Journal of Applied Social Psychology, 8,* 355-365.

Ford, M.E. & Linney, J.A. (1995). Comparative analysis of juvenile sexual offenders, violent nonsexual offenders, and status offenders. *Journal of Interpersonal Violence, 10,* 56-70.

Garcia, L.T. (1986). Exposure to pornography and attitudes about women and rape: A correlational study. *Journal of Sex Research, 22,* 378-385.

Gentry, C.S. (1991). Pornography and rape: An empirical analysis. *Deviant Behaviour, 12,* 277-288.

Glass, G.V., McGaw, B., & Smith, M.L. (1981). *Meta-Analysis in Social Research.* Sage Publications: Beverly Hills, California.

Gray, S.H. (1982). Exposure to pornography and aggression toward women: The case of the angry male. *Social Problems, 29,* 387-398.

Gunther, A.C. (1995). Overrating the X-rating: The third-person perception and support for censorship of pornography. *Journal of Communication, 45,* 27-38.

Harris, M.A., Jacobson, C.K., & Chadwick, B.A. (1995). Pornography and premarital sexual activity among LDS Teenagers. *American Sociological Association.* Department of Sociology. Ohio State University, Columbus.

Hui, C.H. (1986). Fifteen years of pornography research: Does exposure to pornography have any effects? *Bulletin of the Hong Kong Psychological Society, 16-17,* 41-62.

Hunter, J.E. & Schmidt, F.L. (1996). Cumulative research knowledge and social policy formulation: The critical role of meta-analysis. *Psychology, Public Policy, and Law, 2,* 324-347.

Hunter, J.E. & Schmidt, F.L. (1990). *Methods of Meta-Analysis: Correcting Error and Bias in Research Findings.* Sage Publications: Newbury Park, California.

Jaffe, Y. & Berger, A. (1977). Cultural generality of the relationship between sex and aggression. *Psychological Reports, 41,* 335-336.

Jaffe, Y., Malamuth, N., Feingold, J., & Feshbach, S. (1974). Sexual arousal and behavioral aggression. *Journal of Personality and Social Psychology, 30,* 759-764.

Jenks, R.J. (1985). A comparative study of swingers and nonswingers: Attitudes and beliefs. *Lifestyles, 8,* 5-20.

Johnson, T.P. & Moore, R.W. (1993). Gender interactions between interviewers and survey respondents: Issues of pornography and community standards. *Sex Roles, 28,* 243-261.

Kutchinsky, B. (1973). The effect of easy avilability of pronography on the incidence of sex crimes: The Danish experience. *Journal of Social Issues, 29,* 163-181.

Leonard, K.E. & Taylor, S.P. (1983). Exposure to pornography, permissive and nonpermissive cues, and male aggression toward females. *Motivation and Emotion, 7,* 291-299.

Lopez, P.A. & George, W.H. (1995). Men's enjoyment of explicit erotica: Effects of person-specific attitudes and gender-specific norms. *Journal of Sex Research, 32,* 275-288.

Lottes, I., Weinberg, M. & Weller, I. (1993). Reactions to pornography on a college campus: For or against? *Sex Roles, 29,* 69-89.

McKenzie-Mohr, D., & Zanna, M.P. (1990). Treating women as sexual objects: Look to the (gender schematic) male who has viewed pornography. *Personality and Social Psychology Bulletin, 16,* 296-308.

Meyer, T.P. (1962). The effects of sexually arousing and violent films on aggressive behavior. *The Journal of Sex Research, 8,* 324-331.

Mosher, D.L. (1988). Pornography defined: Sexual involvement theory, narrative context, and goodness-of-fit. *Journal of Psychology and Human Sexuality, 1,* 67-85.

Mueller, C.W. & Donnerstein, E. (1981). Film-facilitated arousal and prosocial behavior. *Journal of Experimental Social Psychology, 17,* 31-41.

Padgett, V.R., Brislin-Slutz, J.A., & Neal, J.A. (1989). Pornography, erotica, and attitudes toward women: The effects of repeated exposure. *Journal of Sex Research, 26,* 479-491.

Rosenthal, R. (1995). Writing meta-analytic reviews. *Psychological Bulletin, 118,* 183-192.

Rosenthal, R. (1994). Parametric measures of effect size. H. Cooper and L.V. Hedges (Eds.). *The Handbook of Research Synthesis.* New York: Russell Sage Foundation, 231-260.

Rosenthal, R. (1991). *Meta-Analytic procedures for social research.* Revised Edition. Newbury Park: Sage Publications.

Sapolsky, B.S. & Zillmann, D. (1981). The effect of soft-core and hard-core erotica on provoked and unprovoked hostile behavior. *Journal of Sex Research, 17,* 319-343.

Saunders, R.M., & Naus, P.J. (1993). The impact of social content and audience factors on responses to sexually explicit videos. *Journal of Sex Education and Therapy, 19,* 117-130.

Violato, C. & Russell, C. (1994). Effects of nonmaternal care on child development: A meta-analysis of published research. *Paper presented at the 55th Annual Convention of the Canadian Psychological Association,* Penticton, British Columbia: Canada.

Vogt, P. (1993). *Dictionary of statistics and methodology.* Sage Publications: Newbury Park, California.

White, L.A. (1979). Erotica and aggression: The influence of sexual arousal, positive affect, and negative affect on aggressive behavior. *Journal of Personality and Social Psychology, 37,* 591-601.

Wilson, W.C., & Abelson, H.I. (1973). Experience with and attitudes toward explicit sexual materials. *Journal of Social Issues, 29,* 19-39.

Wolf, F.M. (1986). *Meta-Analysis. Quantitative Methods for Research Synthesis.* Sage Publications: Beverly Hills, California.

Zillmann, D., Bryant, J., & Carveth, R.A. (1981). The effect of erotica featuring sadomasochism and bestiality on motivated intermale aggression. *Personality and Social Psychology Bulletin, 7,* 153-159.

Zillmann, D., Bryant, J., Comisky, P.W., & Medoff, N.J. (1981). Excitation and hedonic valence in the effect of erotica on motivated intermale aggression. *European Journal of Social Psychology, 11,* 233-252.

Zillmann, D. & Sapolsky, B.S. (1977). What mediates the effect of mild erotica on annoyance and hostile behavior in males? *Journal of Personality and Social Psychology, 35,* 587-596.

Zillmann, D. (1971). Excitation transfer in communication-mediated aggressive behavior. *Journal of Experimental Social Psychology, 7,* 419-434.

Zillmann, D., Hoyt, J.L., & Day, K.D. (1974). Strength and duration of the effect of aggressive, violent, and erotic communications on subsequent aggressive behavior. *Communication Research, 1,* 286-306.

Zillmann, D. & Bryant, J. (1982). Pornography, sexual callousness, and the trivialization of rape. *Journal of Communication, Autumn,* 10-21.

5 Parent-Child Interdependence in Chinese Families: Change and Continuity

QI WANG AND YEN HSUEH

Abstract

With rapid economic growth, the parent-child relations in Chinese families have shifted from an emphasis on material reciprocity to an emphasis on psychological interdependence. Western academia and media tend to believe that interdependence is associated with economic hardship and to view individualism as the end of family transformation. However, based on cross-cultural and indigenous studies, we argue that the transformation of Chinese intrafamilial relationships preserves the essence of the Confucian doctrine of filial piety and the philosophical view of a relational self. The transformed parent-child interdependence facilitates the child's adaptation to the present and future Chinese society.

Introduction

As the title indicates, we are going to talk about the transformation of Chinese parent-child relations over the past few decades, a process of both change and continuity. First, we are going to discuss the change in parent-child relations from an emphasis on material reciprocity to an emphasis on psychological interdependence. Then, we will argue that the essence of the Confucian ethic of filial piety and selfhood conception still persists in this new pattern of Chinese parent-child relations, so that it differs from the within-family individualism, due to societal modernization, predicted by some Western scholars.

Change

During the past few decades, great socioeconomic changes have taken place in Chinese society. In response to societal development, the Chinese parent-child relations have been going through some transformations which appear mainly in two related aspects. On the one hand, with economic prosperity, the material needs from intrafamilial interdependence are largely reduced. On the other hand, psychological components in parent-child relations become more salient and tend to be strengthened. The newly emerged pattern of Chinese parent-child relations, which we will name psychological interdependence, is characterized by parents and children mutually supporting each other's psychological needs, respecting and helping each other's personal pursuits, and openly displaying affection toward each other (Figure 5.1).

In traditional Chinese families, children were viewed as possessions or property of parents, and filial piety was perhaps the most important goal of family socialization (Ho, 1981). Absolute obedience and subservience to their parents were required from children, whose life course, including education, marriage, occupation, and even daily life, were subject to parents' wishes. Parents provided care for their children with explicit expectations that later in their lives the children would support and assist them both physically and financially. Although there were also emotional factors in this pattern of parent-child interdependence, especially between the mother and the child, it was masked by material reciprocity. Such a relationship involved protectiveness and physical caring to a greater extent and required less psychological sensitivity and overt affective expressiveness (Ho, 1989, 1986). The traditional Chinese parents had little psychological need to hold on to the child and the psychological needs of the child tended to be largely ignored.

With rapid economic development, it is now possible for both parents and their adult children to be financially self-sufficient, so that the material reciprocity and its associated absolute filial piety is no longer necessary. Recent indigenous studies provide evidence that although the significance of filial piety, so deeply rooted in Chinese society, still remains among Chinese in diverse sociopolitical locations, filial piety no longer commands the same degree of absolute observance it once did (Ho, 1996). Notable departures from the traditional pattern of parent-child relations appear especially in urban families, among the intellectuals and younger people, and are associated with family modernism. In these families, parents no longer tend to subjugate children's needs and interests to those of their own or demand children's absolute obedience. Instead, they place more emphasis on their children's expression of opinions, independence, and self-reliance (Ho, 1989). Also, many young people tend to reject the absolute form of filial obligations, such as sacrifice of their personal wishes, and advocate "cultivating an independent personality" (Li, 1989).

These changes highlight an important feature of psychological interdependence in Chinese families. That is, exclusive loyalty to the family is no longer required, but rather, children are allowed some freedom to develop individual values and to achieve personal goals. This is now very unlikely to endanger the survival of the family, but will help the child adapt to the rapid development of the Chinese society. In a study on Chinese parenting and the related behavioral traits of the child, Xu and others (1991) found that although many Chinese parents do not give up control over their children, they encourage independence of the child and respect the child's individuality. This parenting style was found to be the best predictor for the development of positive character and behavior of the child.

Similarly, Lin and Fu (1990) found in a comparative study of parenting in Chinese, immigrant Chinese, and Caucasian-American families that the two Chinese groups rated higher on both parental control and encouragement of independence than the Caucasian group. They further found that this combination of both traditional and modern attitudes in child-rearing was closely associated with Chinese parents' greater emphasis on achievement of the child than their American counterparts. Interestingly, these researchers did not find any group differences between the Chinese and American parents in open expression of affection. This is in contrast with previous findings that traditional Chinese parents, especially fathers, who emphasize family harmony through emotional restraint (Bond & Wang, 1983; Wu, 1996), are less emotionally expressive and less emotionally involved with their children than American parents (Hsu, 1981). This result suggests another important feature of psychological interdependence, that is, emotional communication in contemporary Chinese families tends to be more open than before.

Therefore, the loosening of the controlling grip that Chinese parents exercise over their children has not only removed traditional constraints on the development of individuality, but has also provided the context where the affectional function in parent-child relations plays an increasingly important role in contemporary Chinese families (Ho, 1996; 1972). In fact, today's Chinese parents are found to be more affectionate and rewarding with their children and are more inclined to use love-oriented than power-assertive modes of discipline (Ho, 1989). As David Ho (1989) claimed, as the traditional forces binding the family together are weakened, new cohesive bonds must be present to avert its disintegration, and a greater emphasis on paternal love may assume its rightful place in the redefinition of parent-child relations in the Chinese family.

The strengthened emotional bonds are especially evidenced by the transformation of father-child relations in Chinese families. Traditionally, emotional distance, tension, and even antagonism dominated the Chinese father-child relationship. Fathers were stern disciplinarians of whom their children were fearful. They were concerned more with the demands of propriety and necessity than with feelings. In contrast, mothers were nurturing caregivers, who provided children with affection and attended to children's daily needs (Ho, 1989, 1986, 1981). However, recent studies conducted in mainland China (Stevenson et al., 1992; Wu, 1996), Hong Kong (Ho & Kang, 1984), and Taiwan (Yuan, 1972) indicated a redistribution of parental authority in Chinese families, where mothers appeared to assume a more active and decisive role as disciplinary agents, while fathers went beyond their roles as disciplinarians and educators to take up many of the caregiving duties, and were even perceived as more lenient than mothers. This new father-child relationship is characterized by less emphasis on obedience and filial obligations and more emphasis on the open expression of affection. Chinese fathers are becoming more emotionally involved and more permissive with their children, and the father-child relationship tends to show greater warmth and emotionality in the modern Chinese culture (Jankowiak, 1992).

Continuity

So far, we have talked about the changes in Chinese parent-child relations in the era of societal modernization and have described the characteristics of the newly emerged psychological interdependence within the Chinese family (Figure 5.2). We stress that this transformation of intrafamilial relationships does not agree with some popular beliefs in Western academia and media which view family transformation as a type of evolution. As we know, ideas about sociocultural evolution can be traced to the nineteenth century when many scholars such as Edward Tylor and Herbert Spencer believed that the development of human societies followed Darwin's principles of evolution and declared some European societies to be the most highly evolved. This belief has permeated many areas of psychological studies. For example, some Western psychologists believe that paralleling societal evolution, intrafamilial relationships are transformed from interdependence -- which characterizes the family relations in "primitive" societies -- to the within-family independence in industrialized, "developed" societies. They claim that parent-child interdependence (e.g., in the Chinese family), is a result of long-term poverty, and that economic growth will eventually diminish this pattern of parent-child relations and lead to individualism within the family (e.g., Stevenson et al., 1992; Triandis, 1989).

However, this belief that regards affluence as the antecedent of individualism suffers from four weaknesses. First, it is based on the assumption that intrafamilial interdependence is inferior to personal independence within the family and is maladaptive to the development of future societies. Second, it ignores the macro sociocultural environments where family interdependence exists, and over-exaggerates the influence of economic factors. Third, it contrasts interdependence with independence in a dichotomous way, while in fact the two could co-exist and even harmonize with each other. Fourth, and finally, it treats the nature of interdependence within the family as fixed and unique, so that this type of relationship only exists because of poverty and becomes extinct with economic prosperity.

The continuous and steady economic growth of Japan and other newly industrialized Asian countries during the past few decades is widely attributed to both management styles and work attitudes that are rooted in the Confucian ethic of which familism is an important component. It is believed that familism is indispensable in providing the support base for the coordination activities of the entrepreneurial role which is vital to economic development (Bond, 1988; Kao & Hong, 1988; Yang, 1988). This indicates that Confucian familism and its best preserved aspect -- intrafamilial mutual dependence (Yang, 1988) -- will not impede socioeconomic development, but instead, can act as an impetus.

Moreover, the Western concept of individualism is hardly tolerated in present Chinese society which is still dominated by hierarchical social relations (Figure 5.3). Although some Chinese educators advocate Western-style family education and emphasize that parents should encourage autonomy and self-direction of their children, many parents have doubts and concerns (Li, 1989). They argue that an adult too open and individualistic will get nowhere in today's Chinese society, since the strict social hierarchy requires each and every individual to have a strong sense of authority and to be sensitive to related others. As David Ho (1996) pointed out, filial piety is a potent determinant of not only intergenerational relationships in the family but also superior-subordinate interactions in the society. To some extent, authoritative control by Chinese parents may actually prepare the child for the strict regimentation of the society. Although Chinese democracy has made some progress in recent years, the hierarchical authority relations which are rooted deeply in the Confucian doctrine of filial piety are still intact. This makes the idea and practice of Western individualism impossible and undesirable in Chinese society in general and in the Chinese family in particular.

The interdependence in the Chinese family is deeply rooted in Confucian philosophy and its conception of selfhood, which is defined as "two persons being together". In other words, a person is a relational being, whose humanism is achieved through interaction with others, and whose identity is determined by the web of a relational network where he is situated. This conception of selfhood and the Confucian principles of filial piety make family the center of a Chinese individual's life and the most primary unit in which he conducts behavior. In his book, *My Country and My People* (1939), Chinese scholar Lin Yutang articulated a notion of the Chinese family as "This form of social immortality, which the Chinese prize above all earthly possessions, has something of the character of a religion, which is enhanced by the ritual of ancestor worship, and the consciousness of it has penetrated deep into the Chinese soul" (p. 34).

Cultural studies have demonstrated that social values related to family and intrafamilial relationships are among those most resistant to social-economic influences (LeVine, 1982; Li, 1985; Lum & Char, 1985; Wolf, 1970). Indigenous research has suggested a general persistence of familism (whose central concept is filial piety), especially parent-child mutual dependence, in Chinese society across different sociopolitical regions, in spite of the impact of modern industrial life and acculturation (Bond, 1988; Chin, 1988; Hsu, 1985; Kao & Hong, 1988; Yang, 1988). Based on theoretical analyses and empirical evidence, Yang (1988) concluded that societal modernization will not eliminate traditional values such as filial piety which will instead coexist with modern attitudes.

Although, as we mentioned earlier, absolute filial piety and its associated material reciprocity is on the decline due to socioeconomic development, Confucian principles in intrafamilial relations persist. This is evidenced in the relative consistency of socialization practices in the Chinese family. Diverse literature on Chinese family socialization has indicated that although Chinese culture is full of variations (such as dramatic social-political changes, important regional and social class differences), undeniable effects of acculturation among overseas Chinese, and substantial rural-urban differences, continuity with the traditional pattern of parent-child interactions in Chinese families is highly discernible among the Chinese today (Ho, 1989).

Despite the official denouncement of Confucian teachings on early education during the early years of Communist China, and in spite of rapid socioeconomic changes and the practice of the single-child policy over the past fifteen years, parents in Mainland China today still manifest strong beliefs in the ancient teachings and act accordingly in raising their children (Wu, 1996). Comparative studies (Kao & Hong, 1988; Wu, 1996, 1985; Yang, 1988) conducted in Mainland China, Hong Kong, Taiwan, Singapore, and other overseas Chinese communities further confirmed the cultural continuity in socialization patterns and intrafamilial mutual dependency. The continuity in traditional family values and practices reflects the perseverance of the essence of the Confucian ethic in today's Chinese families.

Conclusion

In summary, with societal modernization, a new form of parent-child relationship has emerged in the Chinese family. It is characterized by economic self-sufficiency, respect for personal values and psychological needs, encouragement of independence and self-realization, and strengthened intrafamilial emotional bonds. Unlike individualism, suggested by some Western scholars, independence and individuality encouraged in this relationship are still bonded within the family relational network and limited by the macro sociocultural structure, that will serve to better fulfill one's social-familial role. Psychological interdependence retains the essence of traditional family values and responds adaptively to the new requirements arising from modernization of the Chinese society. This new form of parent-child mutual support and its corresponding socialization practices can prepare the child to achieve his personal values and goals, and also the values and goals of his family, in a changing culture of relatedness.

Table 5.1   Change in Chinese parent-child relations

Material reciprocity in traditional Chinese families	Psychological interdependence in contemporary Chinese families
Poverty	Financial self-sufficiency
Absolute filial piety: • Extended and hierarchical family structures • Sacrifice of personal wishes • Honoring ancestors • Financial support of aged parents	Parent-child mutual support of each other's psychological needs Encouragement of children's interdependence and self-realization
Intergenerational emotional distance father-child tension	Strengthened emotional bonds among family members

Table 5.2   Continuity in Chinese parent-child relations

A. Filial piety - The central concept of Confucian familism • Family as the basic social unit and center of a Chinese person's life • Respect for parents and parental authority • Mutual dependence among family members
B. Concept of selfhood • Relational self in one's social-familial network

Table 5.3   Western individualism vs. Chinese psychological interdependence

Individuals as the basic unit to conduct behavior	Family as the basic unit to conduct behavior
Separate Self	Relational Self
One-sidedness of parent-child relations	Parent-child mutual support

References

Bond, M.H. (1988). Invitation to a wedding: Chinese values and global economic growth. In D. Sinha & H.S.R. Kao (Eds.), *Social Values and Development: Asian Perspectives* (pp. 197-209). Sage Publications.

Bond, M.H. & Wang, S. (1983). China: Aggressive behavior and the problems of maintaining order and harmony. In A.P. Goldstein & M.H. Segall (Eds.), *Aggression in Global Perspective* (pp. 58-74). New York: Pergamon.

Chin, A.P. (1988). *Children of China: Voices from Recent Years.* Cornell University Press.

Ho, David Y.F. (1996). Filial piety and its psychological consequences. In M.H. Bond (Ed.), *The Handbook of Chinese Psychology* (pp. 155-165). Hong Kong: Oxford University Press.

Ho, David Y.F. (1989). Continuity and variation in Chinese patterns of socialization. *Journal of Marriage and the Family, 51,* 149-163.

Ho, David Y.F. (1986). Chinese patterns of socialization: A critical review. In M. H. Bond (Ed.), *The Psychology of the Chinese People* (pp. 1-37). Hong Kong: Oxford University Press.

Ho, David Y.F. (1981). Traditional patterns of socialization in Chinese society. *Acta Psychologica Taiwanica, 23,* 81-95.

Ho, David Y.F. (1972). The affectional function in contemporary Chinese families. In *Mental Health and Urbanization: Proceedings of the 24th Annual Meeting* (pp. 131-137). Hong Kong: Mental Health Association of Hong Kong.

Ho, David Y.F. & Kang, T.K. (1984). Intergenerational comparisons of child-rearing attitudes and practices in Hong Kong. *Developmental Psychology, 20,* 1004-1016.

Hsu, F.L.K. (1981). *Americans and Chinese: Passages to Differences.* Honolulu: University Press of Hawaii.

Hsu, J. (1985). The Chinese family: Relations, problems, and therapy. In W.S. Tseng & D.V. Wu (Eds.), *Chinese Culture and Mental Health* (pp. 95-112). Academic Press, Inc.

Jankowiak, W. (1992). Father-child relations in urban China. In B. S. Hewlett (Ed.), *Father-Child Relations: Cultural and Biosocial Contexts.* New York: Aldine de Gruyter.

Kao, H.S.R. & Hong, N.S. (1988). Minimal 'self' and Chinese work behavior: Psychology of the grass-roots. In D. Sinha & H.S.R. Kao (Eds.), *Social Values and Development: Asian Perspectives* (pp. 254-272). Sage Publications.

Kessen, W. (1975). *Childhood in China.* Yale University Press.

LeVine, R.A. (1982). *Culture, Behavior, and Personality.* Chicago: Aldine.

Li, X. (1989). Parents and children. *China Reconstructs, June,* 8-11.

Li, X.T. (1985). The effect of family on the mental health of the Chinese people. In W.S. Tseng & D.V. Wu (Eds.), *Chinese Culture and Mental Health* (pp. 85-93). Academic Press, Inc.

Lin, C.Y.C. & Fu, V.R. (1990). A comparison of child-rearing practices among Chinese, immigrant Chinese, and Caucasian-American parents. *Child Development, 61,* 429-433.

Lin, Y.T. (1939). *My Country and My People.* The John Day Company, Inc.

Lum, C. & Char, T. (1985). Chinese adaptation in Hawaii: Some examples. In W.S. Tseng & D.V. Wu (Eds.), *Chinese Culture and Mental Health* (pp. 215-226). Academic Press, Inc.

Parish, W.L. & Whyte, M.K. (1978). *Village and Family in Contemporary China.* Chicago: University of Chicago Press.

Stevenson, H.W., Chen, C., & Lee, S. (1992). Chinese families. In J. L. Roopnarine and D.B. Carter (Eds.), *Parent-Child Socialization in Diverse Cultures* (pp. 17-33). NJ: Ablex Publishing Corporation, Norwood.

Triandis, H.C. (1989). The self and social behavior in differing cultural contexts. *Psychological Review, 96,* 506-520.

Wolf, M. (1970). Child training and the Chinese family. In M. Freedman (Ed.), *Family and Kinship in Chinese Society* (pp. 37-62). Stanford, CA: Stanford University Press.

Wu, D.Y.H. (1996). Chinese childhood socialization. In M.H. Bond (Ed.), *The Handbook of Chinese Psychology* (pp. 143-154). Hong Kong: Oxford University Press.

Wu, D.Y.H. (1985). Child training in Chinese culture. In W.S. Tseng & D.V. Wu (Eds.), *Chinese Culture and Mental Health* (pp. 113-134). Academic Press, Inc.

Xu, Z.Y., Shen, J.X., Wan, C.W., Li, C.M., Mussen, P., & Cao, Z.F. (1991). Family socialization and children's behavior and personality development in China. *The Journal of Genetic Psychology, 152,* 239-253.

Yang, C.F. (1988). Familism and development: An examination of the role of family in contemporary China Mainland, Hong Kong and Taiwan. In D. Sinha & H.S.R. Kao (Eds.), *Social Values and Development: Asian Perspectives* (pp. 93-123). Sage Publications.

Yang, K.S. (1988). Will societal modernization eventually eliminate cross-cultural psychological differences? In M.H. Bond (Ed.), *The Cross-Cultural Challenge to Social Psychology* (pp. 67-85). Sage Publications, Inc.

Yuan, S.S. (1972). Family authority patterns, rearing practices, and children's sense of political efficacy. *Thought and Word, 10,* 35-55. (In Chinese)

6 Psychosocial Factors Influencing Breastfeeding: A Stepwise Discriminant Analysis Employing a Sample of Italian Women

ALDO ZANON AND CLAUDIO VIOLATO

Abstract

A total of 358 post-partum women with neonates, some who breastfed (77.9%) and some who didn't (21.5%), participated in the present study. The mean age of the subjects was 29.34 years (SD = 4.64; min = 15; max = 43). While the majority (77.9%) of women breastfed their infant at birth, 48.6% had stopped at 6 months and 70.0% stopped by 10 months. The number of months sisters breastfed, the interval of breastfeeding immediately post-partum, and the number of visits to the pediatrician in the first year of the infant's life all were significantly different between the groups. A stepwise backward discriminant analysis revealed that correct group classification could be achieved at nearly 82% between groups who breastfed and those that didn't.

Introduction

The major purpose of the present study was to investigate empirical factors that influence breastfeeding behavior in women with infant children. There are at least four classes of factors that influence decision-making about breastfeeding (Beutovim, 1976): (1) attitudes of mother towards breastfeeding, (2) sociocultural variables (e.g., income, employment), (3) family factors (e.g., support from family members, and (4) physiologic factors (e.g., lactation status). In the present study we focused on all four classes of variables employing multivariate procedures in order to better understand breastfeeding behavior.

The many benefits of breastfeeding have been well documented (e.g., Littman, Mendendorp & Goldfarb, 1994; Alexy & Martin, 1994; Bauer, Ewald, Hoffman & Dubanoski, 1991). Breastfeeding as the preferred method of feeding infants has been endorsed by many including the American Academy of Pediatrics (American Academy of Pediatrics, 1988). The benefits include physiologic, nutritional, immunologic and economic factors. Notwithstanding the many benefits of breastfeeding, rates of breastfeeding continue to be low.

In the United States and Canada breastfeeding rates are about 60% or less at birth, 25% at 6 months and 12% after 10 months (Richardson & Champion, 1992). These rates have remained stable since 1982. In Italy while the overall percentages are somewhat higher (about 74% at birth, 42% at 6 months and 18% at 10 months), the pattern of breastfeeding is very similar to that in North America (Zanon, Bolesani, Lago, Cecchetto, Zanardo, & Formentin, 1988). Since the maximum benefit to breastfeeding is achieved after 1 year (American Academy of Pediatrics, 1982), most children are not achieving the benefits from breastfeeding that they should. It is certainly desirable to increase the rate of breastfeeding.

Encouraging breastfeeding requires understanding the factors that influence women's decision to breastfeed. The four major factors influencing breastfeeding behavior include attitudes, social influence, sociocultural variables, and physiologic status of lactation.

Attitudes towards breastfeeding include perceived benefits (i.e., to the infant and mother) and perceived barriers (e.g., embarrassment at expressing milk, inconvenience of breastfeeding). Numerous studies have documented the relationship between attitudes of mothers with respect to breastfeeding and feeding choice, as attitudes towards infant feeding methods are accurate predictors of infant choice (Black, Blair, Jones & DuRant, 1990). A ten-item scale administered to 102 white and black American women revealed that overall there was a prevalent positive attitude about breastfeeding and few barriers (Richardson & Champion, 1992). With this feedback, why are the rates of breastfeeding in North America in a state of decline? The belief that attitudes are culturally linked seems to be incorrect, as various studies indicate that women from a variety of cultures hold the same fears and beliefs.

In a recent study that measured exclusively the attitudes of Hispanic women regarding breastfeeding, it was discovered that the same results were acquired in a similar study with white women being the participants. Of the 268 Hispanic women surveyed, over half responded that they had never breastfed their children, but more than 95% believed that breastfeeding is best for children (Gorman, Byrd, & Vanderslice, 1995). The most significant barrier in attitudes regarding breastfeeding is quite often reported to be a lack of confidence in milk supply (Houston, Howie, and McNeilley, 1983). As could be expected, an interest in breastfeeding usually results in more perceived positive factors and less perceived negative factors (Alexy & Martin, 1994). Moreover, rural and urban differences do not seem to influence perceived barriers regarding breastfeeding (Alexy & Martin, 1994). When examining attitudes of women regarding breastfeeding their second child, it appears that the experiences and beliefs that were held during the first experience remain consistent in making a decision regarding infant feeding with their second child. Breastfeeding is not instinctual but is a learned behavior. Accordingly, the attitude of the mother is pivotal to the success of breastfeeding attempts.

Social influence includes family, friends, and professionals (e.g., physicians, nurses). In the Littman, Mendendorp and Goldfarb (1994) study, for example, father's approval of breastfeeding resulted in high instances of breastfeeding (98.1%) among their mates. This same study indicated that only 11% of the sample found that talking to their doctor influenced their decision to breastfeed. Matich and Sims (1992) studied the impact of friends on the infant feeding decision of new mothers. Such impact appears to be minor when the mother reported that she cared little about what her friends thought. These women were more likely to breastfeed than those who put importance on their friends' opinions. Reciprocally, women who cared a great deal about what their friends thought were less likely to breastfeed than their counterparts who gave less weight to their friends' opinions (Matich & Sims, 1992).

Several studies have provided conflicting results on the influence of mothers, husbands, sisters, and professionals. In the Kaufman and Hall (1989) study, for example, the father of the infant was a major source of support, as indicated by 75% of mothers, followed by the support of nurses, own mother, doctor or family (25%). Mothers with no social support were six times more likely than those with support to stop their breastfeeding attempts (Kaufman & Hall, 1989). Despite these findings, other researchers have found conflicting results indicating that social and psychological variables are not significant in the early termination of breastfeeding.

Other researchers have suggested that the early termination of breastfeeding is related to postpartum depression (Cooper, Murray & Stein, 1993). Factors such as labor process, complications, obstetric intervention, method of delivery, and maternal and neo-natal health were not found to be related in some studies (Cooper, Murray & Stein, 1993). In contrast to these findings, a 1990 study done at Ohio State University found that there was a significant difference in the likelihood of breastfeeding depending on the method of delivery; a baby born by Cesarean was far less likely to be breastfeed (Grossman, Fitzsimmons, Larsen-Alexander, Sachs, & Harter, 1990). However, like the Cooper, Murray and Stein (1993) study, Grossman et al. (1990) reported that Cesarean delivery did not deter mothers from breastfeeding. The results remain inconclusive and inconsistent.

Education is frequently cited as a predictor of infant feeding choice made by the mother. In one study, researchers compared the feeding choices of two groups from two different hospitals. One of the groups was exposed to the services of a Certified Lactation Consultant (CLC), and the other group was not. The group with exposure to this resource had significantly longer durations of breastfeeding that did the group that did not have a CLC. As well, easily accessed programs such as Lamaze classes increased the likelihood of breastfeeding, especially if the mother had graduated from high school (Grossman et al., 1990). According to Hawkins, Nichols, and Tanner (1987), longer duration of breastfeeding among low-income women can be achieved through educational programs such as access to a CLC. Richardson and Champion (1992), however, employing a 15-question test formulated to assess knowledge regarding breastfeeding, concluded that even when equipped with educational programs, there is no correlation between test performance and duration of breastfeeding.

Breastfeeding in the workplace continues to be an issue for many mothers. Four major themes are often at the core of concern regarding breastfeeding while employed: 1) employer's attitude, 2) time available, 3) privacy, and 4) storage. There is evidence to suggest that mothers often terminate breastfeeding due to employment. White, married mothers often wean their children from breastfeeding before the child turns one year of age so that they can return to work. This is the case for more than half of mothers. There is generally very little provision in the workplace (e.g., private areas, attitude of co-workers) for breastfeeding in the workplace. Often there is little support or information to continue breastfeeding in the workplace. Ridicule or disapproval from co-workers can be major factors in not attempting breastfeeding by the mother.

Richardson and Champion (1992) had contrasting findings. They found that there was no difference as to whether the woman was returning to work or not in her decision to initiate breastfeeding. Proponents of breastfeeding in the workplace have argued that benefits extend to the employer as well. Employers who fund lactation programs in the workplace may accrue more benefits than drawbacks. Lactation programs have been demonstrated to decrease infant illness, reduce medical cost for employers, and decrease employee absence. Nevertheless, the empirical evidence on the role of sociocultural variables such as education, employment, and ethnicity on breastfeeding behavior continues to be equivocal.

Physiologic factors are often sited as a major medical reason for the early termination of breastfeeding. Of 150 participants in a 1991 breastfeeding study, 44% of mothers who were unsuccessful breastfeeding identified lack of milk as the primary reason (Rentschler, 1991). Hill (1991) also found similar feedback from women. Despite these findings, Caldwell (1991) reported that nursing measures to improve the nipple graspability increases the success of breastfeeding. Equally, educational programs about the physiology of breastfeeding and early intervention and lactation consulting can often eliminate common problems for lactating mothers (Moore, 1991). Overall, knowledge about physiologic factors and the mother's status seem to have little bearing on breastfeeding behavior.

The foregoing discussion suggests that further empirical investigation using multivariate approaches is required to explicate more precisely the role of various factors and their interrelationship in breastfeeding behavior. Accordingly, we employed a multivariate approach to the investigation of breastfeeding behavior in the present study.

Method

Subjects

A total of 358 post-partum women with neonates participated in the present study. The mean age of the subjects was 29.34 years (SD = 4.64; min = 15; max = 43). A minority of the subjects (n = 130; 36.3%) had high school graduation or post-secondary studies, while the remainder (n = 228; 63.7%) did not. More than one-third (n = 135; 37.7%) were homemakers, while 180 (50.2%) described their occupation as clerical or laborer. Only 43 (12.1%) women indicated their employment status as professional, managerial or self-employed.

Instruments and procedures

Each subject was asked to complete a questionnaire that included items on demographics, breastfeeding attitudes, knowledge and behavior, family background, home visits, and lactation health status.

Results

More than three-fourths (n = 279; 77.9%) of the subjects indicated that they breastfed their child, while 21.5% (n = 77) said they did not (2 did not respond). The mean number of months breastfeeding was 6.21 (SD = 4.07; min = 1; max = 24). Nearly half of the sample (48.6%) stopped breastfeeding after 6 months; by 10 months 70.0% had stopped. Slightly more than one-fifth (21.1%) breastfed beyond 12 months. Nearly one-third (30.4%) had birthing courses, while the remainder did not (68.4%).

The women were asked to indicate the number of months that important other women (mother, sister, important friend, mother-in-law, sister-in-law, other) in their lives had breastfed. These data were factor analyzed into principal components and then rotated to the normalized varimax criterion. Five cohesive, theoretical meaningful factors which accounted for 68.3% of the common variance emerged: 1) Significant Others, 2) Sisters-in-Law, 3) Sisters, 4) Friends, and 4) Maternal (mother and mother-in-law).

Several exploratory analyses indicated that there were some significant differences between women who had breastfed and those who had not. The women who had breastfed had less total number of visits to their pediatrician in the infant's first year (mean = 7.43, SD = 3.54) than did those who had not breastfed (mean = 8.57, SD = 4.87; $F(1, 349) = 5.22, p < .05$). These group differences were also explored on the five factors: only one significant difference emerged (on Factor 3 - Sisters). Those women who breastfed had sisters who breastfed for longer periods of time than those women who did not breastfeed ($F(1, 354) = 4.44, p < .05$). The feeding intervals during the post-partum hospital stay was also significantly different between the groups. The mean hour interval for the breastfeeding group was 4.00 (SD = .62) while for the non-breastfeeding group was 4.45 (SD = 1.53) ($F(1,314) = 12.03, p < .001$).

In order to attempt to discriminate between the two groups, a stepwise backwards multiple regression analysis was conducted. The results from this are summarized in Table 6.1.

From these results it is clear that the feeding interval in the few days immediately following birth is the most powerful discriminator of between the two groups (loading = .86) followed by the Sister factor (loading = .52). The number of home visits or visits to the pediatrician are not significant in the discriminant function (they are essentially zero). The discriminant function correctly classifies the groups at 81.33% (see Table 6.1).

Discussion

The major findings of the present study may be summarized as follows: 1) the majority (77.9%) of women breastfed their infant at birth but 48.6% had stopped at 6 months and 70.0% stopped by 10 months, 2) the number of months sisters breastfed, the interval of breastfeeding immediately post-partum, and the number of visits to the pediatrician in the first year of the infant's life all were significantly different between the groups, and 3) stepwise backward discriminant analysis revealed that correct group classification could be achieved at nearly 82%.

In the present study as in other research, most women stop breastfeeding well before the maximum benefits of 1 year are achieved (American Academy of Pediatrics, 1982). The social and psychological factors that appear to influence breastfeeding behavior include family influence (at least that of sisters), interval of feeding immediately after birth as well as number of visits to the pediatrician in the first year after birth. Interestingly, it is the women who have fewer visits to their physician that are more likely to breastfeed than those who have more visits. This may indicate that the non-feeders are experiencing more medical or psychological difficulties and are seeking medical intervention more frequently than the breastfeeders. The feeding interval immediately post-partum is also an indicator of breastfeeding behavior. Perhaps it is an indicator of commitment to breastfeeding. The correct classification into breastfeeding and non breastfeeding groups with one discriminant function is substantial (81.33%). The present study indicates that there are several social-psychological variables that influence breastfeeding behavior.

Table 6.1   Summary of stepwise backwards discriminant analysis

Canonical Correlation	Wilks' Lambda	Chi-square	df	Significance
.221	.95	15.42694	2	.0004

Variable	Loading on Function
Feeding Interval	.86
Factor 3 (Sisters)	.52
Home visits	.05
Visits to Pediatrician	-.02

Classification Results

Number of Actual Group	Predicted Group Membership	
	Breastfeeding	Not Breastfeeding
Breastfeeding (n=256)	255 (99.6%)	1 (.4%)
Not Breastfeeding (n=60)	58 (96.7%)	2 (3.3%)

Percent of cases classified correctly: 81.33

References

Alexy, M. & Martin, A. (1994). Breastfeeding: Perceived barriers and benefits/ enhancers in a rural and urban setting. *Public Health Nursing, 11*, 214-218.

American Academy of Pediatrics. (1982). The promotion of breast-feeding. *Pediatrics, 69,* 654-661.

American Academy of Pediatrics. (1988). *Guidelines for perinatal care*, (2nd ed). Elk Grove Village IL: American Academy of Pediatrics, Committee on Fetus and Newborn.

Bauer, G., Ewald, J., Hoffman, R., & Dubanoski, R. (1991). Breastfeeding and cognitive development of three-year-old children. *Psychological Reports, 68,* 1218.

Beutovim, A. (1976). *Shame and other anxieties associated with breastfeeding: A systems theory and psychodynamic approach*, (pp. 159-172). Amsterdam: Elsevier.

Black, R., Blair, J., Jones, V. & DuRant, R. (1990). Infant feeding decisions among pregnant women from a WIC population in Georgia. *Journal of American Dietetic Association, 90,* 255-259.

Cooper, P., Murray, L. & Stein, A. (1993). Psychosocial factors associated with the early termination of breast-feeding. *Journal of Psychosomatic Research, 37*, 171-176.

Gorman, T., Byrd, T. & Vanderslice, J. (1995). Breast-feeding practice, attitudes, and beliefs among Hispanic women and men in a border community. *Family and Community Health, 18*, 17-27.

Grossman, L., Fitzsimmons, S., Larson-Alexander, J., Sachs, L. & Harter, C. (1990). The infant feeding decision in low and upper income women. *Clinical Pediatrics, 29*, 30-37.

Hawkins, L., Nichols, F. & Tanner, J. (1987). Predictors of the duration of breastfeeding in low-income women. *Birth, 14,* 204-209.

Houston, M., Howie, P. & McNeilly, A. (1983). Midwifery forum 2: Breast feeding. *Nursing Mirror, 156,* viii.

Kaufman, K. & Hall, L. (1989). Influences of the social network on choice and duration of breast-feeding in mothers of preterm infants. *Research in Nursing & Health, 12*, 149-159.

Littman, H., Mendendorp, S. & Goldfarb, J. (1994). The decision to breastfeed: The importance of father's approval. *Clinical Pediatrics, 4,* 214-219.

Matich, R. & Sims, L. (1992). A comparison of social support variables between women who intend to breast or bottle feed. *Social Science & Medicine, 34,* 919-927.

Rentshler, D. (1991). Correlates of successful breastfeeding. *Image, 23*, 151-154.

Richardson, V. & Champion, V. (1992). The relationship of attitudes, knowledge, and social support to breast-feeding. *Issues in Comprehensive Pediatric Nursing, 15*, 183-197.

Zanon, A., Bolesani, C., Lago, F., Cecchetto, G., Zanardo, V. & Formentin, P. (1988). Allattamento al seno in tre comuni limitrof; nella provincia di Padova nel 1986. *Minerva Pediatrica, 40*, 349-354.

Section II:

Family Adjustment and Transitions

7 Spiraling Up and Spiraling Down: A Longitudinal Study of Adjustment

CHRISTOPHER BAGLEY AND KANKA MALLICK

Abstract

A longitudinal study of 565 children from birth to age 9 supports the Thomas-Chess model: later adjustment reflects the complex interaction of early temperament profiles, CNS disability, parental interactions with the child, family disruption, and external stressors (particularly, economic poverty). A regression model predicted 28% of variance in conduct disorder measured at age 9. Variables in this model are difficult temperament at age 2, CNS disability at age 6, maternal stress when child aged 6, and child's parental separation > 6 months, at ages 2 to 9. Statistical models rarely demonstrate causal pathways beyond reasonable doubt. Intuitive insights gained from statistical analyses can however lead to collection of detailed case material as a basis for understanding causal pathways, and offering individualized intervention and therapy. This is illustrated by two case histories.

Introduction

Social work is both an integrative and an applied discipline. It seeks to integrate various disciplines (sociology, psychology, economics, social philosophy, policy studies, administration and social history) in the understanding, management and alleviation of social and interpersonal problems of individuals, couples, families and communities (the discipline of medicine likewise integrates and applies a number of "pure" disciplines in the management and cure of physical and psychological ills). The "medical model" is often criticized by social workers as a rigid and sometimes dehumanizing method of dealing with people. Nevertheless, in some branches of medicine (particularly in social psychiatry) models of diagnosis and practice are flexible and humane, recognizing the powerful influences which external factors have on how an individual presents him or her self as a person with physical, social and interpersonal problems. The work of the English psychiatrist Michael Rutter (e.g. Rutter, 1987) exemplifies this humane and flexible approach, which nevertheless serves high standards of scientific rigor.

Another medical group has elaborated a flexible model for understanding child development in ways which do justice to other disciplines (in particular, interactive social psychology), while at the same time attending to the needs of children and their parents in ways which recognized the powerful influence which the family environment can have on children and their problems. This group of New York neuropsychiatrists was originally led by Herbert Birch whose book *Brain Damage in Children* (Birch, Chess & Thomas, 1964) was a major influence on our study of children with epilepsy, in which (following Birch) it was argued that behavioral outcomes for children reflect a combination of underlying central nervous system (CNS) problems, family environments and interactions, and reactions of peers and teachers to a child having seizures (Bagley, 1972). We have retained this interactive perspective in analyzing data from the British Child Development Study (Bagley, Young & Scully, 1983). Temperament (the idea that a child has relatively fixed propensities in reacting to stress and stimuli which are apparent early in life, has proved to be valuable in parent counseling and support (Birch, Thomas & Chess, 1964) and in providing support for adoptive parents - adopted children are particularly likely to include young children with atypical combinations of temperamental style, CNS problems, and earlier dysfunctional parenting (Bagley et al., 1983).

Another striking model for social work research and practice has been the later work from the New York Longitudinal Study (NYLS), which owes much to the influence of Herbert Birch on interaction of biological and social systems. These studies (Chess and Thomas, 1984) are of children with and without various central nervous system (CNS) impairments in infancy, following an epidemic of scarlet fever which caused CNS impairments in a number of New York children. In the early work with a cohort of 141 children, these researchers first observed how the children, as infants, reacted to external stimuli, including interactions with parents and siblings (Graham, Rutter and George, 1973). From these observations it was found that temperament is a relatively stable aspect of personal functioning established early in life, and is probably genetic in origin (Chess & Thomas, 1984). Three main types of temperament have been identified. The first (comprising about 20 percent of all children) is that of *easy temperament* - these children are characterized by "... regularity, positive approach responses to new stimuli, high adaptability to change, and mild or moderate mood intensity ... These children quickly develop regular sleep and feeding schedules, take to most new feeds easily, accept most frustration with little fuss ... such a child is aptly called the easy child, and is usually a joy to his parents, pediatricians and teachers " (Chess & Thomas, 1984 p. 43).

The second type of personal functioning is found "... in the group with irregularity in biological functions, negative withdrawal responses to new stimuli, non-adaptability or slow adaptability to change, and intense mood expressions which are frequently negative. These children show irregular sleep and feeding schedules ... prolonged adjustment periods to new routines, people or situations, and relatively loud periods of crying. Laughter also is characteristically loud. Frustration typically produces a violent tantrum. This is the difficult child, and mothers and pediatricians find such youngsters difficult indeed. This group comprises about 10 percent ..." (Chess & Thomas, 1984 p. 43).

The third main type of personality functioning in infancy and early childhood "... is marked by a combination of negative responses of mild intensity to new stimuli with slow adaptability after repeated contact. In contrast to the difficult children, these youngsters are characterized by mild intensity of reactions, whether positive or negative, and by less tendency to show irregularity of biological functions. [This is] the slow-to-warm-up child ... about 15 percent of our NYLS sample falls into this category." (Thomas & Chess, 1984 pp 43-4). The residual 35 percent in the NYLS had personality styles which could not be easily classified, partly because CNS problems impinged on their personal functioning.

Despite the implicit potential for the development of behavioral problems (both conduct disorder, and emotional disorder) "difficult" temperament (intense mood reactions and difficulty in adapting to change) and "slow to warm up or sluggish temperament" (mild reaction but slow adaptability) do not by themselves predict later problems of behavior and adaptation unless they are combined with stressors such as central nervous system (CNS) trauma and/or inappropriate parenting (a "lack of fit" between parenting style and the child's temperamental needs). Temperament in this interactive model can influence the development of problems of behavior and self-esteem in later years (Chess, Thomas & Birch, 1965; Chess & Thomas, 1984 & 1986; Bagley, 1972 & 1991).

The hypothesis of the present research, derived from the work of Chess and Thomas with the NYLS is that behavior problems in childhood and adolescence reflect the complex interactions of a variety of factors, including those within the child (difficult temperament, CNS impairment including hyperactivity, attention deficit, neurologically based learning problems, epilepsy, hemiplegia, etc., and those external to the child (the interpersonal environment). The assumed process of interaction is complex, with cause and effect difficult to detect at any point in time; a child's negative behavior may become self-confirming as adults despair at the failure of their methods of discipline, care and control. These parents then become punitive and rejecting towards a child whose needs are for acceptance and understanding. Parents who are themselves stressed by external factors, or who have limited conceptual models for coping with problems, parents who have poor self-esteem, who are often depressed, and whose own childhoods were punitive, abusive and unrewarding are particularly likely to be unable to give their "difficult" or CNS-impaired child appropriate feedback which could prevent the evolution of serious behavior disorders, and delinquency (e.g. Patterson, 1986; Thomas & Chess, 1977).

However, the process of interaction between variables in human development in producing a particular psychosocial outcome is difficult to describe in terms of the standard methodologies of social science. As Olson, Bates and Bayles (1990) have noted in trying to predict impulsive behavior at age six from data on temperament at age two, it is virtually impossible to know whether parental strategies were unsuccessful (and uninfluential) attempts to cope with a child's difficult temperament, or were punitive or inappropriate reactions to the child's temperament which influenced the evolution of a difficult temperament into a behavior disorder. The intense mood reactions of the "difficult temperament" child, combined with dislike of change or novelty, periods of crying and bursts of temper are not in themselves signs of behavior disorder. But the added vulnerability of CNS-disorder, and/or angry rejection or punishment by a caretaker may direct the evolution of a behavior disorder.

Although as Chess and Thomas (1984) have urged, "goodness of fit" between child temperament and parenting style is essential for healthy child outcomes (in terms of mental health), it may be a matter of luck, social skill, good professional advice, or family support, or an otherwise unpressured lifestyle more available to middle-class parents, which facilitates this positive feedback. We assume however (as Rutter, 1987 has argued in his review of psychosocial resilience and protective mechanisms in development) that when "variables" interact in human development the process is a dynamic one, so that different combinations of variables create new vulnerabilities, new strengths, and new outcomes at different stages of development. Moreover, the process becomes more complex, and more dynamic as the child becomes older and an increasing number of social, personal and biological variables become involved in this interaction process.

Background of the present study

Our study is strongly influenced in concept and design by the New York Longitudinal Study of a cohort of young children, some of whom had CNS-impairment (Birch et al., 1964; Thomas & Chess, 1977; Chess & Thomas, 1984 & 1986). We identified a cohort of children born in Calgary, Canada born in a 6-month period in the early 1980s (Bagley, 1988 & 1990). Two contrasted groups of children were randomly sampled from health clinics following mandatory registration of the child's birth. The first group were 500 "at risk" newborns according to criteria established in the British National Child Development Study (Alberman & Goldstein, 1970). The second group of 500 infants were controls with exact matching for age, sex and clinic attended (thus broadly controlling for neighborhood factors and socioeconomic background).

Initial data were collected by community health nurses in standard monitoring of all newborns and their mothers in health clinics. None of the controls was considered to be at risk in terms of the criteria used (birthweight < 2,000 gms; problems of pregnancy and delivery; neonatal health problems; mother a teenaged single parent; mother living in poverty; mother's drug/alcohol problems). Largest sample loss occurred in the follow-up when the children were aged, on average, 2.7 years.

At first follow-up, 12.0 percent of those retained had a physical or mental disability ranging from mild to severe; at the second follow-up (when children aged 6 to 7) the portion of children with CNS-disability (defined by the school boards' decision that the child had a CNS disability likely to interfere with behavior and/or learning) was 6.2 percent, due to spontaneous remission of symptoms or medical reassessment. Mothers' ratings of temperament using the Carey scales (Carey & McDevitt, 1978 & 1980; Sostek, 1978; Bagley, 1991) were made when children were aged 2 to 3. At this time mothers also completed the Home Screening Questionnaire (HSQ) devised by Frankenberg and Coons (1986). The HSQ measures lack of quality in parent-child relationships, material poverty in child care, and punitiveness in child-rearing. In this and later sweeps, all interviews and testing took place in the mother's home, and were conducted by women graduates in social work, nursing and education. No direct interview or test data on fathers was collected, because of their unavailability in some families and/or limitations of research funding.

The children were studied in the third data sweep at mean age 6.7 years, and completed the Peabody Picture Vocabulary Test (PPVT - Altepeter, 1985). At this time mothers completed the Parenting Stress Index (Abidin, 1983) measuring parenting difficulty, depression and discouragement in child care roles. Mothers also completed a number of mental health measures, as well as details of any history of neglect and abuse in their own childhood: 41 mothers with very neglectful and abusive childhoods, and currently very poor self-esteem were enrolled at this stage in an experimental study designed to reduce social isolation and improve self-esteem, with an enhancement of child care skills (Bagley and Young, 1990 & 1997). These 41 women and their children have not been included in the present study, since the counseling offered including a focus on adult-child relationships. Thus of the 606 children with complete data-sets in the third follow-up (when the cohort had a mean age of 9.9 years), 565 are included in the present report. Additional measures included family structure, and parental absences.

The dependent measure in the study reported here, completed by teachers when the children were on average aged 9.9 years is the conduct disorder sub-scale of the Rutter behavior disorder measure (Rutter, Tizard & Whitmore, 1970). This scale measures emotional disorders, hyperactivity, and aggressive or conduct disorder. The conduct disorder sub-scale used is a 9-item scale with a description of the child's classroom and school behaviors on the items: steals, lies, has temper tantrums, quarrelsome, destructive, fights, disliked, irritable, disobedient. Each item coded as 0=not present, 1=sometimes present, 3=often present. We also asked mothers to give a detailed and discursive history of family interactions, time and nature of onset of children's problems, and onset date of external stressors.

As in many longitudinal studies, there has been considerable sample loss (some 40 percent over nine years). Sample loss and retention implies two biases: loss of highly mobile and/or unstable parents (who were usually in the "at-risk" category); and retention of parents perceiving problems in their children (who were also predominantly in the "at-risk" category). This latter group was both interested in the research and often also hoped that the research could give advice and referral with regard to child problems, which we were ethically obliged to do. The two types of sample loss have thus worked in opposite directions, losing some parents (especially Aboriginal people, and young, single mothers) whilst retaining others. Those retained are disproportionately represented by children with neurological and other health problems, and parents living in intergenerational poverty, a group in which parents were often born in Calgary, and had lived all their lives (often with or close to their parents) in poor quality or public housing.

The ecological setting of the research

Calgary is the North American center of several oil and natural gas companies, and oil wells exist even within the city limits. Calgary's income per head places it as the fifth most prosperous city in North America (and thus in the world). Despite this, Calgary has a substantial population who experience chronic, and often intergenerational poverty (incomes at or below the public financial assistance rate for Alberta, including those earning the minimum wage: see Bagley, 1992a for definitions). Chronically poor mothers have, according to this longitudinal study, greatly elevated rates of parenting stress, and chronic or intermittent depression (Bagley, 1992a). Economically poor residents of Calgary tend to live in zones of poor quality or subsidized housing, areas which have significantly higher rates of juvenile and adult crime, proportion of children removed into government care following neglect or abuse, adults who experienced physical and sexual abuse as children, and proportion of children injured or killed by motor vehicles (Bagley & Kufeldt, 1989; Bagley, 1992b & 1995). Children with problems of conduct disorder, poor scholastic achievement, poor attention span, and underlying neurological problems are particularly likely to live in areas where they have to cross busy roads in journeys to school, park and playground: such children are significantly more likely than others to be hit, injured and killed by traffic (Bagley, 1993).

Methods of data analysis

Three types of quantitative analysis have been conducted, with conduct disorder scores as the dependent or predicted variable. Stepwise multiple regression (Table 7.1) assigned numerical value (in the form of partial and multiple correlations) to antecedent factors in the potential emergence of serious behavioral problems. Complex predictions can be measured in various ways, and one important but often neglected aspect of measurement is the identification of *sub-types* at new stages of development (Bagley, 1988). This technique has proved valuable, for instance, in identifying the nature and prognosis of childhood autism (Bagley & McGeein, 1989). As Caspi and Silva (1995) point out, much research on personality is "variable-focused" ; but, as they argue, "person-centered" research (e.g., using cluster analysis techniques for classifying individuals rather than variables) is often more appropriate in tracking stability and change in personality and adaptation over time. One good example of this is Magnusson's (1988) study of person-environment interaction.

In the present study cluster analysis has been employed in order to see if different causal patterns can fit into distinct sub-types of cases. Cluster analysis used when the cohort was aged six did identify sub-groups of children experiencing different kinds of stress, with different emotional and behavioral outcomes (Bagley, 1988).

An attempt has also been made to describe the interaction process (the combination of different types and amounts of predictor variables as antecedent to the dependent variable) using an "interaction table" (Maxwell, 1975). The variables entered into this analysis (Table 7.2) were selected on the basis of their contribution to regression analysis, as well as their presumed theoretical importance: presence or absence of CNS handicap at children's mean age 2.7; child's "difficult temperament" (median split, as near as possible) at children's mean age 2.7; mother's parenting stress score (Abidin's instrument, with median split) when children's mean age 6.7; absence of a parent for 6 months or more when child aged 2 to 9 (this was a measure of separation from bonded figures, and did not include fathers who had no contact with the child since the time of the child's birth).

Hypotheses and methods of research

Following the work of Thomas, Birch, Chess and Robbins (1961) we expect that conduct disorder in our cohort of 9-year-olds can best be predicted or understood by the interaction of biological, interactional and social factors in producing different types (and therefore different sub-groups) of outcome in terms of behavioral profiles. The variables chosen for analysis all have a sound underpinning from previous work in terms of their potentially negative impact on family interactions, and maternal and child behavior. The methodologies chosen assume that both quantitative and qualitative methods are needed to elucidate the complex, interacting strands which underlie the development of conduct disorder (and its later sequels including school drop-out, delinquency and other problem behaviors).

Summary of quantitative and qualitative findings

Multiple regression

We mention here only variables which were significant predictors of conduct disorder both before and after regression (partial r of 0.10, p <.05 - see Table

7.1). Strongest predictor was Abidin's Parenting Stress Index, completed by mother when child was 6 (r=.33), followed by CNS disability (r=.25 before regression, partial r=0.22); Difficult Temperament at age 2 (r=.21, partial r=.19); Home Screening Questionnaire when child aged 2 (r=.23, partial r=.14); separation from parent > 6 months, after child 2 (r=.30, partial r=.14); family's sole income public welfare cheque (or dollar equivalent in low wage-earning families) when child 6 and 9 (r=.27, partial r=0.12). Multiple r for these six items is 0.53, explaining 26% of variance in conduct disorder scores.

The picture which emerges from regression analysis points to the complex combinations of temperament, biomedical problems, maternal stress and reactions to child, and environmental stressors, particularly chronic poverty. It remains difficult however to say that any one factor has causal significance in the absence of the other factors: indeed, the complex interactive, loop-back model outlined by Chess and Thomas (1986) probably requires a qualitative elaboration before it can be understood properly.

Interaction table based on branching analysis

Mean conduct disorder score for the entire sample is 3.76 (Table 7.2 and 7.3), which breaks into 2.4 vs. 5.2 (p <.001) for low and high parenting stress children. High parenting stress breaks into dichotomization of difficult temperament (means 3.8 vs. 6.5, p<.01). The Difficult Temperament group breaks down into No-Separation vs. Separation, with further branchings by presence or absence of CNS disorder. Overall, there are 16 sub-groups, with highest mean conduct disorder score for any sub-group of 11.2. This last group includes only four children for whom all four of the antecedent (and perhaps causal) factors are present - Difficult Temperament; High Parenting Stress; CNS Disorder; Parental Separation. In 22 children three of these factors are present: the mean conduct disorder score of this group is of 8.43. The clear implications of this model are that the more stress factors are present (internal to the child, in parental-child interaction, and external to the family) the more likely it is that a child (particularly a male child) will exhibit conduct disorder. Thus the 129 children with none of the stressors present have a conduct disorder score of 0.90, while the 26 children with 3 or 4 stressors have a conduct disorder score of 8.85, an odds-ratio of 1:9.8 (t=17.9 p<.001).

Cluster analysis

For the present cohort we initially hypothesized that the variables previously identified as important for development of conduct disorder could identify distinct clusters of individuals, with contrasted antecedents (and perhaps causes) of behavioral outcome. This hypothesis assumes (as argued by Hope, 1968) that complex interactions in analysis of variance, distinct groupings of variables in a principal components analysis, and unique grouping of individuals in a component or cluster analysis, all reflect aspects of the same basic realities of data identified by the general linear model.

In analysis of data when the cohort was aged 6.7, cluster analysis identified ten distinct sub-types of individuals with particular profiles on family and child characteristics (Bagley, 1988). These 10 clusters (when collapsed into five groups) bear a strong resemblance to the five clusters obtained when the children were 9; indeed much of the data used for clustering at mean ages 6.7 and 9.9 are identical. What is striking however is the degree to which these sub-types differentiate groups of children who have markedly different behavioral outcomes (Table 7.4). This analysis gives a picture which is somewhat different from the regression and interaction table analysis: in part, this reflects the fact that maternal stress and child's difficult temperament have been scored by a dichotomy at the highest quartile, rather than at the median - this seems to give the most clearly differentiated group structure, in terms of conduct disorder scores.

The five clusters extracted by k-means cluster analysis using the BMDP program (Engelman & Hartigan, 1993) are labeled: A "Advantaged homes, few stressors": children's conduct disorder mean 0.98. B "Highly stressed mothers, often in poverty, with CNS impaired children, as well as family disruption": child's conduct disorder mean 8.51. (Additional qualitative data indicate that these women were frequently depressed, and sometimes had personal difficulties in parenting reflecting their own abusive childhoods). C "Mothers with lower stress scores in stable, non-poverty homes, but with a CNS impaired child at nearly three times the average rate": children's conduct disorder mean 2.20. D "Children with higher scores on measure of difficult temperament, but usually unstressed mothers": children's conduct disorder mean 2.75. E "Often stressed mothers more often in chronic poverty, and often with a 'difficult' child": children's conduct disorder mean 4.53.

Qualitative data from open-ended interviews indicated that the coping skills of parents in Clusters B and E were often inadequate, and they frequently reacted with exasperation, despair and anger at apparently intractable naughtiness in their child. The use of emotional rejection and physical punishment was common in both groups. Given the generally poor lack of fit between parenting style and child's behavior in these two groups, we would expect that without intervention and help, the behavior of these children might deteriorate over time, with serious problems of delinquency developing.

Discussion and case histories

The presentation of a mass of statistical data will likely leave the reader (and the authors) somewhat frustrated: we have identified many statistically significant relationships which are consistent over time, and between different types of analysis. Yet we remain uncertain about clear patterns of cause: much more frequent measurements would be needed than the 3-year intervals in collecting data used in this study. Indeed, for the establishment of causal patterns we would probably have to interview respondents about every six months: but such frequent interviewing would likely influence behavioral outcomes for children, given that mothers often sought advice on children's problems from the research interviewers. With no certainty of cause, we merely stress the importance of at least five key factors which interact, as Chess and Thomas (1984; 1986) have argued, in a dynamic manner.

Like Chess and Thomas in their psychiatric practice, we turn to individual case studies to arrive at a qualitative or intuitive understanding of how key variables, identified in statistical analyses, interact and influence outcomes which are either unique, or apply to relatively small groups of children. In this respect, cluster analysis could be particularly useful since it allows us to contrast sub-groups in which causal pathways may be dissimilar (e.g. Bagley, 1996).

Two case histories1 illustrate well the different outcomes which apparently similar children can have when faced with different family and interpersonal environments.

Tom (in Cluster C) was born ten weeks prematurely, weighing less than 2 pounds at birth. He spent 6 weeks in an intensive care nursery. In his first year of life he had several febrile convulsions, and after age two had minor seizures with a focus in the left temporal lobe. He was overactive, lively and inquisitive, but reacted loudly and aggressively to change and difficulty, and had a high score on the "difficult child" temperament profile at age 2. He has one older sister. Tom's mother (owner of a clothing store) and father (a senior executive) aggressively organized available medical and social services on their son's behalf, and he received optimum care including speech therapy, and physical therapy for a right-sided movement co-ordination problem. His PPVT scores at age 6, and WISC scores at age 9 were in the normal range. Tom's parents consulted a psychologist, who developed an interactive, behavioral regime (based on Patterson's model) which allowed them to give optimum feedback to their son, and reinforcement for good behavior. The parents eagerly accepted the "goodness of fit" model. Tom was enrolled in a private school which specialized in relatively bright children with learning problems (dyslexia, etc.), and received individual attention for his learning and attention problems.[2] The school co-operated with the psychologist in devising a learning and interpersonal environment which positively rewarded and channeled Tom's lively, active behavior into constructive channels. By the age of nine he was achieving at a grade appropriate level, and had a conduct disorder score of 2. His seizure problems had long since been controlled by medication: withdrawal of medication two years earlier had not been followed by further seizures. Tom had slight, unilateral hemiplegia which restricted his ability in sports, but this was tolerantly accepted by his peers. In class, he was according to his teacher's report, a cheerful and popular boy.

Mark (in Cluster B) was also born prematurely, and spent time in the intensive care nursery. Like Tom, he had febrile convulsions, and later was diagnosed with left-sided, temporal lobe epilepsy. His PPVT score was in the normal range at age 6; at age 9 his WISC-R IQ score was 104. Unlike Tom he did not have any motor problems. However he was overactive, constantly complaining or crying, had frequent temper tantrums and was rated as having an extremely difficult temperament at age two. Mark was the youngest of three children. His father was absent from home for long periods and gave little support to his wife over child care. Mark's mother was markedly depressed, and coped with his overactive and aggressive behavior by alternately ignoring him (he was shut in a bare room for many hours at a time - the room was stripped of furniture and toys, to prevent Mark from destroying them), and then by smacking or beating. No kind of punishment had any positive effect, and Mark's behavior continued to deteriorate.   His seizure problem and his overactivity were controlled to some extent by medication. But on a regime of Carbamazepine and Ritalin Mark became sullen and withdrawn, or "sneaky" as his mother said. In school he stole and bullied, and was in turn rejected by other children. By age nine he could barely read, and was extremely unpopular because of unpredictable aggression. Mark's father left the family when the boy was seven. Then his older brother then aged 12, took on the function of belting Mark with a strap when he was particularly naughty. His still depressed mother seemed to scapegoat Mark, and she blamed him (perhaps correctly) for his father's departure.

The family moved neighborhoods several times as their economic position deteriorated, but in each new school Mark's behavior seemed worse. He took to leaving school during the day and roaming the neighborhood, and was apprehended whilst shoplifting. Child welfare services became involved, and Mark's mother requested (in Mark's presence) that he be removed to a foster home. This request was unsuccessful, but reinforced Mark's feelings of marginality and rejection. Mark's score on the measure of aggressive behavior was 15, the maximum scored by any child in this cohort.

These two cases of apparently similar children in terms of birth and infant problems, early temperament and intelligence, illustrate how one environment may be reflected in a normal outcome, and another by a situation where major delinquency seems to be a likely outcome. Statistical analyses point to, but cannot prove the causal and interactive nature of variables predicting high levels of conduct disorder. Extensive case histories can in fact give more clues as to which variables are antecedent in time, and how parents and children caused or reacted to various stressors over time, in ways which even the most systematic path analyses, LISREL modeling, and latent structure analysis cannot properly identify. Nor can these techniques (all of which we have applied to the data set) explain much more than a quarter of the variance in the predicted outcome, of conduct disorder.[3]

However, both statistical and case study analyses seem to support the Chess and Thomas (1984) concept of lack of fit between parental intervention strategies and the child's developmental needs, as indicated by type of personality or temperament. In terms of social and psychological strategies, we need to intervene at *all* levels, since it is impossible to be certain for any particular child which factors are likely to be dominant in causing negative behavioral outcomes.

In a somewhat similar study to our own, Caspi, Henry, McGee, Moffitt and Silva (1995) could reach no firm *causal* conclusions from statistically significant links of data in a longitudinal study predicting behavior problems at age 15 from temperament at age 3: but they do point to one possibility: "... behavioral disorders may represent the cumulative consequences of early behavioral styles that are elaborated through evocative, reactive and proactive person-environment interactions, culminating in psychopathological problems later in life ... These specific pathways need to be documented." (p. 66). These pathways can involve "spiraling up" (in the case of Tom), and "spiraling down" (in the case of Mark).

The researchers made a special referral for Mark's mother to social services; but all of this early intervention was ineffective. Mark's mother had problems keeping appointments, and became terrified of social workers since she had worked for a short time whilst receiving a social assistance cheque (technically, a criminal offense, and one which would have cut her off welfare). She was also terrified that social workers would remove her other children, and that she would never see them again. What Mark's mother needed was a child care worker who would give daily support, supervision and training in behavioral management and "goodness-of-fit" strategies for moving Mark into an upward spiral. At a time of severe cutbacks in social services in Alberta, such potentially effective strategies for Mark's family were unavailable.

Special follow-up for these two boys when they were aged 15 indicated both predicted and unpredicted outcomes. Tom's mother continued to defend her son against external stressors, but in ways which now appeared to the researchers to be overprotective. Tom was certainly not aggressive, but he was now somewhat isolated in his secondary school, and although he had two good friends he was rather marginal in wider peer networks in school. When tested at age 15 he displayed signs of sub-clinical anxiety, quite similar to those we have observed in adopted adolescents and young adults (Bagley, Young & Scully, 1983).

Mark's outcome at age 15 confirmed the downward spiral identified at age 9. He had been convicted of a number of offenses, and was serving a term in a young offenders' institution.

Conclusions

The present study points to the following strategies, attempted simultaneously, as a simulation of Tom's "spiraling up" : behavioral training for both child and parents to ensure a "goodness of fit" in matching parenting strategies with child's reactions, on the lines suggested by Patterson (1986) and Chess and Thomas (1986); full neuropsychiatric investigation and treatments, but with a conservative reliance on drug regimes; educational interventions to reduce scholastic failure, and classroom unpopularity; and social work intervention to diminish poverty and parenting stress, and the negative effects of family dysfunction and breakdown. *All* of these strategies need to be employed simultaneously: multiple strategies can, according to our qualitative analyses, reinforce one another and make the other strategies effective.

An additional type of intervention is at the neighborhood or community level, focusing on schools and working with teachers in identifying children with current behavioral and learning problems, and stressed home backgrounds. This focus has been identified by ecological work showing that in some urban districts there is a disproportionate number of families in chronic poverty, with children who often display symptoms of behavioral and emotional disorders, and learning problems.

A final comment, on "experimenter effects" : many mothers in this study came to expect a visit from research interviewers about every three years, and a number contacted us in between interviews for advice on parent-child problems. This we gave, as well as referrals to appropriate agencies.[4] While some of the advice given by research interviewers was ineffective, other advice and referrals may well have helped children and families, so that the research process itself may have influenced results in a positive direction. This is particularly likely since one of the strategies employed with vulnerable sub-groups was to link them with successful parents and peers in social support and peer-counseling networks (Bagley & Young, 1990 & 1997; Bagley & Mallick, 1996).

Table 7.1   Factor predicting conduct disorder in 565 9-year-olds regression analysis

Predictor	Original r	Partial r	Multiple r	Variance Explained
Parenting Stress when child 6	0.33	0.33	0.33	11%
CNS Disability	0.25	0.22	0.41	18%
Difficult temperament at age 2	0.21	0.19	0.49	24%
Home screening questionnaire when child age 2	0.23	0.14	0.50	25%
Separation from parent > 6 months since child age 2	0.30	0.14	0.52	27%
Parent's sole income, welfare cheque when child 6 & 9	0.27	0.11	0.53	28%

Note Since a higher score on the behavior disorder measure indicates more disturbed behavior, positive initial correlations indicate an association with negative behaviors. Partial correlations of 0.1 or greater are significant at the 5 percent level, or beyond. Variables significant at the outset, but insignificant after regression analysis (partial r less than 0.10) were not included in the above set of predictors. Their original correlations with aggressive behavior at age 9, were:
Physical disability not involving CNS, 0.14; male sex, 0.19; mother's years of education, -0.25; household income when child aged 9, -0.18; child's "easy" temperament at age 2, -0.21; child attended pre-school daycare continuously from infancy, 0.11; child's score on Peabody Picture Vocabulary Test at age 6, -0.17. Regression analysis used the SPSS program (Nie et al, 1975).
"Externalizing behavior scale" based on factor analysis of Rutter et al's (1971) scale completed by teachers, and groups the items: destructive; fights; disliked; irritable; disobedient; lies; steals; resentful; bullies.

Table 7.2   **Breakdown of mean conduct disorder scores by parenting stress scores, child's difficult temperament, parental separation, and central nervous system disability measured at earlier points in time**

Entire Sample (N= 565) *Mean conduct disorder score 3.8*															
Parenting stress low 2.5								Parenting stress high 5.0							
Difficult temperament -1.2				Difficult temperament +4.2				Difficult temperament - 4.3				Difficult temperament +6.1			
Sep -		Sep +		Sep -		Sep +		Sep -		Sep +		Sep -		Sep +	
CNS		CNS		CNS		CNS		CNS		CNS		CNS		CNS	
-	+	-	+	-	+	-	+	-	+	-	+	-	+	-	+
Mean conduct disorder scores:															
1.1	1.4	1.5	7.0	4.3	5.3	3.4	5.0	3.9	8.7	4.9	8.7	5.6	9.2	8.2	11.2
Numbers in each group:															
129	5	6	1	125	7	8	1	124	7	8	3	119	7	11	4

Note: Range of scores on the 9-item behavior disorder measure is 0 to 15, with a theoretical maximum of 18. The scale was completed by teachers on the dimension "never" (scored 0); "sometimes" (scored 1); "frequently" (scored 2) for the items: steals; lies; has temper tantrums; quarrelsome; destructive; fights; disliked by others; irritable; disobedient. "Parenting stress" scores divided at the median point. "Difficult temperament" defined by scores above the median for the measure of temperament

Table 7.3   Mean scores on measure of conduct disorder in 9-year-olds by number and type of stress and development factors

Number of factors	Number of children	Mean score on measure of conduct disorder (SD)	Ratios
None	129	1.10(1.8)	1.0
One	260	3.99(3.1)	3.5
Two	150	5.58(2.7)	5.1
Three/Four	26	8.85(3.6)	8.0

Note: This table is based on a condensation of Table 2. The four factors predicting outcome at age 9 (i.e. conduct disorder measure) are: child's "difficult temperament" at age two; disability involving central nervous system, identified at age two; scores on Abidin's parent stress index completed by mother when child aged 6; and separation from a parent for 6 or more months when child aged 0 to 9. Bonferroni post-hoc analysis: no stressors vs. one, two or three+ stressors, $p < .001$ in all comparisons.

Table 7.4   Cluster analysis of family and child variables with differential scores on measures of conduct disorder or aggression

Group Maternal Stress	CNS Disorder	Difficult Temperament	Poverty 6 & 9	Parental Absence 2-9	Conduct Disorder mean
A (104) 3.5%	1.9%	19.2%	0.0%	0.0%	0.98
B (98) 29.6%	30.1%	24.5%	36.7%	10.2%	8.51
C (119) 39.7%	0.0%	11.8%	0.0%	0.0%	2.20
D (101) 8.9%	1.0%	40.6%	2.0%	8.9%	2.75
E (143) 29.4%	1.4%	30.1%	26.6%	0.7%	4.53

Note: Conduct Disorder means were not used for clustering purposes, and are used as external validators of the clusters. Proportions are those of the number in each group, and are calculated horizontally. Indicators of Maternal Stress and Difficult Temperament based on proportions in highest quartile.

References

Abidin, R. (1983). *Parenting Stress Index.* Richmond, VA: University of Virginia, Institute of Clinical Psychology.

Alberman, E. & Goldstein, H. (1970). The 'at risk' register: a statistical evaluation. *British Journal of Preventive and Social Medicine, 24,* 129-135.

Alterpeter, T. (1985). Use of the PPVT-R for intellectual screening with a preschool pediatric sample. *Journal of Pediatric Psychology, 10,* 195-198.

Bagley, C. (1972). *The Social Psychology of the Child with Epilepsy.* London: Routledge.

Bagley, C. (1988). Day care, maternal health and child development: evidence from a longitudinal study. *Early Child Development and Care, 39,* 134-161.

Bagley, C. (1990). *A Long-Term Study of Temperament, Disability, Mental Health and Family Structure: Phase One.* London: McDonald.

Bagley, C. (1991). Factor structure of temperament in the third year of life. *Journal of General Psychology, 118,* 291-297.

Bagley, C. (1992a). Psychological dimensions of poverty and parenthood. *International Journal of Marriage and the Family, 1,* 37-49.

Bagley, C. (1992b). The urban setting of juvenile pedestrian injuries: a study of behavioral ecology and social disadvantage. *Accident Analysis and Prevention, 24,* 673-678.

Bagley, C. (1993). The urban environment and child pedestrian and bicycle injuries: interaction of ecological and personality characteristics. *Journal of Community and Applied Psychology, 2,* 1-9.

Bagley, C. (1995). *Child Sexual Abuse and Mental Health in Adolescents and Adults: Canadian and British Perspectives.* Brookfield, VT: Avebury International.

Bagley, C. (1996). A typology of child sexual abuse: addressing the paradox of interlocking emotional, physical and sexual abuse as causes of adult psychiatric sequels in women. *Canadian Journal of Human Sexuality, 5,* 101-112.

Bagley, C. & Kufeldt, K. (1989). Juvenile delinquency and child pedestrian accidents: an ecological analysis. *Perceptual and Motor Skills, 69,* 1281-1282.

Bagley, C. & McGeein, V. (1989). The taxonomy and course of childhood autism. *Perceptual and Motor Skills, 69,* 1264-1266.

Bagley, C. & Mallick, K. (1996). Towards achievement of reading potential in mainstreamed 13-year-olds: peer counseling strategies. *Disability and Society, 11,* 83-90.

Bagley, C., Wood, L. & Young, C. (1994). Victim to abuser: mental health and behavioral sequels of the sexual abuse of males in childhood. *Child Abuse and Neglect, 18,* 683-697.

Bagley, C. & Young, L. (1990). Depression, self-esteem and suicidal behavior as sequels of sexual abuse in childhood: research and therapy. In M. Rothery & G. Cameron (Eds.). *Child Maltreatment: Expanded Concepts of Helping,* 183-219. Hillsdale, NJ: Lawrence Erlbaum.

Bagley, C. & Young, L. (1997). Sexual abuse and suicidal behaviors in adult women: a controlled intervention. In C. Bagley & R. Ramsay (Eds). *Suicidal behavior in adolescents and adults: Research, taxonomy and prevention,* 220-243. Brookfield, VT: Avebury International.

Bagley, C., Young, L. & Scully, A. (1983). *Transracial and international adoption: Mental health perspectives.* Brookfield, VT: Avebury International.

Birch, H., Chess, S. & Thomas, A. (1964). *Brain Damage in Children: Biological and Social Aspects.* Baltimore, MD: Williams and Wilkins.

Carey, W. & McDevitt, S. (1978). Stability and change in individual temperament diagnoses from infancy to early childhood. *Journal of the American Academy of Child Psychiatry, 17,* 331-337.

Carey, W. & McDevitt, S. (1980). Minimal brain damage and hyperkinesis. *American Journal of Diseases of Children, 134,* 926-929.

Caspi, A., Henry, B., McGee, R., Moffitt, G.H., & Silva, P. (1995). Temperamental origins of child and adolescent behavior problems: from age three to age 15. *Child Development, 66,* 58-68.

Caspi, A. & Silva, P. (1995). Temperamental qualities at age three predict personality traits in young adulthood: longitudinal evidence from a birth cohort. *Child Development, 66,* 486-498.

Chess, S. , Thomas, A. & Birch, H. (1965). *Your child is a person: A psychological approach to parenthood without guilt.* New York: Viking Press.

Chess, S. & Thomas, A. (1984). *Origins and Evolution of Behavior Disorders.* New York: Brunner-Mazel.

Chess, S. & Thomas, A. (1986). *Temperament in Clinical Practice.* New York: Guilford Press.

Engelman, L. & Hartigan, J. (1993). K-means clustering, in: W. Dixon (Ed.) *BMDP statistical software,* pp.462-472. Berkeley, CA: University of California Press.

Frankenberg, W. & Coons, C. (1986). Home screening questionnaire: its validity in assessing home environment. *Journal of Pediatrics, 108,* 624-626.

Graham, P., Rutter, M. & George, S. (1973). Temperamental characteristics as predictors of behavior disorders in children. *American Journal of Orthopsychiatry, 43,* 328-339.

Hope, K. (1968). *Methods of Multivariate Analysis.* London: University of London Press.

Magnusson, D. (1988). *Individual Development from an Interactional. Perspective* Hillsdale, NJ: Erlbaum.

Maxwell, A. (1975). *Analyzing Qualitative Data.* London: Chapman & Hall.

Olson, S., Bates, J. & Bayles, K. (1990). Early antecedents of childhood impulsivity: the role of parent-child interaction, cognitive competence, and temperament. *Journal of Abnormal Child Psychology, 18,* 317-334.

Patterson, G. (1986). Performance models for antisocial boys. *American Psychologist, 41,* 432-444.

Rutter, M. (1987). Psychosocial resilience and protective mechanisms. *American Journal of Orthopsychiatry, 57,* 316-331.

Rutter, M., Tizard, J. & Whitmore, K. (1970). *Education, Health and Behavior.* London: Longman.

Sostek, A. (1978). Infant scales in the pediatric setting: the Brazelton neonatal behavioral assessment scale and the Carey Infant Temperament Questionnaire. *Journal of Pediatric Psychology, 3,* 113-121.

Thomas, A., Birch, H., Chess, S. & Robbins, L. (1961). Individuality in responses of children to similar environmental situations. *American Journal of Psychiatry, 117,* 434-441.

Thomas, A. & Chess, S. (1977). *Temperament and Development.* New York: Brunner-Mazel.

Wyatt, G., Newcomb, M. & Riederle, M. (1993). *Sexual Abuse and Consensual Sex: Women's Development Patterns and Outcomes.* London: Sage.

Notes

1   Rather than using the psychiatric model of trying to define "caseness" , we have used the psychological technique of using continuous distributions on the measures of temperament, using median and quartile cut-off points in some cases (e.g. Tables 7.2, 7.3 & 7.4), or the mean score for the temperament sub-types (as in Table 7.1).

2   In this school classes have a maximum size of ten. Each child has a personal work station, with individualized learning strategies programmed into the interactive computer console. Each work station is several feet from any other, avoiding problems of distraction for overactive children. In a study of self-esteem development in this school, we found that children often had devastated self-esteem on admission, but after a year had fully recovered positive self-appraisal -gains not made in similar children whose parents could not afford fees for a private school of around $10,000 a year.

3   Some "advanced" statistical techniques such as latent structure analysis seem to both mystify the problem they seek to elucidate, and obscure what seem to be common sense interpretations of data - see for example Wyatt, Newcomb & Riederle (1993) who claim to show from latent structure analysis that there is a causal link between incestuous abuse of a child, and development of good self-esteem later in life. We argue from analysis of cases (using cluster analysis) rather than from analysis of variables (which are often dehumanized abstractions, moving us away from the real world) that a sub-group of children who experience incest may have benign mental health outcomes, but incest is certainly not beneficial in its effects - see Bagley (1996).

4   In a final phase of this research, when the children are aged 17, we are interviewing children separately from parents, asking questions *inter alia* about physical, emotional and sexual abuse within and outside of the family, using a format programmed for a portable computer (Bagley, Wood & Young, 1994).

8   What Happens to the Sibling Subsystem Following Parental Divorce?

MADELEINE BEAUDRY, MARIE SIMARD, SYLVIE DRAPEAU, AND CÉCILE CHARBONNEAU

Abstract

Parental divorce can lead to two patterns of organization in the sibling subsystem: it may remain intact (all siblings live together under the same roof) or it may be split (siblings don't all live together). Moreover, physical custody can take different forms: to the mother, to the father, or to both parents. This paper has three objectives. First, we will explore the two patterns of organization in the sibling subsystem (intact/split) in relation to the custody form (mother/father/both) and to certain characteristics of the child and of his sibling relationship(s). Second, for each custody form, we will verify if these characteristics vary with the patterns of organization in the sibling subsystem. Third, we will examine how the previously-analyzed characteristics may vary within a model where the status of the sibling group (intact/split) and the custody form (mother/father/both) are considered simultaneously. For each sibling group (N=144), a parent answered questions concerning each of his or her children, particularly, the arrangements that were made for each of them, the quality of the sibling relationship(s) for each child and the modifications in their relationships consequent to the transition. Results show differences when siblings live apart. The discussion will highlight what impact modifications in the sibling subsystem consequent to parental divorce may have on child development.

Introduction

This present research is part of a larger project dealing with the sibling relationship within family transitions. Until now, studies focusing on family transitions have overlooked the conditions that prevail when these transitions occur and their effects on parents, on children, and on the parent/child relationship. Thus, few have examined the modifications that occur within the sibling subsystem, yet its structure is often modified by these transitions. Studies on child development allow us to hypothesize that, when changes occur within the family structure, the sibling subsystem plays an important role in the child's adjustment to the transition (Cloutier, Beaudry, Drapeau, Samson, Mireault, Simard, & Vachon, 1997).

In Canada, 78,152 divorces were registered in the 1990 census. Results from a recent study in Quebec (Beaudry, Beaudoin, Cloutier, & Boisvert, 1993) and the records from a mediation center in Montreal indicate that approximately 10% of children are separated from their siblings when their parents divorce. Thus, following parental divorce, a great number of children are subject to changes that can affect their sibling relationships.

Parental divorce can bring about two patterns of organization in the sibling subsystem: it either remains intact or it is split. The sibling subsystem is considered intact when all the children that are living together at the time of the divorce were still living together at the time of study. The subsystem is considered split when at least one of its members was living apart from the others at the time of the study and had been living with them at the time of the divorce; however, this separation must necessarily have been a consequence of the parental divorce. Physical custody can take different forms: to the mother, to the father, or to both parents (joint). A custody is considered joint when a child spends the same amount of time at each parent's domicile or when he spends 4 or 5 days per week at one place and 2 to 3 days at the other. Custody is considered only to the mother or to the father when a child lives mainly at one parent's home while he goes to the other parent's only on a visitation basis.

The study of sibling relationships is faced with the challenge of accurately determining the unit of observation. Thus, children are considered part of the same sibling subsystem when they have the same mother and when they have lived together for at least one year. Excluded from this definition, are all children descending from a father's former or later union. The following example will show the complexity of defining the unit of "siblings" . Two children, A and B, have the same mother but different fathers. From a subsequent union, A's father has a new born child while B's father had a child from a previous union. Thus, if we need to identify A and B's siblings, we find that the sibling group is not the same for both children. In order to obtain an operational definition of a sibling group, the previously-stated definition was adopted for the study.

In this study, we first explored the status of the sibling group (intact or split) in relation to the custody form (mother, father, joint) and certain characteristics of the family, the children, and the relationship between siblings. Then, we verified if these characteristics vary with custody form (mother, father, joint). Finally, the sibling group (intact or split) is considered alongside the custody form (mother, father, joint).

Method

Participants

Parents (n=144) who participated in the study came from the metropolitan region of Quebec. They were recruited either from an advertisement in newspapers or from a list of participants in a prior study. In order to collect the data, telephone contact was made with each parent who had accepted to participate in the study, the mother in 70 percent of the cases. In order to familiarize themselves with the content of the questionnaire, parents had been sent a copy by mail.

Questionnaire

Data were collected using a questionnaire developed specifically for this study. One of the parents answered the questionnaire verbally. Questions deal with characteristics concerning the family, each child and each child's relationship with his sibling(s). Questions on family characteristics included the number of children that make up the sibling group, the length of time since the divorce, the number of custody changes that have occurred since the divorce and the length of time since the last custody modification. Questions on children dealt with their sex, their age, the age gap between them and each of their sibling(s), and the custody form attributed to each child. Regarding the characteristics of sibling relationships, the parent was asked his perception concerning the quality of the relationship that each of his children has with each of his sibling(s) (ranging from 0 "not at all harmonious " to 4 "very harmonious") and their perception of the extent of the change in this relationship since the divorce (ranging from 0 "not at all modified" to 4 "greatly modified").

Results

Data comparing each child (n=283) based on the status of the sibling group and on the custody form were analyzed using *t*-tests, chi-squares, and analysis of variance.

When the different features investigated are compared on the basis of the status of the sibling group, as we can see in Table 8.1, we find that children who are separated from their sibling(s) have a greater number of custody modifications since the divorce of their parents [$t(153) = 4.7$; $p<0.0001$], and that the last of these modifications occurred more recently [$t(265) = 2.1$; $p<0.04$] than the children who live with all of their brothers and sisters. Moreover, children in split sibling groups tend to be older [$t(281) = 3.0$; $p<0.003$], to live with their fathers and not to be in joint custody [$X2(2, N = 283) = 50.4$; $p<0.0001$]. The parents more often perceive sibling relationships as less harmonious [$t(198) = 2.8$; $p<0.005$] and they consider that the relationship has undergone greater modifications since the divorce [$t(209) = 4.4$; $p<0.0001$] than children who live with all of their siblings.

Custody form

When these same characteristics are compared on the basis of custody form, as Table 8.2 indicates, the length of time since the divorce of the parents [$F(2,280) = 5.97$; $p<0,003$], the number of custody modifications since the divorce [$F(2,280) = 8.68$; $p<0.0002$], the length of time since the last change in custody [$F(2,276) = 6.1$; $p<0.003$], the number of children in the sibling group [$F(2,280) = 7.8$; $p<0.0005$], the mean age of the children [$F(2,280) = 11.4$; $p<0.0001$], the sex of the children [$X2(2, N = 283) = 10.1$; $p<0.006$], the quality of the relationship between the children [$F(2,279) = 9.6$; $p<0.0001$] and the degree of modification in their relationships [$F(2,278) = 4.5$; $p<0.01$] vary with the form of custody. In order to specify these differences, *a posteriori* analyses were conducted. These analyses reveal that, for *joint custody*, the divorce generally occurred more recently, the children were younger, and the quality of the relationship between siblings was perceived by the parent as being more harmonious than with the other custody forms. When the *mother had custody*, the children generally lived with the same arrangement for longer without change and the sibling group included a greater number of children than in the other forms of custody. The children in their *father's custody* generally underwent a greater number of custody modifications, were more often boys, and their relationship with their sibling(s) was perceived by the parent as having changed more since the divorce than for children in other custody forms.

In order to verify if the characteristics previously analyzed vary when the status of the sibling group and custody form are considered simultaneously, analysis of variance 2 (status of sibling group) X 3 (custody form) was performed separately on each variable.

As we can see when we compare Table 8.3 with Table 8.1, when the custody form is taken into account, the number of custody modifications since the divorce [$F(1,277) = 9.77$; $p<0.002$], the quality of sibling relationships [$F(1,276) = 6.51$; $p<0.01$] and the extent of change in sibling relationships since the divorce [$F(1,275) = 8.50$; $p<0.004$] still vary along with the status of the sibling group; however, the length of time since the last custody modification [$F(1,273) = 2.38$; $p<0.12$] and the age of the children [$F(1,277) = 0.19$; $p<0.67$] are no longer significant, while the age gap between siblings increases in significance [$F(1,277) = 12.93$; $p<0.0004$]. Therefore, when the custody form is taken into account, *a posteriori* analyses tell us that when children are separated from their sibling(s), they undergo more custody modifications, the age gap with their siblings tends to be greater, and their parents consider that their relationships with their siblings are less harmonious and more subject to change than when the children still lived with all of their brothers and sisters.

Mediating variables

The next step was to examine the effects of the custody form on these different variables while considering the status of the sibling group. When we compare Table 8.3 with Table 8.2, we see that the length of time since the divorce [$F(2,277) = 3.14$; $p<0.05$], the age of the children [$F(2,277) = 7.29$; $p<0.0008$], and the sex of the children [$X2(2, N = 283) = 8.55$; $p<0.01$] still vary along with the custody form. However, the number of custody modifications since the divorce [$F(2,277) = 2.76$; $p<0.06$], the amount of time since the last custody modification [$F(2,273) = 2.67$; $p<0.07$], the number of children in the sibling group [$F(2,277) = 2.67$; $p<0.07$], the quality of sibling relationships [$F(2,276) = 1.00$; $p<0.37$] and the modifications in these relationships [$F(2,275) = 1.29$; $p<0.28$] are no longer significant, while the age gap between siblings increases in significance [$F(2,277) = 4.83$; $p<0.009$]. Therefore, when the type of organization of the sibling subsystem is taken into account, *a posteriori* analysis informs us that, when children lived mainly with their father, they were usually older and they were more often boys, than in other custody forms. When children lived in joint custody, the divorce of their parents was generally more recent, the age gap with their sibling(s) was greater and they were younger than those in the other custody forms.

The interaction effects obtained from these analyses concern mainly the children who live in joint custody; those who were separated from their siblings have a greater age gap between them than is the case for the other children, while those who lived with their brothers and sisters had a more harmonious relationship with their sibling(s) than the other children generally did.

Several authors have noted that, in adolescence, the quality of sibling relationships deteriorates (Anderson & North, 1988; Anderson & Rice, 1992; Brody, Stoneman & McCoy, 1994; Buhrmester & Furman, 1990; Lempers & Clark-Lempers, 1992; Stoneman & Brody, 1993). In order to verify if the perception of parents concerning the quality of the relationships between their children and the modification of such relationships since the divorce is not influenced by the age of their children, a two-way analysis of covariance, 2 (status of the sibling group) X 3 (custody form) with the age of the children as co-variate were performed separately on these two variables. The results of these analysis show that the quality of sibling relationships [$\underline{F}(1,275) = 6.30$; $\underline{p}<0.01$] and the degree of modification they undergo [$\underline{F}(1,272) = 5.91$; $\underline{p}<0.02$] as perceived by the parent, still vary along with the status of the sibling group. These results maintain that, for children separated from their sibling(s), parents tended to feel that they had less harmonious relationships with their siblings and that they had experienced greater changes in their sibling relationships since the divorce than for children living with their sibling(s).

Discussion

Our findings highlight the fact that children who are separated from their siblings following parental divorce are older, have had more custody changes, and, as perceived by their parents, they have less harmonious relationships with their siblings and the relationships have changed more since the divorce than children who live with their brothers and sisters. Moreover, split custody necessarily brings about an increase in the proportion of fathers who get custody. When we consider which children live more with their fathers, we find that they are more often boys. These results indicate that the quality of sibling relationships seem to deteriorate when the sibling group is split. However, we do not know what the quality of the relationship was prior to the parental divorce and in which direction the change occurred. The separation of siblings can be the result of poor relationships between children or it can simply be an arrangement made by the parents. Thus, in future research, we should verify the quality of sibling relationships prior to parental divorce. Moreover, we should examine if the relationship between ex-spouses brings about conflicts between the children and incites them to take sides with parents.

In spite of the fact that conflicts tend to increase between siblings after parental divorce (Anderson & Rice, 1992; Hetherington, 1993; MacKinnon, 1989), children express their preference for having brothers and sisters rather then being an only child (Shapiro & Wallace, 1987; Springer & Wallerstein, 1983). Moreover, in family transitions, siblings can play an important role in a child's adjustment to the transition. In fact, according to Combrinck-Graham (1988), Jenkins (1992), Kempton, Armistead, Wierson and Forehand (1991), following parental divorce, children who live with brothers and sisters are healthier, have less behavioral problems, and show better adjustment. Brothers and sisters can represent an important source of emotional support, assistance and companionship for one another in everyday life and during stressful periods (Dunn & Kendrick, 1982; Goetting, 1986; Lamb, 1982). Thus, separating siblings can bring about a loss in certain roles specific to brothers and sisters and induce more conflict and tension between children. Following separation from their siblings, do children feel liberated or do they feel deserted? When do these feelings appear and how long do they last? Future research will have to take children's perceptions into account in order to answer these questions.

Table 8.1   Status of the sibling group in relation to custody form and certain characteristics

Status of the Sibling Groups

Characteristics	Intact (n=168)	Split (n=115)		df	p <
FAMILY					
Time since divorce	4.8	5.3	$t = 1.5$	281	.15
Number of custody modifications	0.23	0.65	$t = 4.7$	153	.0001
Time since last modification	4.4	3.6	$t = 2.1$	265	.04
Number of children under 18	2.4	2.4	$t = 0.5$	281	.6
CHILDREN					
Age	11.4	12.8	$t = 3.0$	281	.003
Age gap	3.5	4.0	$t = 1.74$	281	.08
Sex			$X^2 = 0.04$	1	.85
Boys	55.4%	56.5%			
Girls	44.6%	43.5%			
Custody form:			$X^2 = 50.4$	2	.0001
Mother	57.1%	47.8%			
Father	10.1%	43.5%			
Joint custody	32.7%	8.7%			
RELATIONSHIP WITH SIBLINGS					
Quality of the relationship (0 to 4)	3.02	2.70	$t = 2.8$	198	.005
Relationship modifications (0 to 4)	2.06	2.75	$t = 4.4$	209	.0001

Table 8.2 Custody form in relation to certain characteristics

Characteristic	Custody form				df	p <
	Mother (n=151)	Father (n=67)	Joint Custody (n=65)			
FAMILY						
Time since divorce	5.2	5.6	3.8	$F = 6.0$	2	.003
Number of custody modifications	0.3	0.7	0.3	$F = 8.7$	2	.0002
Time since last modification	4.7	3.4	3.2	$F = 6.1$	2	.003
Number of children under 18	2.6	2.4	2.2	$F = 7.8$	2	.0005
CHILDREN						
Age	12.0	13.4	10.2	$F = 11.4$	2	.0001
Age gap	3.7	3.6	3.8	$F = 0.2$	2	.82
Sex				$X^2 = 10.1$	2	.006
Boys	47.7%	70.2%	60%			
Girls	52.3%	29.5%	40%			
RELATIONSHIP WITH SIBLINGS						
Quality of the relationship (0 to 4)	2.8	2.7	3.3	$F = 9.6$	2	.0001
Relationship modifications (0 to 4)	2.2	2.7	2.2	$F = 4.5$	2	.01

Table 8.3   Status of the sibling group and custody form considered simultaneously in relation to certain characteristics

Characteristics	Sibling status (intact/split)	Custody form (mother/father/joint)	Status X Custody
FAMILY			
Time since divorce	$F=0.09$	$F=3.14$*	$F=0.01$
Number of custody modifications	$F=9.77$**	$F=2.76$	$F=0.26$
Time since last modification	$F=2.38$	$F=2.67$	$F=0.64$
Number of children under 18	$F=0.06$	$F=2.67$	$F=2.07$
CHILDREN			
Age	$F=0,19$	$F=7.29$***	$F=1.67$
Age gap	$F=12.93$***	$F=4.83$**	$F=6.28$**
Sex	$X^2=0.08$	$X^2=8.55$**	$X^2=0.18$
RELATIONSHIP WITH SIBLINGS			
Quality of the relationship (0 to 4)	$F=6.51$**	$F=1.00$	$F=3.77$*
Relationship modifications (0 to 4)	$F=8.50$**	$F=1.29$	$F=0.20$

* $p < .05$
** $p < .01$
*** $p < .001$

References

Anderson, E.R., & North, A.M. (1988). *Competition and Cohesion in Sibling Relations during the Adaptation toRemarriage.* New-Orleans, LA: Paper presented at the Annual Meeting of the Southeastern Psychological Association.

Anderson, E.R., & Rice, A.M. (1992). Sibling relationships during remarriage. *Monographs of the Society for Research in Child Development, 57,* 149-177.

Bank, S.P., & Kahn, M.D. (1982). *The Sibling Bond.* New York: Basic Books.

Beaudry, M., Beaudoin, A., Cloutier, R., & Boisvert, J.M. (1993). Étude sur les caractéristiques associées au partage des responsabilités parentales à la suite d'une séparation. *Revue Canadienne de Service Social, 10,* 9-26.

Brody, G.H., Stoneman, Z., & McCoy, J.K. (1994). Forecasting sibling relationships in early adolescence from child temperaments and family processes in middle childhood. *Child Development, 65,* 771-784.

Buhrmester, D., & Furman, W. (1990). Perceptions of sibling relationships during middle childhood and adolescence. *Child Development, 61,* 1387-1396.

Cloutier, R., Beaudry, M., Drapeau, S., Samson, C., Mireault, G., Simard, M., & Vachon, J. (1997). Changements familiaux et continuité: Une approche théorique de l'adaptation aux transformations familiales. In G.M. Tarabulsy, & R. Tessier (Eds.), *Enfance et familles: Contextes et développement* (pp. 31-56). Montréal, Qc: Presses de l'Université du Québec.

Combrinck-Graham, L. (1988). When parents separate or divorce: The sibling system. In M.D. Kahn, & K.G. Lewis (Eds.), *Siblings in therapy: Life span and clinical issues* (pp. 190-207). New York: W. W. Norton and Co.

Dunn, J., & Kendrick, S. (1982). *Siblings: Love, envy and understanding.* Cambridge, MA: Harvard University.

Goetting, A. (1986). The developmental tasks of siblingship over life cycle. *Journal of Marriage and the Family, 48,* 703-714.

Hetherington, M.E. (1993). An overview of the Virginia Longitudinal Study of Divorce and Remarriage with a focus on early adolescence. *Journal of Family Psychology, 7,* 39-56.

Jenkins, J. (1992). Sibling relationships in disharmonious homes: Potential difficulties and protective effects. In F. Boer, & J. Dunn (Eds.), *Children's sibling relationships: Developmental and clinical issues* (pp. 125-138). Hillsdale, NJ: Lawrence Erlbaum.

Kempton, T., Armistead, L., Wierson, M., & Forehand, R. (1991). Presence of a sibling as a potential buffer following parental divorce: An examination of young adolescents. *Journal of Clinical Child Psychology, 20,* 434-438.

Lamb, M.E. (1982). Sibling relationships across the lifespan: An overview and introduction. In M. Lamb, & B. Sutton-Smith (Eds.), *Sibling relationships: Their nature and significance scross the lifespan* (p.1-11). Hillsdale, NJ: Lawrence Erlbaum.

Lempers, J.D., & Clark-Lempers, D.S. (1992). Young, middle, and late adolescents' comparisons of the functional importance of five significant relationships. *Journal of Youth and Adolescence, 21*, 53-96.

MacKinnon, C.E. (1989). Sibling interactions in married and divorced families: Influence of ordinal position, socioeconomic status, and play context. *Journal of Divorce and Remarriage, 12,* 221-234.

Shapiro, E.K., & Wallace, D.B. (1987). Siblings and parents in one-parent families. *Journal of Children in Contemporary Society, 19*, 91-114.

Springer, C., & Wallerstein, J.S. (1983). Young adolescents 'responses to their parents' divorces. In L.A. Kurdek (Ed.), *New directions for child development: Children and divorce* (pp. 15-27). San Francisco, CA: Jossey-Bass.

Stoneman, Z., & Brody, G.H. (1993). Sibling temperaments, conflict, warmth, and role asymmetry. *Child Development, 64,* 1786-1800.

9 Parental Self-Efficacy and Characteristics of Mother and Father in the Transition to Parenthood

WILMA BINDA AND FRANCA CRIPPA

Abstract

The main aim of this longitudinal project was to examine how normal couples cope with the transition to parenthood. In this paper the principal goal was to examine parental self efficacy during this family life phase. Self-efficacy - which in this research was conceived as a level of beliefs which concern judgments of one's ability to perform competently and effectively during pregnancy and afterwards with the new child - is the mediating link between beliefs, knowledge and behavior. Perceived ability to be able to deal with the complex needs associated with the new role means to feel able to respond to the necessity of a baby, one's own needs and those of partner (Bandura, 1986). The sample was composed of 60 couples (60 mothers and 60 fathers, in total 120 subjects) expecting their first child, in North Italy. In this longitudinal research project data were to be collected twice (6-8 month of pregnancy and 3-4 months postpartum). Parallel versions of a self-report questionnaire were administered to husband and wife. Data were analyzed by LISREL.

Introduction

Performing the new parental role competently and effectively - and therefore presumably being able to behave appropriately - sets up a parental alliance (Cohen & Weissman, 1984). This alliance shows common and shared investment for the future of the new family. This will create the style of parenting.

Many studies have demonstrated that the transition to parenthood is a key transition for the family. From the moment of birth, the partners may define the new relational couple identity more now than at the moment of the formation of the couple; and in addition they decide what they - as parents - are prepared to accept and invest in this new voyage. More factors are important for the couple's togetherness, because after the birth the couple is not only a marital couple but also a parental couple. The child breaks into the couple and gives rise to the birth of a family, making the marital bond visible and the newly created parental bond permanent (Bradt, 1980; Cowan & Cowan, 1988; La Rossa, 1986; Lewis, 1989; Scabini, 1995; Walsh, 1993). Notwithstanding this research, a great deal of work is still required to determine the reciprocal dynamics between husband, wife and neonate in the transition to parenthood.

Accordingly, we undertook a longitudinal study of such transitions. The main aim of our longitudinal project was to examine how couples cope with the transition to parenthood. In particular we wanted to investigate: 1) marital functioning in concurrence with the birth event: (bonds, roles, area of satisfaction and area of conflict); 2) the relationship with the family of origin for both the new parents: (changes on perceptions, attitude and reciprocal behavior); 3) the relationship with the external world: emerging needs, relationships between sociosanitary services and mothers who work outside the home.

In this research, many questions have led us to consider various relevant aspects of the birth event, because it consists not only in the birth of a baby, but also in the birth of the parental relationship and the reality of a new family. Specifically, the principal aim of the present report was to examine parental self-efficacy during this family life phase.

As Bandura (1986, 1993) has indicated that, self-efficacy is the mediating link between, beliefs, knowledge and behavior. In our research, it was conceived as a level of beliefs concerning judgments of one's ability to perform competently and effectively with the new child during pregnancy and afterwards. During the transition to parenthood, perceived parental self-efficacy is shown to be a crucial mediating variable.

Perceived ability to be able to deal with the complex needs associated with the new role means to feel capable of responding to the needs of one's baby, to one's own needs and those of the partner. Performing such a new role competently and effectively - and therefore, presumably, to be able to behave appropriately - sets up a parental alliance (Cohen & Weissman, 1984). This alliance shows a common and shared investment for the future of the new family. The construction of this parental alliance may be slow and risky, meanwhile creating the style of parenting.

Method

Sample and procedures

Our larger study is a multimethod project in two parts, quantitative and qualitative[1]. This paper focuses only on some quantitative results. First-time parents were administered self-report questionnaires in two versions, one for the husband, and one for the wife. Data were collected twice: 1) when the expectant mother was 6 - 8 months pregnant, and again when the baby was 4 months old. Our sample included 60 community sample couples, 60 fathers and 60 mothers. There were, therefore, a total of 120 subjects.

The first time data was collected between the 6th and the 8th month of pregnancy. They included self-report questionnaires for mothers and fathers attending prenatal courses for expectant couples at several health districts in northern Italy, mainly in the outskirts of Milan. The second time data was collected in the immediate post-birth period when the baby was 4 months old, we employed two self-report mailed questionnaires. Each couple, therefore was administered four questionnaires: two for the mother and two for the father, (two collected during the pregnancy and two after the birth).

In this paper we reported only the relevant results of some scales. The first scale, which expresses the perceived parental self-efficacy, was developed based on Bandura's self-efficacy concept. This scale measures the level of beliefs which concern judgments of one's ability to perform competently and effectively. In particular, in the pre-birth questionnaire (pregnancy self-efficacy) we included 15 items related to pregnancy, labor and delivery; in the postpartum questionnaire (parental efficacy) we had 23 items related to parental experience and mutual support between the partners. The alpha reliability coefficients for each of the two is .75. The self-esteem scale by Rosemberg measures the level of confidence in oneself was also included.

The Family Environment Scale (FES) by Moos and Moos (1981), assessed the new parent's perception as to the function of the extended families. Four subscales were used: cohesion, expressiveness and conflict subscales concerning relational perspective and a commitment subscale for individual aspects. Finally, an overall satisfaction scale, composed of 4 items using a 4-point Likert scale, was adopted. This scale assessed the level of satisfaction with one's own life, marriage, work and the relationship with a new baby.

Results

Descriptive data

Expectant mothers ranged in age from 17-37 years, with a mean age of 29.5 years, new fathers from 26 to 44 years, with a mean age of 32. All couples were married, with a modal marriage length of two years. Employment status was an important variable throughout our analysis, as dual-earner families compose the majority of the sample. Only 7.1% of women considered themselves housewives. Moreover, while 10% of women were unemployed during their pregnancy, the same percentage rose to 27.4 % when the baby was 4 months old, with mothers declaring they did not want to return to work.

The average yearly net income among sampled families is approximately 30 million lira (middle class); 46% of couples owned their homes at the time of the study. In the majority of cases (86.2%), the extended families lived close to the new parents, usually living in the same area of the town or in the same village. Therefore, it was possible and typical for the new parents to access help from the new grandparents.

Pregnancy and parental self-efficacy

The perception of efficacy increased, for mothers and fathers, during the transition to parenthood and, after childbirth. (Figure 9.1). During the time when the first questionnaire was administered, mothers in the study were assessed as having medium or high efficacy. At the time of the second questionnaire, the percentage increased to 64.4%. At the time of the first questionnaire, 33.3% of fathers perceived themselves as having medium or high efficacy; postpartum this percentage rose to 55.2 %.

T-tests were conducted to explore differences between the self-efficacy at different times. The t-value estimate for mothers was $t_2(56) = -4.35$, p<.001, and the estimate for fathers was $t(57) = -2.92$, <.005. Such changes indicate that a high number of new parents who - after the direct impact with the reality of parenthood - perceived themselves, or believed that they were fairly competent in the new role as parent. Usually, these parents should experience increased success in establishing a warm and harmonious relationship with their children.

Fathers demonstrated an increase in their perception of self-efficacy. It is interesting to note that for 43.6% of the couples both partners declared a high level of self-efficacy after the birth compared to 17.3% during pregnancy.

Based on these and other results, we hypothesized that the perceived self-efficacy plays a central role in building the parental characteristics for both mothers and fathers, in a more crucial way for the parental alliance between the new parents. To test this hypothesis we analyzed longitudinal data with structural equation modeling techniques employed linear structure relations (LISREL).

Formulation of the LISREL models

Our analyses were based on both individuals' and couples' changes after the birth of their first child. Consequently, we constructed three models concerning respectively, the new mother, the new father and the parents together as new parents. Data was longitudinal and the correlation matrix is summarized in Table 9.1. In particular, two-wave models explored stability of attitudes in the transition to parenthood. In addition, they focused on relationship patterns at both stages, so as to account for parental alliance. Such an explanatory framework was tested in three structural equation models using LISREL analyses (Joreskog & Sorbom, 1989).

Such models included (Figures 9.2, 9.3, & 9.4), in the case of single new parents, eight endogenous variables, two of which, strictly latent, expressed the relationship with her or his family of origin. The latent constructs were measured by means of data of four FES subscales: cohesion, conflict, commitment and expressiveness. The remaining endogenous variables, directly observable, may be considered latent variables with zero measurement errors. Four of them, in pairs, were repeated measures of self-esteem and global satisfaction in the occasions mentioned above. On the contrary, pregnancy self-efficacy and parental self-efficacy were distinct variables and not merely repeated observations. Exogenous variables, which are directly observable, were total years of education, age and length of marriage. They did not appear in conclusive models and consequently in any figure, not being statistically significant. In effect, models with no independent variables may still be tested in LISREL analyses. To provide a metric for the latent constructs and to identify the measurement model, the first indicator, loading for each latent construct was set equal to 1.0 in the unstandardized version.

The three models

On the whole, each model fits the data well, as shown in Table 9.2. Ratios between chi squared-test values and their degrees of freedom are close to 1, leaving the ratio from 1 to 3 for non-falsification. Besides, both Goodness of Fit

Indexes (G.F.I.) and Adjusted Goodness of Fit Indexes (A.G.F.I.) results are approximately 0.8.

Because the model-to-date fit was assessed through chi-squared-tests, sample size is an issue. Small samples reduce the probability of rejecting a hypothesized model. Therefore, the hypothesized model was also tested against the null model, which assumes no structural relations. The difference of the null from the hypothesized model (nested models) resulted in a chi-squared distribution, with a degree of freedom equal to the difference of the compared models. In all cases, models were significant at the .05 or .01 levels.

In order to provide a metric for the latent construct and to identify the measurement model, the first indicator loading had been set for each latent construct equal to 1.0. Parameters and paths presented estimated in the models were significant at .05 level of significance. The models together with the parameter estimates are summarized in Figures 9.2, 9.3, & 9.4.

Figure 9.2 contains the model of the mother's data. The FES data, (perception of the climate of the extended family of mothers), produced a direct impact upon pregnancy self-efficacy. After the birth, the FES data affected global satisfaction. Global satisfaction, (as measured after the birth), directly affected parental self-efficacy. Finally, there is a direct relation between perception of pregnancy self-efficacy and parental self-efficacy. The mother starts becoming a parent during the pregnancy, and this contributes to the perception of her self-efficacy.

In the model for fathers (Figure 9.3), the only relation linking the prenatal and post-birth period was between the two measures of global satisfaction. Self-esteem has a direct effect on pregnancy self-efficacy: As in the mothers' model, satisfaction has effects upon parental self-efficacy. Fathers' perception of self-efficacy during the transition to parenthood changes, its only link being with his self-esteem in the expectancy period. Having a child and managing the initial problems of the future family is related to their identities and confidence in themselves.

After the birth, the perception of self-efficacy affects the fathers' satisfaction relating to some aspects of their lives and of their relationship. When these new young fathers were satisfied with their life, it was possible for them to cope with the reality of a new baby. With regard to fathers perceiving self-efficacy, their transition to parenthood was not a smooth sequence, but a jump into the unknown.

In the new parents model (Figure 9.4), we dealt with the complexity of life as a new parent. Four key variables become central: paternal and maternal self-efficacy and paternal and maternal global satisfaction. These variables in reciprocal association, revealed the presence of the reciprocal effects between mothers and fathers. These effects were only evident after the birth of the baby. In addition, the mother's parental self-efficacy produced double effects upon her partner's parental self-efficacy and global satisfaction.

On the other side, the father's variables affected only the mother's global satisfaction after the birth. Moreover, building these new links was important for the two key variables (self-efficacy and satisfaction). Only after the birth did parental alliance become evident and the shared beliefs of the two new parents existed. Mothers play a central role both before and after the birth, because of the relationship they have enjoyed and experienced with their extended family.

Discussion

We have clarified how one's perception of one's own relationship with one's own family creates a protective umbrella for the relationship between the mother and her child. Maternal self-efficacy influences both paternal self-efficacy and paternal satisfaction, but paternal satisfaction affected maternal satisfaction in such a way that the marital bond strengthened through this positive loop together with the partners' perception of the ability to cope with their baby's needs.

The perceived couple efficacy may be a protective factor in coping with the potentially stressful events of parenting. Consequently, this may create some important shared beliefs in the couple for further developmental reactions when faced with both minor and serious difficulties.

Rutter (1990) has also underscored the importance of this resilience: The ability to actively cope with internal stresses and external events is enhanced with resilient people. High self-efficacy creates shared beliefs in new parents and these may be a good protective factor to assist in managing and coping with every family transition now and in the future. As Rutter indicated (1994), protective factors extend over time and work indirectly through their effects on the interpersonal relationships and not through direct changes in the individual.

The construction of a parental alliance by means of shared self-efficacy beliefs of the couple, protects the parenting style of this couple with their child and at the same time the marital bonds and the functioning of the couple as Belsky's research has demonstrated so clearly (Belsky, 1990; Belsky & Rovine, 1990).

Becoming parents solidifies the relationship between the two partners and also improves other aspects of their family life. However, there does exist (and we have collected some relevant characteristics in the qualitative part of our research) a group of couples who live with the risk of experiencing difficulties, strains and worries due to the complexity of the task of childbearing and these new parents live in a disharmonious relationship with each other and with their baby. They find it hard to build a strong, efficient, and effective shared style of parenting.

Usually every partner becomes more able and more specialized with the new family needs, even if they encounter considerable difficulty.

In conclusion, the birth event creates the parental couple. Our results suggest that the experience of the birth of one's child constitutes crucial points for the couple's fusion and so it becomes a critical turning point to the transition to adulthood.

Figure 9.1 Pregnancy and parental self-efficacy for mothers and fathers

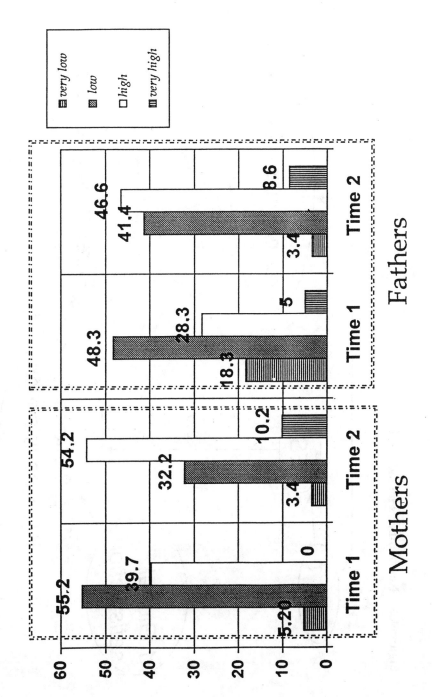

Figure 9.2   New mother's model

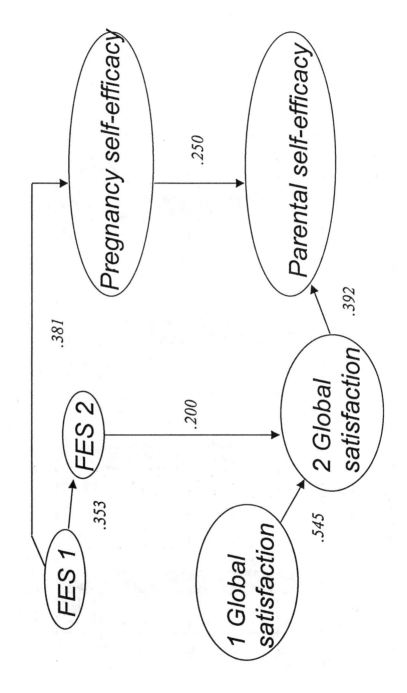

Figure 9.3   New father's model

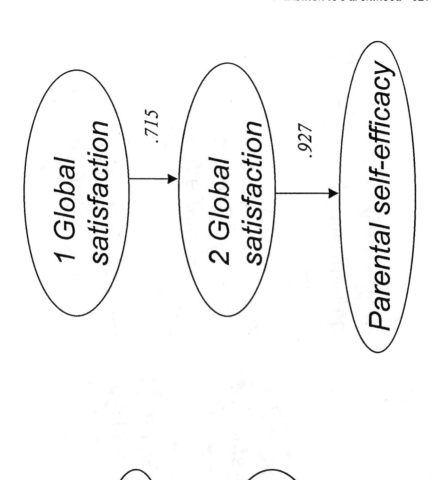

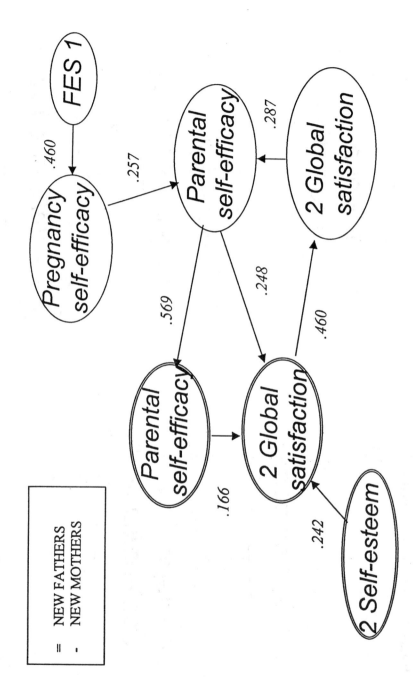

Figure 9.4   Both parents' model

= NEW FATHERS
- NEW MOTHERS

Table 9.1 Goodness of fit of three models

	X2	DF	X2/DF	GFI	AGFI
⇨ **New mother**	79.14	73	1.084	.861	.800
⇨ **New father**	67.59	71	0.952	.859	.791
⇨ **Couple of new parents**	129.35	113	1.145	.829	.768

References

Bandura, A. (1986). *Social foundations of thought and action: a social cognitive theory.* Englewood Cliffs, NJ: Prentice Hall.

Bandura, A. (1993). Perceived self-efficacy in cognitive development and functioning. *Educational Psychologist, 28,* 117-148.

Belsky, J. (1990). Children and marriage. In F. D. Fincham & T.N. Bradbury (Eds.). *The psychology of marriage* (pp.172-200). New York: The Guilford Press.

Belsky, J., & Rovine, M. (1990). Pattern of marital change across the transition to parenthood: Pregnancy to three years postpartum. *Journal of Marriage and the Family, 52,* 5-19.

Binda, W. (1997). *Diventare famiglia* (Becoming the family). Milano: Angeli.

Bradt, J.O. (1980). The family with young children. In E. Carter & M. McGoldrick (eds.). *The family life cycle: a framework for family therapy* (pp.122-146). New York: Gardner Press.

Cohen, R.S. & Weissman, S.H. (1984). The parenting alliance. In R.S. Cohen, B.J.Cohler & S.H. Weissman. (Eds.). *Parenthood: A psychodynamic perspective* (pp.33-49). New York: Guilford Press.

Cowan, P.A. & Cowan C.P. (1988). Changes in marriage during the transition to parenthood: Must we blame the baby? In G.Y. Michaels & W.A.Goldberg (Eds.). *The transition to parenthood. Current theory and research* (pp. 114-154). Cambridge: Cambridge University Press, 870-878.

Erikson, D.H. (1982). *The life cycle completed.* A review. New York: Norton.

Fincham, F.D. & Bradbury, T.N. (Eds.). *The psychology of marriage.* New York: The Guilford Press.

Gable, S., Belsky, J. & Crinc, K. (1992). Marriage, parenting and child development progress and prospect. *Journal of Family Psychology, 5,* 276-294.

Joreskog, K.G. & Goldberger, A.S. (1975). Estimation of a model with multiple indicators and multiple causes of a single latent variable, *Journal of the American Statistical Association, 10,* 631-639.

Joreskog, K.G. & Sorbom, D. (1989). Lisrel 7: *A guide to the program and applications* (2nd ed.). Chicago: SPSS.

Kalmuss, D., Davidson, A. & Cushman, L. (1992). Parenting expectations, experiences and adjustment to parenthood: A test of the violated expectations framework. *Journal of Marriage and the Family, 54,* 516-526.

Lavee, Y. (1988). Linear structural relationships (lisrel) in family research. *Journal of Marriage and the Family, 50,* 937-948.

La Rossa, R. (1986). *Becoming a parent.* Beverly Hills: Sage Publications.

Lewis, J.M. (1989). *The birth of the family.* New York: Bunner Mazel Publishers.

Luster, T. & Okagaki, L. *Parenting. An ecological perspective.* Hillsdale: Lawrence Erlbaum Associates.

McDermid, S., Huston, T. & McHale, S. (1990). Changes in marriage associated with the transition to parenthood: individual differences as a function of sex-role attitudes and changes in the division of household labor. *Journal of Marriage and the Family, 52,* 475-486.

Miller, B.C. & Sollie, D.L. (1980). Normal stress during the transition to parenthood. *Family Relations, 25,* 459-465.

Moos, S. & Moos, M. (1981). *Family Environment Scale.* Manual. Palo Alto, C.A: Consulting Psychologist Press.

Rutter, M. (1983). Stress, coping and development: some issues and some questions. In N.Garmezy & M.Rutter (Eds.). *Stress, coping and development in children* (pp.1-42). New York: McGraw-Hill.

Rutter, M. (1990). Psychosocial resilience and protective mechanism. In *AAVV Risk and protective factors in the development of psychopathology.* Cambridge: Cambridge University Press.

Rutter M. (1994). Capacità di reagire di fronte alle avversità (The ability of reacting in front of contrary). *Adolescenza,* 223-252.

Scabini, E. (1978). Una scala di soddisfazione coniugale (A marital satisfaction scale). *Studi di Psicologia,* 1, 171-192.

Scabini, E. (1995). *Psicologia sociale della famiglia* (Social Psychology of the Family). Torino: Bollati Boribghieri.

Shuster, C. (1993). Employed first-times mothers. A typology of maternal responses to integrating parenting and employment. *Family Relations, 42,* 13-20.

Smetana, J.G. (1994). *Beliefs about parenting: Origins and developmental implications.* San Francisco: Jossey Bass Publishers.

Teti, D.M. & Gelfand, M. (1991). Behavioral competence among mothers of infants in the first year: The Mediational Role of Maternal Self-Efficacy. *Child Development, 62,* 918-929.

Wallace, P. & Gotlib, I. (1990). Marital adjustment during the transition to parenthood: stability predictors of change. *Journal of Marriage and the Family, 52,* 21-29.

Walsh, F. (1993). *Normal Family Processes.* New York: The Guilford Press.

Zuo, J. (1992). The reciprocal relationship between marital interaction and marital happiness: a three wave study. *Journal of Marriage and the Family, 54,* 870-878.

Note

1   Data for the quantitative research was collected for all couples contacted during this research, that is 142 mothers and 142 fathers in total 284 subjects. The questionaire sections were: demographic variables regarding the parents; demographic variables on family of origin for both the new parents; expectations and perceptions of the birth event (labor, delivery, first week of the baby and so forth); relationship with the baby (pregnancy and parental efficacy; roles and values; dual earner families with mothers working outside the home; educational resources and difficulties); marital relationship; relationship with both extended families. Overall data and a comprehensive discussion are presented in Binda (1997).

10   From Adolescence to Young Adulthood: A Family Transition

MARGHERITA LANZ

Abstract

Nowadays adolescence is considered a "joint developmental enterprise" between parents and offspring which involves all family members and is characterized by transformation and continuity. Adolescence is a long period whose end is not a "jump" to adulthood but rather involves a new developmental phase called young adulthood. The aim of this study is to verify through a cross sectional study how the parent-child dyad and the whole family modify their relationships from adolescence to young adulthood. The sample is composed of 325 intact families with children aged between 11 and 24. In order to analyze how the distance between parents and child varies according to child's age, a congruence score based on distance measure was calculated. Our results indicated that late adolescence is a critical phase for the whole family. Young adulthood was characterized by a realignment in the relationships.

From adolescence to young adulthood: A family transition

The purpose of the present study was to verify through a cross sectional approach if the different phases in which adolescence has been divided are real moments of transition for family relationships. Specifically we intend to analyze how parent and child modify their perception of communication and family environment throughout various ages. The interest in this topic stems from the virtual discarding of the notion that adolescent development can best be characterized as a period of "storm and stress" (Blos, 1979) and the adoption of a much broader and less problem-centered conception (Jackson & Bosma, 1992). This shift in perspective brought the researchers to consider changes in family relations as part of an adjustment process, through which families adjust to the changing characteristics of one of its members. Terms such as transformation and realignment are used to refer to this process by which close, warm relationships are maintained (Grotevant & Cooper, 1983). At the same time modes of interaction and patterns of influence are gradually adjusted to the changing knowledge, skills, and predilections of adolescent offspring (Collins, 1990).

Adolescence is now considered a "joint developmental enterprise" between parents and offspring which involves all family members and is characterized by transformation and continuity (Cigoli, 1985; Scabini, 1995; Sroufe, 1991; Youniss, 1983). Nowadays adolescence is a long period whose end is not a "jump" to adulthood but rather involves a new developmental phase termed young adulthood (Sherrod, Haggerty & Featherman, 1993). The transition to adulthood is therefore taking on new features. It is no longer a short span of time made up of precise steps, but a long transition characterized by numerous microtransitions (Breunlin, 1988) beginning in late adolescence. In general, researchers focus on the description of the single phase and do not take into account the transition to the different phases (Cowan, 1991). In this way, the moments of transition do not emerge and it is not clear if the different phases of adolescence are characterized by real changes in all the developmental areas or if developmental transition occurs in different moments for different people.

Although in the literature the important role played by the family context during adolescence has been underscored, the works that have considered parents and adolescents together are rather scarce (Gecas & Seff, 1990). In this study we were interested in detecting how the parent-child dyad and the whole family modify their relationships from adolescence to young adulthood.

In research on family functioning, agreement or congruence between family members is studied as a "within-family" phenomenon. The interest in congruence stems from its frequent use as a basis for inference about family patterns and processes. Congruence between parents, for example, has often been proposed as a marker of family cohesion and/or organization, with beneficial consequences for children's development (e.g., Huston & Rampler, 1989; Minuchin, 1985; Simons, McCluskey & Millet, 1985). Parent-child agreement across adolescence has also been regarded as an indication of the extent to which parents monitor for differences between themselves and their children and accordingly modify their perceptions or their expectations (Collins & Luebeker, 1991). Congruence can be considered the result of the re-negotiation process through which parents and children build up a new balance (Collins & Luebeker, 1994; Lanz, Vermulst, Gerris & Scabini, 1998). The study of congruence represents the study of the distance between parents and children and allows us to focus on the dyad.

During the transition periods the study of congruence can be very useful in order to analyze how parents and children re-negotiate their relationship. During adolescence parent-adolescent relationships involve a movement toward separateness to adulthood and simultaneous pulls to remain connected to family members. There is a considerable amount of complex parent-adolescent negotiation, such that adolescents can separate their own point of view from that of their parents, while simultaneously making clear and justifying their views to their parents. On the other side, parents have to allow adolescents the freedom to separate themselves, communicating and reinforcing parental values and perspectives at the same time (Youniss & Smollar, 1989). It is through communication and family relations that the important process of individuation can be supported or inhibited.

The aim of this study was to detect how congruence between parent and child varies during the transition to adulthood. In particular we wanted to analyze if the composition of the dyad and child's age affected the level of congruence. From a methodological point of view, this study followed a family research design because each part of the project was constructed keeping in mind the point of view of the family (Feetham, 1988; Larsen & Olson, 1990). We intended to study families with adolescents using adequate methods to produce and analyze data and techniques that allowed us to consider the family as a unit of analysis. In fact we focused on both the dyad and the entire family, considered as a set of generations. Our research questions consisted of:

1.   Is it possible during adolescence to identify a critical phase in which changes are more significant?
2.   Is there any difference between congruence with mother and congruence with father?
3.   How much does intergenerational distance change during adolescence?
4.   How much does family configuration change during the transition to adulthood?

Method

Participants

The sample was composed of 325 "normal" families (triads of father, mother, and children) with a child aged between 11 and 24 years (M=17.5, SD=3.40) selected with the assistance of public and private schools in Milan. The age of the mothers ranged from 36 to 64 (M=46.9, SD=5.68); the age of the fathers ranged from 37 to 75 (M=50.33, SD=5.9). Approximately 44% of the sample were boys and 54% were girls. All the children were students and lived with their parents.

The sample was divided into four groups according to age and school grade. The four groups included: early adolescence from 11 to 14 years (20% of the sample); middle adolescence from 15 to 16 years (23% of the sample); late adolescence from 17 to 19 years (23% of the sample); and young adults from 20 to 26 years (34% of the sample).

Procedure

After the school headmasters and the teachers provided consent, students were asked to complete a self-report questionnaire at the school with two researchers present. Students gave their parents an envelope including a letter explaining the general purpose of the study and a self-report questionnaire. Parents completed the instruments at home.

Measures

Parents Adolescent Communication Scale (PACS; Barnes & Olson, 1985; Barnes & Olson, 1982) was one of the instruments administered. It is an instrument developed to obtain a description of parent-adolescent communication and to measure its positive and negative aspects. The scale is composed of two subscales: the first deals with openness in communication (10 items) and investigates freedom in communication, comprehension and satisfaction about communication; and the second deals with communication problems (10 items), that is, the absence of sharing in communication and the presence of negative feelings and selectivity of participants. The Italian version of PACS has been standardized by large samples of adolescents and adults (Lanz, in press). The Alpha coefficient for Openess is .87 and for Problems in Communication .76. Respondents were asked to rate their agreement, on a 5-point Likert scale ranging from (1) *strongly disagree* to (5) *strongly agree*. Examples of items regarding openness in communication are: "My father/mother/child is always a good listener" and "When I ask a question, I get an honest answer from my father/mother/child". Examples of items measuring the existence of problems in communication included: "There are topics I avoid discussing with my father/mother/child" and "I don't think I can tell my father/mother/child how I really feel about some things". The adolescents were requested to appraise the communication with their mothers and their fathers separately. The instrument was scored in two subscales.

The Family Environment Scale (Moos & Moos, 1981) is an instrument developed to obtain a family environment description. The original version is composed of 10 subscales. The participants completed a split-half Italian version of four of the original subscales (Cristante & Cusinato, 1995): cohesion, control, conflict, and organization. Each scale consists of 5 items, answered with a 5-point Likert scale ranging from (1) *strongly disagree* to (5) *strongly agree*. The alpha reliabilities were .63 for Cohesion, .73 for Control, .69 for Conflict, and .59 for Organization.

To obtain a congruence measure, congruence scores were computed between mother-child and between father-child based on distance between participants (Vermulst, Lanz & Van Leeuwe, 1998) so that the higher the within-dyad congruence, the smaller the distance. The higher the score, the higher the within dyad congruence.

Building of the triangle was also undertaken. Determining a family means having a mother, a father and a child. The triad is the unit of measurement of the family. Two fundamental relationships of the family are the marital and parent-child relationship. Using the congruence concept as previously defined we can build up (Figure 10.1) a triangle composed by the following elements: a) the base of the triangle represents the marital distance (measure of discongruence); b) the side of the triangle represents the father-child and mother-child distance; and c) the perpendicular height represents the intergenerational distance.

We decided to calculate the elements of the triangle based on family cohesion because it may be considered the background in which marital and parent-child relationships are re-negotiated.

Results

In Tables 10.1 and 10.2, the means and standard deviations for the two measures of communication and the four measures of family environment within the four groups are presented.

As demonstrated by these tables, late adolescents and young adults reported less openness and more problems in communication with their parents than early or middle adolescents. Mothers and fathers did not seem to modify their communication with their children depending on the child's age. As far as the family environment was concerned, the level of family cohesion and family organization results, decreased in late adolescence and young adulthood for the three informants. From these first results, late adolescence emerged as the crucial period above all others for adolescents who reported more problematic communication with parents and less cohesion.

In Table 10.3, the means and standard deviations of congruence on parent-child communication are presented. To verify change, the congruence between parents and children in the four groups was performed using two MANOVAs (father-child and mother-child) for the two variables (openness and problem in communication) with age and gender as the two factors.

For father-child dyads, the results of the analyses indicated that the level of congruence on communication in the overall test was significantly affected by age $(F(6,612)=1.96, p<0.05)$ but not by gender or interaction of age and gender. To investigate the age effects on the individual measures, a series of univariate ANOVAs were additionally performed. The results indicated that only congruence on openness in communication was significantly affected by age $(F(3,306)=3.58, p<0.05)$. The Newman Keuls' test showed that in the group of late adolescents and young adults there was a reduction in the level of congruence on openness in communication. In these two phases fathers and children are more distant regarding the positive aspects of their relationship. Instead congruence on the negative aspects did not change .

For mother-child dyads the results of the analyses showed that congruence on communication in the overall test was significantly affected by the interaction of gender and age $(F(6,614)= 2.45, p <0.05)$. Two univariate ANOVAs were additionally performed to investigate the interaction effects of congruence on open communication and problematic communication. The results of the univariate ANOVA indicated that only congruence on negative aspects of communication was significantly affected by the interaction between age and gender $(F(3,307)=3.32, p <0.05)$. Regarding the problematic aspects of their relationships, mothers and daughters in late adolescence had a higher level of congruence than sons and mothers.

We analyzed the different levels of congruence between mother-child and father-child in the four groups. Considering congruence on openness in communication, the t-test showed that in all groups there was a higher level of congruence in mother-child dyads than that of father-child dyads (early adolescence: $t(59)=2.35, p < 0.05$; middle adolescence: $t(73)=.55$ n.s.; late adolescence: $t(70)=2.29, p < 0.05$; young adulthood: $t(108) = 3.12, p < 0.05$). On the contrary, regarding the problematic aspects of communication, a higher level of congruence was evident in the father-child than the mother-child dyad (early adolescence: $t(58)=4.22, p < 0.05$; middle adolescence: $t(71)=6.53, p < 0.05$; late adolescence: $t(71)=4.32, p < 0.05$; young adulthood: $t(108) = 5.99, p < 0.05$). While mother and child were more involved in the intimate aspects of their relationship, father and child were more able to share the negative aspects of their relationship.

To investigate the effects of child's age and gender on the family environment, two MANOVAs (mother-child and father-child) were performed for the four variables (Table 10.4). The father-child dyad did not show significant effects of age and gender on congruence scores and there was a non-significant interaction between the two factors. The level of congruence results were stable over time. The results of the mother-child dyad analyses showed that congruence with the family environment overall, was significantly affected by age ($F(12,921)=3.64$, $p <0.05$) but not by gender or by the interaction between age and gender. The results of the univariate ANOVAs indicated that congruence on cohesion ($F(3,308)=2.68$, $p <0.05$), control ($F(3,308)=5.57$, $p <0.05$), and organization ($F(3,308)= 5.21$, $p <0.05$) were significantly affected by age. In particular, our findings showed a lower level of congruence for cohesion and control within late adolescence, while in young adulthood the lowest level of congruence concerning family organization was found. From our findings it appears that the level of congruence changes not only according to the child's age, but also according to the dyads considered. The mother-child dyad involved re-negotiating more family environment aspects than the father-child dyad.

To investigate the difference in father-child and mother-child dyads on congruence and family environment, paired t-tests were used. Father-child congruence on family organization was found to be higher in young adult groups ($t(109)=3.25$, $p <0.05$). For the other variables the difference was not significant.

In order to investigate how the intergenerational distance changes in the four groups, the perpendicular height of the triangle, which represents the intergenerational distance, was calculated. It ranged from 0 to infinity. In Table 10.5 the means and standard deviations for the base and the perpendicular heights of the four triangles are displayed.

Two ANOVAs were performed (one for marital distance and one for perpendicular heights) with age as a factor, to analyze the effect of child age. The results indicated a significant effect of age on marital distance ($F(3)=3.98$, $p <0.05$) and on perpendicular height ($F(3)=2.90$, $p <0.05$). The Newman Keuls' showed that intergenerational distance increased in late adolescence while at the same time marital distance decreased. In late adolescence the intergenerational distance reached the maximum point. In the following phase, young adulthood, the perpendicular height decreased, the base of the triangle increased compared to late adolescence, and the triangle was more or less equilateral (Figure 10.2). It may represent the fact that in the family of young adults there are three adults living together.

Discussion and conclusion

The first finding of the present study showed late adolescence as a critical phase in which there are a lot of changes both on a dyadic and family level. On the dyadic level, the relationship between parents and adolescents is characterized by a significant distance on several aspects of family functioning. Parents and adolescents have a different perception of their relationship but also of the family environment. In previous research this lack of congruence has been conceptualized as an index of conflict, but in this study it has been considered a marker of distancing that the adolescent must set and handle to individuate from the family. So the diminishing congruence during late adolescence can be considered an "acceptable disagreement between generations" (Goodnow, 1994) which is necessary for the family to cope with the new needs and point out the individuality of its members (Carlson et al., 1991). What is not clear is when the level of disagreement is no longer acceptable; in other words when the distance between parents and late adolescents becomes so great that it is impossible for adolescents to come back and be "accepted" by parents. During this phase the little oscillation between adequate and inadequate functioning became a significant transition and the separation process became more evident.

On the family level, late adolescence is the phase in which there is maximum intergenerational distance and the smallest marital one. To tolerate the intergenerational distance parents become close to each other; only in this way can the family find a new balance.

Late adolescence is the end and the beginning of a transitional phase which takes place progressively and slowly during young adulthood. Young adulthood distinguishes itself from late adolescence because it is characterized by a realignment of relationships. In fact, during this phase there are not a lot of changes, but there is an adjustment on the previous modification.

Referring to the family level it has been possible to show how the marital couple increases its distance in order to accept their child as a young adult. The young adult's family shows itself as an equilateral triangle in which all sides have the same length and the distance between family members is the same; the family is composed of three adults.

A second finding of our study is that mothers and fathers have different congruence with their children. Although fathers, traditionally and culturally are less involved in the raising of their children, they are able to identify negative aspects of their relationship. From this result we concur with Marta (1998) who stated that fathers, because of their lower involvement, can perceive the negative aspects of their relationships, while mothers, being more involved than fathers in the rearing of their children, have greater difficulty in describing their family situation in objective ways.

From a methodological point of view, this study represents an attempt to study the family, taking into account the different points of view of the family itself. The different levels of analysis enable us to clarify the changes in the family and highlight the different roles played by parents and children. The use of a triangle has permitted us to combine family members and to have a deeper understanding of family transformation.

The present study underscores the importance of investigating the moment of transition on a family level. The complexity of family processes can emerge only when we combine mother, father and child. The results obtained indicate that subsequent research should concentrate on achieving a better understanding of the transition process from the family's point of view. Moreover, greater attention will need to be focused on the methodological aspects of family research in order to find the best way to measure family relations and processes.

Figure 10.1 Congruence between family dyads

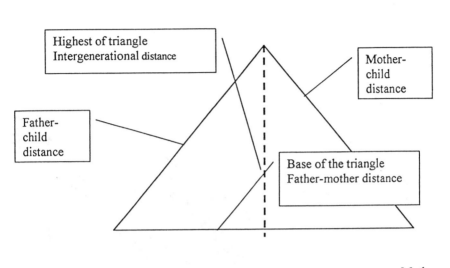

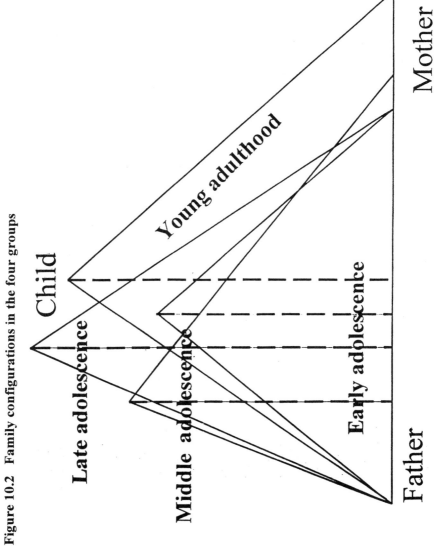

Figure 10.2   Family configurations in the four groups

Table 10.1 **Means and standard deviations of openness and problems in communication for child, mother and father**

	Early adolescence		Middle adolescence		Late adolescence		Young adulthood	
	mean	sd	mean	sd	mean	sd	mean	sd
Children								
Openness vs. mother	42.0	6.4	40.4	6.3	38.7	8.4	38.8	7.1
Openness vs. father	37.6	8.5	36.6	8.1	33.4	9.5	34.2	7.9
Problem vs. mother	22.0	6.1	24.4	8.0	26.1	6.6	23.6	7.3
Problem vs. father	24.1	7.6	25.8	7.3	27.4	7.1	23.8	7.0
Mother								
Openness vs. child	39.1	7.0	39.3	6.13	39.5	6.6	39.9	5.9
Problem vs. child	21.77	6.9	22.85	6.7	24.45	7.1	22.5	6.8
Father								
Openness vs. child	37.7	7.0	39.2	6.1	39.48	5.8	38.29	6.7
Problem vs. child	22.1	6.5	23.2	5.8	24.3	7.0	22.6	6.1

The range is from 10 (lowest) to 50 (highest).

Table 10.2 **Means and standard deviations of cohesion, organization, control and conflict for children, mother and father**

	Early adolescence		Middle adolescence		Late adolescence		Young adulthood	
	mean	sd	mean	sd	mean	sd	mean	sd
Children								
Cohesion	18.8	3.0	18.2	3.4	16.5	4.2	17.5	3.4
Organization	17.8	2.6	18.0	2.8	17.8	3.2	17.0	2.6
Control	15.3	3.6	13.8	3.2	13.7	3.1	13.0	3.1
Conflict	12.1	3.7	12.4	3.9	13.6	4.2	12.8	4.1
Mother								
Cohesion	19.8	2.8	19.2	2.8	18.5	2.7	18.3	3.0
Organization	18.4	2.6	18.7	2.7	19.3	3.6	17.5	2.4
Control	14.1	2.7	13.8	3.0	14.3	3.0	13.7	2.9
Conflict	12.6	2.7	13.81	2.8	13.6	3.0	13.6	2.9
Father								
Cohesion	19.7	3.4	19.0	2.8	18.4	2.4	17.9	3.3
Organization	17.6	2.5	18.6	2.4	18.7	3.3	17.5	2.8
Control	14.7	2.9	15.2	2.6	14.3	3.1	14.4	3.0
Conflict	12.8	2.6	13.0	2.5	13.0	2.7	13.1	2.7

The range is from 5 (lowest) to 25 (highest).

Table 10.3   Mean scores for father-child and mother-child congruence on openness and problem in communication as a function of child's age

	Early adolescence		Middle adolescence		Late adolescence		Young adulthood	
	mean	sd	mean	sd	mean	sd	mean	sd
Father-Child								
Openness	0.74	0.12	0.78	0.11	0.70	0.16	0.73	0.13
Problem	0.71	0.12	0.72	0.11	0.70	0.11	0.71	0.11
Mother-Child								
Openness	0.78	0.10	0.77	0.11	0.76	0.12	0.78	0.10
Problem	0.62	0.10	0.61	0.11	0.61	0.12	0.62	0.12.

The range is from 0 (lowest) to 1 (highest).

Table 10.4   Mean scores for father-child and mother-child congruence on cohesion, control, organization and conflict as a function of child's age

	Early adolescence		Middle adolescence		Late adolescence		Young adulthood	
	mean	sd	mean	sd	mean	sd	mean	sd
Father-Child								
Cohesion	0.77	0.13	0.78	0.11	0.73	0.14	0.74	0.12
Organization	0.77	0.12	0.77	0.01	0.72	0.16	0.74	0.13
Control	0.70	0.13	0.67	0.16	0.65	0.15	0.70	0.13
Conflict	0.73	0.13	0.74	0.13	0.70	0.16	0.71	0.14
Mother-Child								
Cohesion	0.78	0.11	0.76	0.11	0.72	0.13	0.74	0.12
Organization	0.73	0.09	0.76	0.10	0.75	0.14	0.70	0.11
Control	0.69	0.14	0.68	0.13	0.61	0.12	0.68	0.11
Conflict	0.75	0.13	0.74	0.13	0.71	0.13	0.73	0.11

The range is from 0 (lowest) to 1 (highest).

Table 10.5   Means and standard deviations of perpendicular heights (intergenerational distance) and base of triangle (marital distance) for the four groups

	Early adolescence		Middle adolescence		Late adolescence		Young adulthood	
	mean	sd	mean	sd	mean	sd	mean	sd
Intergenerational distance	10.54	11.34	11.59	12.29	16.03	15.02	14.43	13.19
Marital distance	17.38	14.73	18.43	11.42	16.85	10.85	22.41	12.03

References

Barnes, H. & Olson, D.H. (1985). Parent Adolescent Communication and the Circuplex Model. *Child Development, 56,* 438-447.

Barnes, H. & Olson, D.H. (1982). Parent Adolescent Communication. In D.H. Olson, H.I. McCubbin, H. Barnes, A. Larsen, A. Luxxen, & M. Wilson (Eds). *Family Environment,* (pp.29-44). St Pauls: University of Minnesota and the Circuplex Model. *Child Development, 56,* 438-447.

Blos, P. (1979). *The adolescence passage: Developmental issues.* New York: International University Press.

Breunlin, D.C. (1988). Oscillation theory and family development. In C. Falicov (Ed). *Family Transition* (pp.133-155). New York: Guildford Press.

Carlson, C.I., Cooper, C.R., & Spradling, V.Y. (1991). Developmental implication of shared versus distinct perceptions of the family in early adolescence. In R.L. Paikoff, *Shared views in the family during adolescence.* San Francisco: Jossey-Bass.

Cigoli, V. (1985). Adolescenza. Progresso e degrado del processo di individuazione familiare [Adolescence. Progress and deterioration of the family individuation process]. In E. Scabini (a cura di) L'organizzazione Famiglia tra crisi e Sviluppo (pp.202-239). Milano: F.Angeli.

Collins, W.A. (1990). Parent-child relationships in transition to adolescence: Continuity and change in interaction, affect and cognition. In R. Montemayor, G.R. Adams, T.P. Gullotta (Eds.). *Advances in adolescent development: Vol.2. From childhood to adolescence: A transitional period?* (pp.85-106). Newbury Park, CA: Sage.

Collins, W.A. & Luebeker, C. (1994). Parent and adolescents expectancies: Individual and relational significance. In J. Smetana, Beliefs about parenting origins and developmental implications. San Francisco: Jossey-Bass.

Cowan, P.A. (1991). Individual and family life transitions : A proposal for a new definition. In P.A. Cowan, M. Hetherington. (Eds). *Family Transitions* (pp.3-30). Hillsdale: LEA.

Cristante, F. & Cusinato, M. (1995). *La valutazione del clima familiare [Family environment evaluation].* Manuscript in preparation. University of Padua: Padua, Italy.

Feetham, S.L. (1988). *Developing Programs of Research of Families.* Presented at University of Pennsylvania School of Nursing, March, 1, Philadelphia, PA.

Gecas, V. & Seff, M.A. (1990). Families and Adolescents: A review of the 1980s. *Journal of Marriage and the Family, 34,* 941-958.

Goodnow, J. (1994). Acceptable disagreement between generations. In J.G. Smetana, *Beliefs about parenting: Origins and developmental implications.* San Francisco: Jossey-Bass.

Grotevant, H. & Cooper C. (1983). *Adolescent Development in the Family.* New directions of child development. San Francisco: Jossey-Bass.

Huston, T.L. & 'Rampler, J.K. (1989). Interpersonal Attitudes, dispositions, and behavior in family and other close relationships. In H.D. Grotevant (Ed.) *Current*

Issues in Marital and Family Assessment. Special Issue of *Journal of Family Psychology, 3*, 177-198.

Jackson, S. & Bosma, H. A, (1992). Developmental research on adolescence: European perspectives for the 1990s and beyond. *British Journal of Developmental Psychology, 10*, 319-337.

Lanz, M. (in press). La scala di comunicazione genitori-figli: l' applicazione ad un campione italiano [Parent-child communication scale: Results from an italaina sample]. *Bollettino di psicologia applicata.*

Lanz, M., Vermulst, A., Gerris, J. & Scabini , E. (1998). Congruence on parenting inside the family using adolescence and pre-adolescence. (Submitted).

Larsen, A. & Olson, D. (1990). Capturing the complexity of Family Systems: Integrating Family Theory, Family Scores, and Family Analysis. In T. Draper, A. Marcos. *Family Variable. Conceptualization, Measurement and Use* (pp.19-47). London: Sage Publication.

Marta, E. (1999). Parent-adolescent interactions and psycho-social risk in adolescents: An analysis of communication, support and gender. Submitted.

Minuchin, S. (1985). Family and individual development provocations from the files of family therapy. *Child Development, 56*, 289-302.

Moos, R.H. & Moos, B.S. (1981). *Family Environment Scale Manual.* Palo Alto, CA: Consulting Psychologist Press.

Olson, D.H., McCubbin, H.I., Barnes, H.L., Larsen , A.S., Muxen, M.J. & Wilson, M.A. (1983). *Families: What makes them work.* Newbury Park, CA: Sage.

Scabini, E. (1995). *Psicologia Sociale della Famiglia* [The social psychology of the family]. Torino:Bollati Boringhieri.

Sherrod, L., Haggerty, R. & Featherman, D. (1993). Introduction: Late adolescence and the transition to adulthood, *Journal of Research on Adolescence, 3*, 217-226.

Simons, C., McCluskey, K. & Millet, M. (1985). Interparental rating of temperament for high and low risk infants. *Child Psychiatry and Human Development, 15*, 167-179.

Sroufe, L. W. (1991). Assessment of Parent-Adolescent Relationships: Implications for Adolescent Development. *Journal of Family Psychology, 5*, 21-45.

Sroufe, L. & Fleeson, J. (1988). The coherence of family relationship. In R.A. Hinde, & J. Stevenson-Hinde (Eds.). *Towards Understanding Families* (pp.27-48). Oxford: Oxford University Press.

Vermulst, A., Lanz, M., & Van Leeuwe, J.F.J. (1988). *Congruence within dyads, an alternative for inter- and intraclass correlation.* Manuscript submitted for publication.

Youniss, J. (1983). Social construction of adolescence by adolescents and parents. In H. Grotevant, C. Cooper. *Adolescent Development in the Family* (pp.93-109). London: Jossey-Bass.

Youniss, J. & Smollar, J. (1989). Transformation in adolescents' perceptions of parents. *International Journal of Behavioral Development, 12,* 71-84.

Section III:

Child and Adolescent Development

11 Regulation and Its Disorders

DIANE BENOIT

Abstract

A brief review of self-regulation is presented, in addition to current knowledge about the prevalence, classification, etiology, phenomenology, outcome and treatment of regulatory disorders. The role of the environment as external regulator or dysregulator is also described, in addition to the importance of assessing both internal (within the infant) and external (within the environment) aspects of regulation in infants who have clinical problems. The case of an 11-month-old infant with regulatory disorder is used to illustrate the role of the family environment on the perpetuation of regulatory disorders and the impact of regulatory disorders on the family. Future directions for research are discussed.

Introduction

Most parents who expect a new baby imagine the baby will be healthy, adapt easily to the family's routines, sleep well, thrive, and be easily comforted when distressed (in other words, the baby will be able to self-regulate). Most parents never imagine that a baby might not enjoy being held and cuddled, might be unhappy and miserable most of the time, might not want to eat enough to keep hydrated and well nourished, might not sleep enough, or might remain inconsolable despite a loving environment and almost heroic efforts to soothe him or her. Yet, there seems to be a growing number of unhappy and inconsolable babies who cannot self-regulate and suffer from regulation disorders. The purpose of this paper is twofold. First, a brief review of self-regulation and regulation disorders will be presented. Second, the case of an infant with regulatory disorder will be used to illustrate the mutual impact regulatory disorders and the family environment have on each other.

Self-regulation

Most healthy newborns have the capacity to regulate complex physiological processes (e.g., breathing, cardiopulmonary functioning, thermoregulation, swallowing, digestion). This capacity to self-regulate allows them to maintain physiological homeostasis and ensure their survival (Porges, 1996). As they mature, infants' self-regulatory capacities also mature and encompass increasingly complex domains such as emotion regulation, self-consoling, sensorimotor integration, motor planning, regulation of sleep-wake cycles and hunger-satiety cycles (Cichetti & Tucker, 1994; Thompson & Calkins, 1996). It is believed that infants must learn to competently regulate physiological processes before they can engage effectively in complex social, behavioral, and emotional interactions with the environment (Porges, 1996). In essence, a well functioning, maturing nervous system (in particular the autonomous nervous system) is essential for self-regulation even though individual differences in self-regulatory capacity may exist in neurologically intact infants (Porges, 1996).

Various internal (within the infant) and external (in the environment) factors influence infants' self-regulatory capacity (Fox, Schmidt, Calkins, Rubin, & Coplan, 1996; Rogerness & McClure, 1996; Thompson & Calkins, 1996). Examples of internal factors that may negatively influence self-regulatory capacity include prenatal drug and cocaine exposure, prematurity, brain injury, and birth complications (Allessandri, Sullivan, Imaizumi, & Lewis, 1993; Jacobson, Jacobson, Sokol, Martier, & Ager, 1993; Mayes, Bornstein, Chawarska, Haynes, & Granger, 1996; Mayes, Bornstein, Chawarska, & Granger, 1995; Mayes, Granger, Frank, Schottenfeld, & Bornstein, 1993; Porges, 1996; Struthers & Hansen, 1992). External factors that may impair or improve infants' self-regulatory capacity include the quality of the caregiver's response to the infant's signals (Mayes et al., 1996). For instance, a disorganized, unpredictable caregiver who repeatedly fails to feed an infant who shows signs of hunger may interfere with the infant's ability to establish regular hunger-satiety cycles, to feel hunger and/or to communicate feelings of hunger.

The assessment of both internal and external components of regulation has important clinical implications as it guides intervention (Porges, 1996). For example, when a premature infant cannot achieve thermoregulation (i.e., cannot maintain an appropriate body temperature), heating units can be used in special care units. Similarly, when an infant cannot soothe himself to sleep at bed time and during the night, structured bed time routines and behavioral programs can be used (DeGangi, Craft, & Castellan, 1991; Ferber, 1985; Sadeh & Anders, 1993).

Prevalence and classification

The prevalence of regulatory disorders is unknown. However, given that birth complications and pre-maturity are risk factors for regulatory disorders (Porges, 1996), and given the growing number of seriously ill infants who survive because of advances in medical technology, regulatory disorders could be on the rise. Regulatory disorders are not included in the diagnostic nomenclature of DSM-IV but are included in the Diagnostic Classification: 0-3 (Zero to Three, 1994).

The "diagnosis" of regulatory disorder should not be made in infants younger than 6 months because of the high frequency of transient difficulties with self-regulation (e.g., sleep problems that resolve spontaneously by 5 to 6 months of age (DeGangi, DiPietro, Greenspan, & Porges, 1991). Further, in order for a "diagnosis" of regulatory disorder to be made, behavioral and constitutional (maturational) elements must be present and the difficulties in sensory, sensori-motor, or processing capacities must affect daily adaptation and relationships (DeGangi, 1991; DeGangi, DiPietro, Greenspan, & Porges, 1991; DeGangi, Porges, Sickel, & Greenspan, 1993; Greenspan & Wieder, 1993).

Specific subtypes of regulatory disorders have been described based on clusters of symptoms exhibited by the infant. These include (1) Hypersensitive, (2) Under-reactive, (3) Motorically Disorganized, (4) Impulsive, and (5) Other disorders (Greenspan & Wieder, 1993; Zero to Three, 1994). Severity ratings have also been described, ranging from mild (e.g., elimination problems, sleep difficulties) to severe (e.g., irregular breathing, startles, gagging; Greenspan & Wieder, 1993). Examples of moderately severe regulatory disorders include problems with gross and fine motor activity (e.g., abnormal tonus or posture, jerky or limp movements, poor motor planning), attentional organization (e.g., driven or perseverating on small details) and affective organization, including predominantly negative affective tone and moodiness.

Etiology

Regulatory disorders are believed to be due to dysfunctions in the autonomic nervous system (DeGangi, DiPietro et al., 1991; Greenspan & Wieder, 1993), although they are influenced by the environment (Mayes et al., 1996). Specifically, infants with regulatory disorders have been shown to have higher baseline vagal tone and inconsistent vagal reactivity (i.e., heterogeneous response to sensory and cognitive tasks). These findings suggest that infants with regulatory disorders may have autonomic (parasympathetic) hyperirritability caused by defective central neural programs and mediated via neurotransmitters through the vagus nerve (DeGangi, DiPietro et al., 1991; Porges, 1991). However, more research in the field is clearly needed to replicate these findings.

Phenomenology

Regulatory disorders are characterized by a "difficult" temperament, irritability, moodiness, difficulty self-consoling, and lack of cuddliness (DeGangi & Greenspan, 1988). Infants with regulatory disorders also have difficulty regulating physiological processes so that many have sleep problems (regulation of sleep-wake cycles, difficulty falling asleep, frequent night awakenings), feeding problems (regulation of hunger-satiety cycles, refusal to eat a variety of food textures), and elimination problems (constipation, diarrhea). Many have a history of colic. They may present with impaired attentional capacity, impulsivity, negativism, difficulty in making transitions, and impaired reactivity to sensory stimulation (e.g., auditory, visual, tactile, gustatory, vestibular, olfactory, temperature). Many have impaired integrative and processing capacities in the sensorimotor area, for example, they may have impaired motor tone and motor planning, delays in fine motor skills, and impaired capacity to discriminate or integrate auditory-verbal or visual-spatial stimuli (DeGangi, DiPietro, et al., 1991; DeGangi & Greenspan, 1988; DiGangi, Porges, et al., 1993; Greenspan & Wieder, 1993).

Importantly, many domains requiring self-regulation are closely intertwined so that difficulties in one domain may create difficulties in another. For example, sleep, arousal, affect, and attention are known to be such closely intertwined domains. It is well known that difficulties with inadequate sleep are often associated with symptoms of irritability, emotional lability, difficulty concentrating, and fatigue (Dahl, 1996; Derryberry & Reed, 1994; Derryberry & Tucker, 1994; Posner & Dehaene, 1994; Rothbart, Posner, & Rosicky, 1994). This multi-domain involvement might help to explain why infants with regulatory disorders are so difficult for families to cope with. Indeed, because of the regulatory disordered infant's sleep problems, the parents are often sleep deprived and have little reserve for dealing with the irritable, unconsolable, and sleep-deprived infant. The fact that many babysitters also cannot cope with many infants with regulatory disorders only compounds the problems as the parents often cannot have respite (DeGangi, Craft et al., 1991).

Outcome

Few studies have examined the outcome of infants with regulatory disorders. One study showed that infants with regulatory disorders who are left untreated are at risk for later developmental, sensorimotor, and/or emotional and behavioral problems (DeGangi, Porges et al., 1993), including problems in the areas of cognitive abilities, attention span, activity level, emotional maturity, motor maturity, and tactile sensitivity. Another study showed that low regulation, negative emotionality, and general and positive emotional intensity predicted behavior problems in elementary school children (Eisenberg, Fabes, Guthrie, Murphy, Maszk, Holmgren, & Suh, 1996).

Role of the environment as external regulator or dysregulator

Clinical experience and findings from research suggest that the caregiving environment plays an important part in helping a child self-regulate or dysregulate. For example, findings from one study showed that compared to mothers of infants without regulatory disorders, mothers of infants with regulatory disorders showed less contingent responses, less physical proximity, more flat affect during play interactions, and had more negative perceptions of their infant (DeGangi et al., 1991; DeGangi, Porges et al., 1993). Findings from these studies do not point to a causal link between suboptimal caregiving and regulatory disorders. Rather, they suggest that the quality of a caregiver's response to an infant with a regulatory disorder may interfere with clinical improvement of some regulatory disorders.

Treatment

The treatment of regulatory disorders essentially focuses on improving the child's coping strategies (by teaching self-soothing strategies, or targeting the particular sensory processing deficit), helping parents cope with their regulatory disordered child, and re-structuring the environment by "imposing" an external regulation (DeGangi, Craft, & Castellan, 1991; DeGangi, Wietisbach, & Scheiner, 1993; Greenspan, 1992; Greenspan & Wieder, 1993). Direct intervention to improve the sensory, sensorimotor, or processing problems are essential when these problems are identified (typically these treatments are provided by occupational therapists trained in the treatment of sensory integration and processing problems). A structured sensorimotor therapy is particularly helpful in promoting gross motor skills, self-care abilities, and sensory integrative functions (DeGangi, Wietisbach et al., 1993; Williamson & Anzalone, 1997). When the regulatory disorder affects primarily areas of sleep, appetite/feeding, or emotion regulation, interventions by a mental health professional may be helpful. In addition to the general principles of treatment outlined above, intervention by a mental health professional could include educating the parent and referral source about regulatory disorders (as clinical experience suggests that many health and mental health professionals are unfamiliar with regulatory disorders) and correct any distorted perceptions of the child.

Case vignette

J. was an 11 month old who was referred by his pediatrician for an evaluation of feeding problems in the context of failure to thrive. No underlying medical contributor to the feeding problems and failure to thrive was identified. J. had a 4-year-old brother who never experienced any problems, was generally content, and was functioning well. J.'s mother happily stayed at home to care for her two sons and J.'s father was a professional. The family was from an upper middle class background. J. was born after a planned, full term, uncomplicated pregnancy and an easy delivery with Apgar scores of 9 both at 1 and 5 minutes. Within the first 24 hours of his life, J. developed a fever and fast, labored breathing (with "a lot of mucus" which made him gag and vomit when he attempted to feed the first couple of days). Although no cause was identified, he was placed on prophylactic antibiotics. Both J. and his mother went home on day three. J.'s parents continued to notice what they called "upper respiratory congestion" (presence of mucus and congested breathing) for several months but no cause could be identified (a sweat test to rule out cystic fibrosis was even conducted but was negative).

When J. was first seen in the clinic at age 11 months, his parents reported that he had achieved his developmental milestones on schedule with one exception, he still could not crawl. They said that J. had always been a "gassy" baby who always had difficulty burping (although the parents did not think that he had "colic") and always had problems with constipation. They described him as "chronically tired," "moody," "irritable," having "quite a temper," and "being unable to self-soothe". J. was said to be unable to amuse himself and constantly needed someone to entertain him. J. was also unable to tolerate separations from his mother or father, to the point that he was always physically in the presence of one of his parents. J. apparently had no difficulty with olfactory, visual, and auditory stimulation but had a possible tactile hypersensitivity (as he disliked getting dressed and clothing labels would "drive him nuts").

J. had chronic sleep problems. His parents estimated that J. slept a total of six to seven hours per 24-hour period. He typically stayed at the breast for two hours at night before settling (during this time, mother read or did some other activity while sitting and holding J.). Mother said that if she removed him from her breast before the two hours, J. would cry and would not settle. When he was sound asleep after having spent two hours on the breast, J. was taken to his parents' bed where he stayed with his mother. J. would typically wake up several times during the night and his father would hold him in a very specific way while walking (gently but firmly pressing J.'s abdomen on father's left shoulder) in order for J. to settle. Mother nursed J. at least twice during the night. J. has irregular, brief (approximately 30 min.) naps during the day, usually when he was in the car or nursed.

According to his parents, J.'s appetite problems began at birth. Mother said that J. was never as "voracious" a feeder as her other son, that he rarely showed signs of hunger, but that he managed to thrive as he breastfed frequently during the day and night. The problems with food refusal began when solids were first introduced at 6 months old. J. reacted by spitting the food out and appearing mostly disinterested but occasionally distressed with infant cereal. When pureed foods were introduced about 4 to 6 weeks later, the problems with food refusal further deteriorated as J. began to protest more forcefully whenever spoon feeding was attempted. Mother recalled that J. "hated" pureed textures, that he "made faces" and that his entire body was "shaking" when the food was placed inside his mouth. He also gagged and occasionally the gagging led to vomiting. Because of his strong negative reactions to spoon feeding, J.'s mother thought that he simply "was not ready" and she did not push him to eat solids so that J.'s main source of nutrition remained breast milk. However, J.'s mother continued to expose him to the pureed textures. J.'s reaction to the introduction of finger foods at about 6 months old was to refuse to put the food (e.g., biscuits, cookies) to his mouth (at the time of assessment, he still refused to place these food textures into his mouth or to even bring the food to his lips). His parents noted that J. never placed anything in his mouth (either toys or foods). He always refused pacifiers and bottles. He was willing to drink from a glass since age 6 months, but only accepted water in small quantities. By the time J. was first seen in the clinic, he was willing to accept small amounts of clear broth, ice cream, pudding, and pureed vegetables and fruits. In fact, his mother said that over a typical 24-hour period, J. was willing to drink 2 oz. of water and eat 3 oz. of clear broth, 1 oz. of pureed foods but all other liquids and solids were refused. J. was also nursed "on demand," (i.e., every 1-1/2 to 2 hours throughout the day and at least twice during the night). His caloric intake was obviously insufficient to meet the nutritional requirements of an 11-month-old boy and J. was failing to thrive. He had begun dropping off the growth curve at about 6 months old, going from the 75th percentile for age at 6 months to below the 5th percentile at 11 months.

Needless to say, J.'s parents were probably as sleep deprived as J. They said that they found themselves losing patience with J., his brother, and with each other at times. They both admitted that J. was so difficult to deal with that if he had been their first child, they would never have wanted other children. J.'s father admitted that he found himself resenting J. at times for depriving him of sleep as this greatly affected father's functioning at work. J.'s mother admitted that her feelings oscillated between being a "zombie" and being the "worst, most inadequate mom on earth" as she recognized that she could not make her baby happy, feed him or soothe him. She said that seeing her own baby generally unhappy, "starving himself" and refusing her attempts to comfort him created mixed feelings in her (sadness, helplessness, hopelessness, frustration, extreme worry, compassion, love, tenderness, and need to protect her son). Both parents also said that they felt their other son was missing out on experiences with them, as they were so preoccupied with J. and needed to spend so much time to attend to his needs. J.'s mother admitted that she found it difficult to be emotionally available to J. when he needed her (which she felt was constantly), especially given that no babysitter or member of the extended family wanted to babysit him because he "always cried, refused to eat and sleep, and could not be consoled".

J. was believed to have a regulation disorder because of the presence of (1) sleep problems (difficulty regulating sleep-wake cycles, difficulty settling at bed time, frequent night awakenings); (2) feeding problems (difficulty regulating hunger-satiety cycles, refusal of textured foods, extreme food selectivity) - severe enough to be associated with failure to thrive; (3) difficulty self-consoling; (4) difficulty with mood regulation (which obviously could be secondary to the sleep deprivation and his undernourished state); (5) gastrointestinal irregularities ("gassy", constipation problems); (6) possible gustatory hypersensitivity (because of his reactions to foods); (7) tactile hypersensitivity (reaction to lumpy textures, dislike of getting dressed and clothing labels); and (8) possible developmental delays (unable to crawl at 11 months).

To treat the regulatory problems, J.'s parents were asked to "impose external regulation" on J. To accomplish this, the parents tackled the first three problems listed above (all the other problems seemed to improve once the first three problems were treated).

(1) Sleep problems: J.'s father imposed a structured bed time routine and used a behavioral sleep program to teach J. to learn to soothe himself to sleep without needing his mother (breastfeeding and holding) or his father (carrying) to do it for him (DeGangi, Craft et al., 1991; Ferber, 1985; Sadeh & Anders, 1993). All feeds were also eliminated during the night. Within four days of treatment, J. went from sleeping an average of 6-7 hours per 24-hour period to sleeping 11 hours during the night and taking two 60-90 minute naps during the day. Although his general mood and disposition improved dramatically as a result of the improved sleep, the problems with refusal of solids and liquids remained.

(2) Feeding problems - severe enough to be associated with failure to thrive: A four-component feeding program (Benoit, Green, & Arts-Rodas, 1997) was used. The feeding program consisted of (i) a structured feeding schedule and routine with time limited meals, (ii) nutritional guidance (to provide high energy foods), (iii) behavior modification, and (iv) parent training. Only the first two components of the feeding program were used in the first week of treatment as these components are the simplest to use and can extinguish many feeding problems that do not have a behavioral (i.e., learned) component (Benoit et al., 1997). The first two components of the feeding program seemed to help J. begin to establish regular hunger-satiety cycles, to show signs of hunger and satiety and to begin to thrive. However, because J. continued to be very difficult to feed (because he repeatedly pushed the food away, refused to drink anything but water, fussed, squirmed to be put down, etc.), a behavior modification program was started to extinguish these maladaptive feeding behaviors. The behavior modification program consisted of sitting him in the high chair comfortably but restricting his escape attempts (by "tucking" him into the high chair by placing towels on either side of his trunk and in his crotch to prevent him from slouching, sliding, and escaping). J.'s hands (which he used to bat the spoon away) were gently but firmly held down and the spoon was brought to his lips *without ever using feeding techniques that would induce pain or fear*. When the food was on J.'s lips, he licked and swallowed it. Within about 2 weeks, J. was still fussing occasionally at meal times but was willing to open his mouth and swallow the food offered to him and was drinking milk from a cup. Gradually, the need to hold his hands down disappeared as J. stopped pushing the spoon away. He even began to cooperate with self-feeding (although this took several weeks to accomplish).

(3) Difficulty with self-soothing: J.'s parents saw a dramatic improvement in J.'s ability to self-console once he began to sleep better at night. They

attributed this to the fact that because of the sleep program which called for the use of a transitional object, J. now had a strategy for dealing with distress (he chose a cotton-covered stuffed animal as his transitional object).

(4) Difficulty with mood regulation: In J.'s case, it seems that an improved nutritional status and improved sleep patterns greatly improved his overall mood, compliance, and frustration tolerance, an observation that has been made in previous research on the effects of using sleep programs (Minde, Faucon, & Falkner, 1994).

(5) Gastrointestinal irregularities ("gassy", constipation problems): These problems seemed to improve as J.'s diet improved.

(6) Possible gustatory hypersensitivity: This problem seemed to disappear with the use of the behavior modification program, which has previously been compared to the behavioral technique of "flooding." In other words, the repeated exposure to the feared/uncomfortable stimulus (in J.'s case, textured foods) seemed to desensitize him to the "fear" of eating and habituate him to food textures. Within two weeks of behavior therapy, J. could tolerate increasingly coarser textures (although he was still not on an age appropriate diet).

(7) Tactile hypersensitivity: With the exception of J.'s aversion to lumpy textures, no major improvements were reported in this area and the parents did not find that this was a significant problem (they dealt with it by removing clothing labels and getting J. dressed as quickly and efficiently as possible).

(8) Possible developmental delays: J's parents attributed the resolution of this problem to his improved nutritional status and sleep patterns. However, recommendations were made for J. to be assessed by an occupational therapist knowledgeable about regulatory disorders.

Conclusion

The purpose of this paper was to review current knowledge about self-regulation, its disorders, and the mutual impact regulatory disorders and the environment have on each other. Research is clearly needed to elucidate the prevalence, phenomenology, developmental course, prognosis and treatment of regulatory disorders. More research is also needed to examine the interplay of the infant's autonomous nervous system and the caregiving environment on the development and course of regulatory disorders. Although relatively little is known about regulatory disorders compared to other, better known disorders of infancy and childhood, these disorders are highly clinically relevant as they are challenging and occasionally destructive for families, have been associated with negative outcomes, in the child, and can be managed successfully.

References

Allessandri, S.M., Sullivan, M.W., Imaizumi, S., & Lewis, M. (1993). Learning and emotional responsivity in cocaine-exposed infants. *Developmental Psychology, 29*, 989-997.

Benoit, D., Green, D., & Arts-Rodas, D. (1997). Posttraumatic feeding disorders Letter to the Editor. *Journal of the American Academy of Child and Adolescent Psychiatry, 36*, 577-578.

Cichetti, D. & Tucker, D. (1994). Development and self-regulatory structures of the mind. *Development and Psychopathology, 6*, 533-549.

Dahl, R.E. (1996). The regulation of sleep and arousal: Development and psychopathology. *Development and Psychopathology, 8*, 3-27.

DeGangi, G.A. (1991). Assessment of sensory, emotional, and attentional problems in regulatory disordered infants: Part 1. *Infant & Young Children, 3*, 1-8.

DeGangi, G.A., Craft, P., & Castellan, J. (1991). Treatment of sensory, emotional, and attentional problems in regulatory disordered infants: Part 2. *Infant & Young Children, 3*, 9-19.

DeGangi G.A., DiPietro, J.A., Greenspan, S.I., & Porges, S.W. (1991). Psychophysiological characteristics of the regulatory disordered infant. *Infant Behavior and Development, 14*, 37-50.

DeGangi, G.A. & Greenspan, S.I. (1988). The development of sensory functioning in infants. *Physical and Occupational Therapy in Pediatrics, 8*, 21-33

DeGangi, G.A., Porges, S.W., Sickel, R.Z., & Greenspan, S.I. (1993). Four-year follow-up of a sample of regulatory disordered infants. *Infant Mental Health Journal, 14*, 330-343.

DeGangi, G.A., Wietisbach, M.G., & Scheiner, N. (1993). A comparison of structured sensorimotor therapy and child-centered activity in the treatment of preschool children with sensorimotor problems. *The American Journal of Occupational Therapy, 47*, 777-786.

Derryberry, D. & Reed, M.A. (1994). Attention and temperament: Orienting toward and away from positive and negative signals. *Journal of Personality and Social Psychology, 66*, 1128-1139.

Derryberry, D. & Tucker, M.A. (1994). Motivating the focus of attention. In P. Niedenthal & S. Kitayama (Eds.), *The heart's eye: Emotional influences in perception and attention* (pp. 167-196). San Diego, CA: Academic Press.

Eisenberg, N., Fabes, R.A., Guthrie, I.K., Murphy, B.C., Maszk, P., Holmgren, R., & Suh, K. (1996). The relations of regulation and emotionality to problem behavior in elementary school children. *Development and Psychopathology, 8*, 141-162.

Ferber, R. (1985). *Solving your child's sleep problems*. New York: Simon & Schuster.

Fox, N.A., Schmidt, L.A., Calkins, S.D., Rubin, K.H., & Coplan, R.J. (1996). The role of frontal activation in the regulation and dysregulation of social behavior during the preschool years. *Development and Psychopathology, 8,* 89-102.

Greenspan, S.I. (1992). Regulatory Disorders. In: *Infancy and Early Childhood: The practice of clinical assessment and intervention with emotional and developmental challenges* (pp. 601-638). Madison, CT: International University Press, Inc.

Greenspan, S.I. & Wieder, S. (1993). Regulatory disorders. In C.H. Zeanah (Ed.), *Handbook of Infant Mental Health* (pp. 280-290). New York: Guilford Press.

Jacobson, S., Jacobson, J.L., Sokol, R.J., Martier, S., & Ager, J.W. (1993). Prenatal alcohol exposure and infant information processing. *Child Development, 64,* 1706-1721.

Mayes, L.C., Bornstein, M.H., Chawarska, K., & Granger, R.H. (1995). Information-processing and developmental assessments in 3-month-old infants exposed prenatally to cocaine. *Pediatrics, 95,* 539-545.

Mayes, L.C., Bornstein, M.C., Chawarska, K., Haynes, O.M., & Granger, R.H. (1996). Impaired regulation of arousal in 3-month-old infants exposed prenatally to cocaine and other drugs. *Development and Psychopathology, 8,* 29-42.

Mayes, L.C., Granger, R.H., Frank, M.A., Schottenfeld, R., & Bornstein, M.H. (1993). Neurobehavioral profiles of infants exposed to cocaine prenatally. *Pediatrics, 91,* 778-783.

Minde, K., Faucon, A., & Falkner, S. (1994). The effects of treating sleep problems in toddlers on their daytime behavior. *Journal of the American Academy of Child and Adolescent Psychiatry, 33,* 1114-1121.

Porges, S.W. (1996). Physiological regulation in high-risk infants: A model for assessment and potential intervention. *Development and Psychopathology, 8,* 43-58.

Porges, S.W. (1991). Vagal tone: A mediator of affect. In J.A. Garber & K.A. Dodge (Eds.), *The development of affect regulation and dysregulation.* New York: Cambridge University Press.

Posner, M.I. & Dehaene, S. (1994). Attention networks. *Trends in Neuroscience, 17,* 75-79.

Rogerness, G.A., & McClure, E.B. (1996). Development and neurotransmitter-environmental interactions. *Development and Psychopathology, 8,* 183-199.

Rothbart, M.K., Posner, M.I., & Rosicky, J. (1994). Orienting in normal and pathological development. *Development and Psychopathology, 6,* 635-652.

Sadeh, A. & Anders, T.F. (1993). Sleep Disorders. In C.H. Zeanah (Ed.), *Handbook of Infant Mental Health* (pp. 305-316). New York: Guilford Press.

Struthers, J.M. & Hansen, R.L. (1992). Visual recognition memory in drug exposed infants. *Journal of Developmental and Behavioral Pediatrics, 13,* 108-111.

Thompson, R.A. & Calkins, S.D. (1996). The doubled-edged sword: Emotional regulation for children at risk. *Development and Psychopathology, 8,* 163-182.

Williamson, G.G. & Anzalone, M. (1997). Sensory integration: A key component of the evaluation and treatment of young children with severe difficulties in relating and communicating. *Zero to Three, 17*, 29-36.

Zero to Three/National Center for Clinical Infant Programs (1994). Diagnostic Classification: 0-3. Arlington, VI: *Zero to Three*, pp. 19-21.

12 Children's and Parent's Perceptions of Parental Attitudes and Behaviors Pertaining to Academic Achievement

JONATHAN MIDGETT, LAURA BELSITO, BRUCE A. RYAN, AND
GERALD R. ADAMS

Abstract

Children in grades 4 (n=157), 7 (n=151), and 11 (n=99) and a parent (n=407) completed the Inventory of Parental Influence (IPI) (Campbell, 1994). This instrument assessed children's and parent's perceptions of school-focused, parental behaviors from the child's view of each parent, as well as mothers and fathers views of their own behaviors. Prior to this investigation it was unclear whether children and parents views of school-focused parenting behaviors were identical or divergent. Initial analyses for age differences revealed no significant developmental age pattern. Therefore, age was eliminated as a major feature and the sample was examined by collapsing the three age groups into a single total sample of 407 responses for children and for adults. Factor analyses performed separately for each of the four possible perspectives produced five factors for children's viewpoint (Help, Support, Pressure, Press for Intellectual Development, and Monitoring) and five factors for parents (Help, Support, Expectations to Excel, Concern for Child's Motivation, and Management/ Promotion of Learning). The evidence indicates that children and parents share a similar view of help and support; however they diverge in their perceptions of the remaining parenting behaviors and attitudes pertaining to education. The findings suggest that children and parents' perspectives are similar on some perceived parenting behaviors yet different on others. Several explanations are offered to account for these distinctions; the primary explanations being differences in maturity between children and adults and the distinction associated between children and the adult role of parent.

Children's and parent's perceptions of parental attitudes and behaviors pertaining to academic achievement

Ecological theories of social development describe a hierarchy of influence for the multiple layers or contexts of factors affecting a child's progress through school (Ryan & Adams, 1995). Community programs and resources encompass and influence family resources which in turn affect more general parental styles. These general styles then affect specific parenting behaviors focused on school activities which in turn have direct effects on children's academic performance. The closer the influencing factor is to measurable outcomes, such as grades, the stronger its effect on those outcomes. There is growing interest at multiple levels of society to examine the dynamic interaction of these embedded contexts of family, school, and community in determining children's educational success (e.g., see Booth & Dunn, 1996; Ryan, Adams, Gullotta, Weissberg, & Hampton, 1995; Wang, Haertel, & Walberg, 1997).

Educational and social scientists interested in family influences on children's school achievement have investigated family factors such as: parental expectations (Seginer, 1983), attributions, home affective environment, and discipline (Christenson, Rounds & Gorney, 1992); family resources like parental education, occupation, income and attention (Amato & Ochiltree, 1986); parenting styles (Steinberg, Lamborn, Dornbusch, & Darling, 1992); parental involvement such as parental surveillance of homework, reactions to grades, and family style (Christenson, Rounds & Gorney, 1992; Ginsburg & Bronstein, 1993; Grolnick & Slowiaczek, 1994); parental pressuring, helping, and monitoring (Campbell & Mandel, 1990); family structure (Astone & McLanahan, 1991); and parent-child interactions (Scott-Jones, 1995). One recent review of a large number of studies (Wang, Haertel, & Walberg, 1997) indicated that next to teaching practices, the home environment and parental behaviors associated with child-rearing are the second most important influence (after classroom factors), on children's educational success. Wang et al.(1997) suggested that some of the most essential features of children's school success include parenting and relational behaviors such as positive parent-child relationships, family cohesion, reading to children, and selecting or limiting television viewing time.

In most of this research either the perspective of the child is obtained or that of a parent. The failure to compare a child's view against a parent's viewpoint could lead to incorrect conclusions about the nature of influences affecting school achievement. If parents and children have different perceptions of the same issues, these differences could become covert sources of conflict. Given the age difference between children and parents, different levels of social perspective taking skills, and varying life roles, one should expect some different viewpoints about the nature and intention of parenting behaviors. Because the child's point of view may differ from that of the parents, he or she may experience parental action in a manner completely unintended by the parent. This different perception, or different reality, may produce effects also unintended and unforeseen by the parent. Scientists untangling such issues stress the need to consider and compare both the child's and the parents' perspectives (Ginsburg & Bronstein, 1993; Paulson & Sputa, 1996).

What kinds of specific, useful behaviors do parents use during school-focused interactions? Parents may help children by assisting them in remembering assignments, by aiding them with the organization of a task, by promoting the will power to turn off the television set, or by suggesting books that might be interesting or useful to the child's educational activities. In approving of grades and getting children to finish their homework, parents may use basic rewards and punishments (Campbell & Mandel, 1990; Seginer, Cohen, & Zukerman, 1988). When motivating children (or dealing with failure and success) parents may voice their expectations about achievement and aspirations (Amato & Ochiltree, 1986; Astone & McLanahan, 1991). To help children surmount a difficult assignment or learn a new skill, parents may need to help by direct instruction (Chen & Uttal, 1988; Tizard, Schonfield, & Hewison, 1982). Parents also get involved in academics by monitoring how children manage their time (Keith, et al., 1986; Campbell & Mandel, 1990). Along with these actions, parents may further promote a child's academic development by enriching their environment with books, offering educational experiences in and outside of the home, and encouraging them to learn.

In addition to basic reading, writing and mathematical skills, children progressing through formal education have to learn time-management, self-discipline, individual and social responsibility, and self-motivation. Children learn to compete with peers, to accept feedback and criticism, to try new things, and to keep trying even when a task is difficult. As parents guide and help a child to learn these self-disciplines, their own history within educational contexts, as well as attitudes towards success and failure may affect how they interact with their child's academic challenges (Csikszentmihalyi, Rathunde, & Whalen, 1993). In a schooling or learning context, a child's knowledge, self-understanding, and maturity might be bolstered by a parent's guidance.

In general, parental behaviors, family rules, and intellectual habits of the family offer a structure to family time, activities, and expectations of child behavior and academic success. Nonetheless, it remains uncertain as to whether children and parents share a common perception of the nature of school-focused parenting behaviors, rules, and expectations. Is there an isomorphic relationship between perceptions of school-focused parenting behaviors by children and parents? The present investigation focused on this question by comparing the perspectives of parents and children on a measure of school-focused parental behaviors and attitudes.

Sample

The children studied in the present investigation were enrolled in 11 publicly funded Roman Catholic schools in a southern Ontario community of approximately 100,000 inhabitants. As part of a larger study investigating family-school connections and children's academic performance and social adjustment in the schools (Ketsetzis, Ryan, & Adams, in press), children in grades 4 (n=157), 7 (n=151), and 11 (n=99) and a parent from each family (n=407) completed a questionnaire on parenting behaviors. The community was primarily middle class and mainly of English, Italian, Scottish, and German ancestry.

Measurement

Children and parents completed the Inventory of Parental Influence (IPI) (Campbell, 1994). The IPI has two substantially parallel forms, one for children to assess the parents and one for parents to assess themselves. Four sets of responses were obtained: the child's view of mother, child's view of father, mother's view of herself, and father's view of himself. The IPI form for children has 52 items, while the parents form has 54 items. All responses are on a five-point Likert-type scale ranging from (1) strongly disagree to (5) strongly agree and (1) never to (5) always.

Campbell (1994) identified five distinct factors within the IPI. These factors were labeled Help, Support, Pressure, Press for Intellectual Development, and Monitoring/Time Management. An example of a help item is "My [parent] helps me with my math homework" and "When I bring home a test paper, my [parent] goes over my mistakes with me." Support items include: "My [parent] is satisfied if I do my best" and "My [parent] has much patience with me when it comes to my education." Examples of Pressure items are: "My [parent] is never pleased with my marks" and "My [parent] does not feel that I'm doing my best in school." Press for Intellectual Development items cover such topics as providing reading materials and watching educational television. Monitoring/ Time Management items measure parental tracking of time spent on homework, limiting leisure television viewing, and setting aside time for reading.

Analysis

The data were factor analyzed (principal axis factoring) for each grade using an oblique rotation. Screen tests indicated that for children and parent responses at each grade level, a five factor solution best fit the data. Therefore grade levels were combined and analyses were computed separately for children's view of mothers, children's view of fathers, mothers views, and fathers views.

Results

Tables 12.1 and 12.2 summarize the results and include the factor names, significant items, and individual item loadings. Cronbach alphas for the children's factors ranged from alpha = .59 to .90. Likewise, parental factors ranged from alpha = .53 to .88. The factors Help and Support maintained consistent item groupings across children and parents and across children's views of mothers and fathers. Children's views of parental behaviors were divided into an overall factor structure virtually identical to Campbell's (1994) prediction. Children viewed mothers and fathers behaviors according to the dimensions of Help, Support, Pressure, Press for Intellectual Development, and Monitoring/Time Management (see Table 12.1). These findings, using a Canadian sample, essentially replicated the factor structure for children reported by Campbell.

The 12 items for the children's Help factor had loadings ranging from .33 to .69. The 11 Support items had loadings ranging from .30 to .62. Factor loadings for the 14 Pressure items ranged from .33 to .69. Of the two smaller child factors, Press for Intellectual Development loadings (6 items) ranged from .34 to .83 and Monitoring/Time Management loadings (7 items) ranged from .31 to .66. A few items which loaded significantly for the children's view of one parent were found to be significantly loaded on a different factor for the child's view of the other parent. Likewise, a few items failed to load significantly on the same fathers' and mothers' factors, but differences between overall factor structures between parents were unsystematic.

For parents' views of themselves (see Table 12.2), Help had 15 items (range = .31 to .81) and Support had 8 items (range = .31 to .62). Unlike the factor structures of Help and Support, however, which were similar for children and parents, parents divided one of the children's factors (Pressure) into two factors and combined another pair of the children's factors (Press for Intellectual Development and Monitoring/Time Management) into a single factor yielding three new factors. First, the items making up the children's factors of Press for Intellectual Development and Monitoring/Time Management were combined by the parents into a single factor consisting of items dealing with provision of reading materials, reading habits, and family leisure activities, which we called Management/Promotion of Learning. This new parental dimension did not distinguish between attitudes towards reading and attitudes towards time management like the children's factor structure did. Management/Promotion of Learning had 16 items across mothers and fathers with loadings ranging from .35 to .72. Second, the parental items parallel to those in the children's Pressure factor were divided into two parental dimensions, with those items dealing with issues of future success in school, which we called Expectations to Excel, separate from the items concerning issues of motivation, which we called Concern for Child's Motivation. These two new parental dimensions specifically contained the items concerning behaviors children viewed as pressuring. The first new parental factor, Expectations to Excel, had 9 items with factor loadings ranging from .33 to .73 which focused directly on academic performances (e.g., grades, class standing, test performance, and expectations for attending university). The second new parental factor, Concern for Child's Motivation, had loadings ranging from .34 to .94 and contained 8 items. These items focused directly on parental beliefs or concerns about a child's efforts in school (e.g., doing their best, being lazy, trying to avoid homework). The children's parallel items for both of these new parental factors were found in the children's Pressuring factor.

Discussion

Children seemed to perceive parental helping and supporting behaviors in ways similar to their parents. Although extreme levels of parental help have been associated with lower academic performance (Campbell & Mandel, 1990), the present study suggests that children and parents at least view these two parental efforts similarly. Because of this, these interactions are probably less likely to be sources of conflict between children and parents. The three new factors produced by parents, however, could potentially cause conflict because parents may intend something by their actions that the child does not comprehend. The different factor groupings of the same items by parents and children suggested a different perspective of the same parental, school-focused behaviors and attitudes.

First, the parental factor, Management/Promotion of Learning, a combination of two children factors, may indicate that parents viewed 'reading activities' as the same as "monitoring"; that this was all part of their overall goal of promoting their child's intellect. Children, on the other hand, may have differentiated such parental behaviors because these activities involved different activities like reading and watching television. Children may not have appreciated the broader parental goals. Another possible explanation for this difference may be that parents were answering those items in the Monitoring and Press for Intellectual Development factors in a socially desirable manner, while the children reported more truthfully how much parents actually restricted television viewing and promoted reading. Children may be watching far more (or far less) television than their parents notice.

Second, parents seemed to differentiate between concerns about their children's motivation to perform well in school and expectations about succeeding or excelling in school, as indicated by the factor groupings which divided the children's Pressure items. These same concerns and expectations seem to all be perceived similarly by their children because they grouped them all together in the same factor of pressure. Possibly, a child feels equally pressured by both motivational concerns of parents and their parents expectations for high academic achievements. Consequently, a child answering items on the IPI about parental concerns about their achievement ("My [parent] is never pleased with my marks" and "I think I do well, but my [parent] thinks I could do better") may have rated them similarly to items about parental expectations ("My [parent] is only pleased if I get a 100% on a test" and "When it comes to school, my [parent] expects the impossible"). On the other hand, parents may have distinguished the actual history of their child's achievement ("I do not feel my child is doing his/her best in school") from the performance they would desire ("I'll be very upset if my child doesn't make it to the top of the class"). To the child, though, parental concerns and parental expectations appeared to be virtually the same thing; pressure on them to perform.

Perhaps children differentiate kinds of parental attitudes differently because of a developmentally lower level of cognitive complexity. Children may not understand how getting homework done on a daily basis is linked to long-term achievement. They might not see the importance of starting a project more than one day before it is due or may not believe that time spent reading a book instead of watching television can have positive effects on grades. Children may just see the immediate tasks while parents have a more complex picture of education and its potential benefits.

These subtle differences in perspective suggest the possibility of significant mis-communication between parents and children, especially surrounding the pressuring issues. Parents may mean to convey a desire for their children to do their best by trying to convince them of the benefits of being at the top of the class. Parents may not mean to overly pressure their children, but in the process may actually lead the child to think that they want the child to achieve a seemingly impossible goal. Alternatively, parents might think their children are not getting as high marks as they could and in the process of trying to help them improve could be perceived by children as "pushy" and "strict". The potential for conflict and negative outcomes for these understandable and arguably admirable parental goals suggests that parents use caution when attempting to motivate their children. These differences of view could easily intensify given the length of time children spend in school.

Further inquiry into the divergence between children's views of their parent's influences and the parents' views of themselves may provide insights for understanding the development of family processes, the development of children's coping responses to achievement pressures, and the development of children's competence in self-directed academic tasks. It is recommended that research be, focused on whether children's views develop into constructs that are more similar to their parents as they grow older and whether parent's or children's views are more predictive of academic outcomes.

Table 12.1   Child's view of parents: Factors, factor loadings, and items from the IPI (child's form)

Children's Factor: Help

Child's view of Mother (alpha = .87)	Child's view of Father (alpha = .90)	Items
.72	.71	My Mother/Father helps me s tudy before a test.
.72	.77	My Mother/Father helps me with my math homework.
.69	.65	My Mother/Father looks over my homework.
.68	.74	My Mother/Father helps me with schoolwork I don't understand.
.62	.65	My Mother/Father helps me with my school reports.
.60	.65	My Mother/Father goes over spelling words right before a test.
.60	.60	I do well in school mostly because of my Mother's/Father's help.
.60	.64	When I bring home a test paper, my Mother/Father goes over my mistakes with me.
ns	.38	My Mother/Father takes a big interest in my schoolwork.
.35	.35	Before I leave for school, my Mother/Father asks me if I have everything I need.
.34	.44	My Mother/Father wants me to bring home test papers to see how well I did.
ns	.31	My Mother/Father helps me to choose books to read.

Children's Factor: Support

Child's view of Mother (alpha = .69)	Child's view of Father (alpha = .71)	Items
.62	.59	I'm glad my Mother/Father cares so much about my education.
.50	.51	My Mother/Father is proud of me.
.45	.54	My Mother/Father is pleased if I do my best.
.43	.44	I get along very well with my Mother/Father.
.38	ns	My Mother/Father takes a big interest in my schoolwork.
.38	.47	My Mother/Father is excited about my education.
ns	.44	My Mother/Father has much patience with me when it comes to my education.
.36	.32	I feel that children my age need their Mother's/Father's guidance when it comes to school.
.35	ns	My Mother/Father wants me to go to a good university.
.34	.37	I feel happy when I get good marks because I know it pleases my Mother/Father.
.31	.30	My Mother/Father feels it is important not to miss a day of school.

"Ns" denotes non-significance.

Table 12.1 (cont'd)

Children's Factor: Pressure

Child's view of Mother (alpha = .85)	Child's view of Father (alpha = .83)	Items
.69	.60	My Mother/Father pressures me too much with homework.
.66	.61	My Mother/Father does not feel I'm doing my best in school.
.65	.61	My Mother/Father is never pleased with my marks.
.64	.65	I think I do well, but my Mother/Father thinks I could do better.
.62	.57	My Mother/Father is 'pushy' when it comes to education.
.61	.58	My Mother/Father expects too much of me.
.58	.56	My Mother/Father 'bugs' me with my schoolwork.
.57	.55	When it comes to school, My Mother/Father expects the impossible.
.50	.51	School would be more pleasant if my Mother/Father were not as strict.
.45	.39	Mother/Father is pleased <u>only</u> if I get 100% on a test.
.44	.45	I don't think I am as smart as Mother/Father thinks I am.
.38	.34	Mother/Father doesn't believe me when I say I have no homework.
.38	.38	I'm afraid to go home with a failing mark.
ns	.33	I am really lazy and if it were not for Mother/Father, I'd not be doing as well in school.

Children's Factor: Press for Intellectual Development

Child's view of Mother (alpha = .78)	Child's view of Father (alpha = .78)	Items
.83	.75	My Mother/Father wants me to read books.
.81	.76	My Mother/Father likes me to read a lot.
.58	.55	My Mother/Father likes me to read before I go to sleep.
.50	.52	My Mother/Father wants me to go to the library.
.40	.34	My Mother/Father buys me books for presents.
ns	.43	My Mother/Father insists I set aside a certain time for reading.

Children's Factor: Monitoring/Time Management

Child's view of Mother (alpha = .72)	Child's view of Father (alpha = .59)	Items
.61	.66	My Mother/Father decides how much T.V. I can watch.
.45	.32	My Mother/Father makes me watch educational T.V.
.44	.54	My Mother/Father sets rules on the kinds of T.V. shows I can watch.
.39	ns	My Mother/Father expects me to do homework at the same time each night.
.37	ns	My Mother/Father insists I set aside a certain time for reading.
.37	ns	My Mother/Father keeps track of the amount of time I spend on homework.
ns	.31	My Mother/Father wants me to go to a good university.

"Ns" denotes non-significance.

Table 12.2   Parents' views of themselves: Factor, factor loadings, and items from the IPI (parents' form)

Parental Factor: Help

Mothers (alpha = .82)	Fathers (alpha = .87)	Items
.81	.76	I check my child's homework.
.76	.75	I supervise my child's homework.
.71	.70	I help my child study before a test.
.69	.67	I help with my child's math homework.
.62	.54	I help with my child's school reports.
.55	.57	I go over my child's mistakes when he/she brings home a test.
.54	.42	Before leaving for school, I ask if my child has everything needed (homework, books, reports).
.51	.62	I help my child with schoolwork he/she doesn't understand.
.49	ns	I help my child with schoolwork only when asked.
.47	.49	My child does well in school mostly because of my help.
.38	.30	I insist that homework be completed each day.
.34	ns	I feel children need parental guidance when it comes to schoolwork.
.33	ns	I keep track of the amount of time my child gives to homework.
.33	ns	I want my child to bring home test papers to see how well he/she did.
.31	ns	I expect my child to do his/her homework at the same time each night.

Parental Factor: Support

Mothers (alpha = .64)	Fathers (alpha = .53)	Items
.62	.46	I am enthusiastic about my child's education.
.46	ns	I have much patience with my child when it comes to his/her education.
ns	.44	I want my child to go to a good university.
.42	.41	I take a big interest in my child's school work.
.34	.37	I get along well with my child.
ns	.31	I am proud of my child.
.31	ns	The more self-disciplined a person is the more successful he/she will be in life.
.31	ns	I'm satisfied if I know my child does his/her best.

Parental Factor: Expectations to Excel

Mothers (alpha = .69)	Fathers (alpha = .71)	Items
.65	.73	I'll be very upset if my child doesn't make the top of the class.
.60	.71	I am only pleased when my child gets 100% on a test.
.55	.54	It's important that to me that my child select friends from classmates who are the better students.
.53	ns	I want my child to go to a good university.
.46	.53	I expect my child to go to university.
ns	.44	I am never satisfied with my child's grades.
.35	.37	I am pushy when it comes to education.
ns	.37	My child is afraid to come home with a poor grade.
ns	.33	School would be more pleasant for my child if I were not as strict.

Table 12.2   (cont'd)

Parental Factor: Concern for Child's Motivation

Mothers (alpha = .83)	Fathers (alpha = .78)	Items
.94	.84	I do not feel my child is doing his/her best in school.
.91	.81	I don't feel my child does his/her best in school.
.81	.82	I think my child can do better in school than he/she does.
.57	.44	I have my doubts when my child says they have no homework.
.45	.31	My child is basically lazy and without me he/she would not be doing as well in school.
.38	.36	My child is smarter than he/she thinks.
.35	.36	I think my child doesn't get enough homework.
.34	ns	I am never satisfied with my child's grades.

Parental Factor: Management/Promotion of Learning

Mothers (alpha = .85)	Fathers (alpha = .88)	Items
.67	.72	I determine how much television my child can watch.
.59	.76	When my child watches too much T.V. I restrict his/her T.V. time.
.59	.71	I encourage my child to read books.
.59	.67	I set definite rules regarding the <u>kinds</u> of television programs my child can watch.
.54	.56	I encourage my child to read right before going to sleep.
.51	.60	I encourage my child to spend more time in bookstores.
.49	.55	I insist that my child watch educational television programs.
.48	.54	I insist that my child set aside a certain time for reading.
.47	.45	I buy books for presents.
.46	.51	I encourage my child to go to the local library.
.43	.33	We supply lots of reading material for my child.
.41	.43	I help my child select books to read.
ns	.38	I expect my child to do his/her homework at the same time each night.
ns	.36	I keep track of the amount of time my child gives to homework.
ns	.35	I don't allow my child to go out and play until he/she finishes his/her homework.
ns	.35	When my child is absent, I tell him/her to telephone a friend to get the homework.

"Ns" denotes non-significance.

References

Amato, P.R. & Ochiltree, G. (1986). Family resources and the development of child competence. *Journal of Marriage and the Family, 48*, 47-56.

Astone, N.M. & McLanahan, S.S. (1991). Family structure, parental practices and high school completion. *American Social Review, 56,* 309-320.

Booth, A. & Dunn, J.F. (1996). *Family-school links: How do they affect educational outcomes?* Mahwah, NJ: Lawrence Erlbaum Associates.

Campbell, J.R. (1994). Differential socialization in mathematics achievement: Cross-national/cross cultural perspectives. *International Journal of Educational Research, 21.*

Campbell, J.R. & Mandel, F. (1990). Connecting math achievement to parental influences. *Contemporary Educational Psychology, 15*, 64 -74.

Chen, C. & Uttal, D.H. (1988). Cultural values, parents' beliefs, and children's achievement in the United States and China. *Human Development, 31*, 351-358.

Christenson, S.L., Rounds, T. & Gorney, D. (1992). Family factors and student achievement: An avenue to increase students success. *School Psychology Quarterly, 7*, 178-206.

Csikszentmihalyi, M., Rathunde, K., & Whalen, S. (1993). *Talented teenagers: The roots of success and failure.* Cambridge: Cambridge University Press.

Ginsburg, G.S. & Bronstein, P. (1993). Family factors related to children's intrinsic/extrinsic motivational orientation and academic performance. *Child Development, 64*, 1461-1474.

Grolnick, W.S. & Slowiaczek, M.L. (1994). Parents' involvement in children's schooling: A multidimensional conceptualization and motivational model. *Child Development, 65*, 237-252.

Keith, T.Z., Reimers, T.M., Fehrmann, P.G., Pottebaum, S.M., & Aubey, L.W. (1986). Parental involvement, homework, and T.V. time: Direct and indirect effects on high school achievement. *Journal of Educational Psychology, 78*, 373-380.

Ketsetzis, M., Ryan, B.A., & Adams, G.R. (In press). Family processes, parent-child interactions, child characteristics influencing school-based social adjustment. *Journal of Marriage and the Family.*

Paulson, S.E. & Sputa, C.L. (1996). Patterns of parenting during adolescence: Perceptions of adolescents and parents. *Adolescence, 31*, 369-381.

Ryan, B.A. & Adams, G.R. (1995). The family-school relationships model. In B. Ryan et al (Eds.), *The Family-School Connection: Theory, Research, and Practice* (pp. 3-28). California: Sage Publications.

Ryan, B.A., Adams, G.R., Gullotta, T.P., Weissberg, R.P. & Hampton, R.L. (1995). *The family-school connection: Theory, research and practice.* California: Sage Publications.

Scott-Jones, D. (1995). Parent-child interactions and school achievement. In B. Ryan et al (Eds.), *The Family School Connection: Theory, Research, and Practice* (pp. 75-107). California: Sage Publications.

Seginer, R. (1983). Parents' educational expectations and children's academic achievements: A literature review. *Merrill-Palmer Quarterly, 29,* 1-23.

Seginer, R., Cohen, Y.B., & Zukerman, S. (1988). Mothers' characteristics and first grade boys' performance: Testing an academic achievement path model. *Journal of Genetic Psychology, 149,* 349-361.

Steinberg, L., Lamborn, S.D., Dornbusch, S.M. & Darling, N. (1992). Impact of parenting practices on adolescent achievement: Authoritative parenting, school involvement, and encouragement to succeed. *Child Development, 63,* 1266-1281.

Tizard, J., Schonfield, W.N., & Hewison, J. (1982). Collaboration between teachers and parents in assisting children's reading. *British Journal of Educational Psychology, 52,* 1-15.

Wang, M.C., Haertel, G.D., & Walberg, H.J. (1997). Fostering educational resilience in inner-city school. In H. J. Walberg, O. Reyes, and R.P. Weissberg (Eds.), *Children and Youth: Interdisciplinary Perspectives* (pp.199-140).Thousand Oaks, CA: Sage Publications.

13 A Stepwise Discriminant Analysis of Delinquent and Nondelinquent Youth

ELIZABETH ODDONE-PAOLUCCI, CLAUDIO VIOLATO, AND
CHRIS WILKES

Abstract

The purpose of the present research was to determine the similarities and differences between nondelinquent and delinquent youth, and to investigate the impact of family variables on delinquency. Based on a review of 285 records of institutionalized youth, patient demographic and developmental life history variables were examined. A stepwise discriminant analysis revealed that several variables distinguish between delinquent and nondelinquent adolescents. In comparison to nondelinquents, more delinquent youth were diagnosed as conduct disordered, had histories of prenatal complications, reached developmental milestones at unpredictable rates, performed poorly in school, experienced physical abuse, reported maternal psychopathologies, and were insecurely attached to both parents. These results are discussed and interpreted within the delinquency research.

A stepwise discriminant analysis of delinquent and nondelinquent youth

Despite the media's role in highly publicizing and sensationalizing youth violence and crime, the frequency of these debates coupled with scientific evidence, suggest that concern for youth may be warranted. Studies indicate that "delinquent behavior is a common occurrence during adolescence, with prevalence rates peaking between the ages of 15 and 17" (Hurrelmann & Engel, 1991, p.119; Rutter & Giller, 1984). Roberts and Hudson (1993) reported that crime rates for several offence categories have recently risen steadily in Canada. Similarly, Violato and Travis (1994) asserted that millions of people are victimized yearly by delinquency, when "property is stolen or destroyed and people are injured or killed" (p.1).

Because discretion is utilized by parents, communities, and the authorities, it is difficult to know with any certainty just how serious and frequent adolescent delinquency and crime is. In fact, many lawbreakers never come to official attention, or are spared legal processing through police discretion; of those who are arrested, only about 20% are ever adjudicated (Bartol & Bartol, 1989; Elliott, Ageton, & Canter, 1979; Giallombardo, 1982; Santrock, 1990; Thompson, 1986). Studies of hidden lawbreaking have shown that many youth who are believed to be nondelinquent, later admit to delinquent involvement (Gibbons, 1976). It has been argued that more studies are needed to understand which youth are at the greatest risk for developing behavioral problems (Jensen, Koretz, Locke, Schneider, Radke-Yarrow, Richters, & Rumsey, 1993).

Correlates of delinquency

Several family process variables have been identified as related to the phenomenon of delinquency. For instance, lack of parental supervision, parental rejection, and minimal parent-child involvement, are among the most powerful predictors of delinquency, while medium-strength predictors include parents' marital relations and parental criminality, and weaker predictors are lack of parental discipline, parental health, and parental absence (Henggeler, 1989; Hirschi & Gottfredson, 1988; LeBlanc, 1992; Loeber & Stouthamer-Loeber, 1986; Mussen et al., 1990; Rutter & Giller, 1984). Evidently, as the number of family 'handicaps' increases, the potential for child behaviour problems also increases. According to LeBlanc (1992, p.349), "structural and family environmental factors are distant explanatory factors of offending while constraints are proximal factors, and bonding is the 'hyphen' between them."

Like adults, youth seek the approval of significant others in the world in which they live in order to reinforce their sense of belonging. If this approval is denied, then they may feel powerless, alienated, hostile, bored, or personally inadequate (Gibbons, 1976). While these feelings may lead some youth to become social isolates, others may search for delinquent groups that will provide them with approval and self-confirmation. Alone and alienated, many youth gravitate to gangs in the hopes of filling the voids in their lives, and finding people who will give them the respect and refuge they may not experience at home. According to Ellis (1987), delinquency "has the dual advantage of being exciting and conferring status within the group of adolescent peers" (p.191). Moreover, as discovered by Palenski and Launer (1987), the peer group can also provide its members with survival information and techniques on how to 'make it' once they reach a state of independence.

Like the family and peer system, however, the school system is not always successful in socializing its members, and consequently, has come under scrutiny as potentially promoting delinquent behaviour. According to the 'school deficit hypothesis', the educational system is seen as cultivating a sense of failure, by employing negative labels and treating some children as slow or special learners. As the school becomes aversive and frustrating, children are predicted to violate its rules and regulations (Bartol & Bartol, 1989; Elliott, 1982). Several researchers have discussed the relationship between poor school performance, dropping out of high school, and high rates of delinquent conduct (Henggeler, 1989; Hirschi & Gottfredson, 1988; Smith et al., 1995; Violato & Travis, 1994).

Support has also been found for the argument that a child abused at a younger age is at a higher risk for subsequent delinquent behaviours than a nonabused child (Scudder, Blount, Heide, & Silverman, 1993). Cicchetti and Olsen (1990) have contended that maltreated infants are significantly more likely to be insecurely attached to their caregivers, and when they grow up, they tend to suffer from poor peer relations, cognitive deficits, and low self-esteem. Esbensen and Huizinga (1991) found a remarkably strong relationship between the variety of delinquent involvement and the likelihood of victimization. Relative to control subjects, abused and neglected youth tend to have a larger mean number of offenses, and at an earlier mean age (Scudder et al.,1993). According to Smith et al.'s (1995) study, about 82% of all respondents stated they had been victimized at school within the past year. Moreover, among those victimized, there were substantially more youth who reported also engaging in acts of delinquency. According to Letourneau (1994), this position suggests that delinquent behaviour patterns may develop in response to victimization, especially when there is a need for the offender to master his or her own feelings of powerlessness and being controlled.

Consistent with these findings, is the report by many incarcerated youth that they have been victims of parental abuse and neglect (Simons et al., 1989). Brown's (1984) study revealed that physical abuse is not positively correlated with any form of delinquency, but neglect and emotional abuse is with all forms of self-reported delinquent behavior. Thus, although child maltreatment has been typically viewed as less problematic than physical abuse, in actuality it may have more serious social consequences than originally assumed.

Defining delinquency within developmental psychopathology

Delinquency in the present study is approached from a developmental perspective. Delinquent behaviors are viewed as quantitative variations on normal characteristics that may be evident at other developmental periods, in less intense degree and across fewer situations. Four criteria are included in the present study's operational definition of delinquency. Delinquency refers to: (1) any act of an individual, male or female, and of any socio-cultural-economic background, who is under the age of 20; (2) who has violated a law or social norm; (3) that has caused or could cause liability for adjudication or treatment (Santrock, 1990); (4) whether or not it has been brought to the attention of a social or law-enforcing agency (Tappan, 1982).

As can be evidenced by this definition, the "liability for adjudication or treatment" is included, thereby not limiting the investigation of delinquency solely to legal labeling and processing. Rather, this study attempts to explore combined "hidden" and "official" delinquent behaviors, by fusing the legal component of delinquency with the psychiatric category of conduct disorder and self-report data. It seems that only a few studies have been conducted in Canada that examine both reported and unreported delinquent and criminal incidents involving youth (Smith, Bertrand, Arnold, & Hornick, 1995). Finally, since there are no direct negative repercussions on the youth from this sample as a result of labeling them delinquent, the definition adopted for the present study considers any youth who reported engaging in a status or criminal offence, even once, as delinquent.

Purpose of the present study

The present study attempts to empirically investigate the differences between male and female delinquent and nondelinquent young adults. The main purpose of the present study, then, was to compare and contrast delinquent and nondelinquent youth on a number of life history, demographic, and psychological variables. The results are expected to contribute to the further specification of a developmental model of delinquency, so that a step toward greater understanding, prediction, and management of youth behavior may occur.

Method

Subjects

Two hundred and eighty-five in-patients files of youth (n=285) ranging in age from 10 to 19 years with a mean age of 15, treated at the Calgary Foothills Hospital's Young Adult Program (YAP) were utilized.   Residents ranged in their length of stay on the psychiatric unit anywhere from 1 to 107 days, with an average stay of 34 days.   In order to reconstruct the life histories of these youth, files were accessed from the Foothills Hospital Health Records Department.   Records were included in the investigation if patients had been admitted for psychiatric concerns, had consented to research involvement and publication, and had spent the majority of their hospital stay on the YAP floor.

It was known that some of the patients had engaged in acts of delinquency to varying degrees without necessarily incurring legal action or retribution (i.e., hidden delinquency, or no record or arrests).   To meet the current study's objectives, subjects were divided into the group of delinquent or nondelinquent based on documented evidence of the youth's involvement in 'official' or 'hidden' delinquency.   Any documented evidence within patient records that indicated the commission of status or criminal offenses with or without coming to official attention, or having received a discharge diagnosis of conduct disorder, resulted in the youth being considered a member of the delinquent group.   Consequently, of the 285 patients, 155 (54%) were identified as delinquents and 130 (46%) comprised the comparison nondelinquent group.

Instrumentation and procedure

Prior to beginning the data collection phase, the researchers identified the primary domains for measurement based on previous research.   A protocol was designed with the intent of collecting information drawn from admission assessment interviews and records detailing the progress and disposition of each youth up until discharge, and when possible with follow-up summaries.   The protocol included the two areas of patient demographics (e.g., age, gender, race, living arrangements) and developmental life history variables (e.g., history of family psychopathology, physical and sexual abuse, attachment to parents and peers, academic performance, nature of delinquent involvement).

Results

The results are presented in two sections: (1) descriptive and chi-square results on demographic and developmental life history variables, and (2) discriminant analysis between nondelinquent and delinquent youth.

Descriptive analyses

Comparisons between nondelinquents and delinquents were made on several demographic, developmental, family psychopathology, and attachment variables. Approximately 46% were nondelinquent and 54% of the sample were delinquent, with over 85% of the youth describing themselves as caucasian. No statistically significant differences emerged between the two groups on the variables of gender (X2=.01, df=1, p=.94), race (X2=.07, df=1, p=.78), and household composition (X2=10.9, df=6, p=.09), although the majority of youth reported living with their biological parents (41.2% of nondelinquent and 31% of delinquent youth). Socioeconomic comparisons based on maternal and paternal occupation between youth indicated that 40.5% of nondelinquents' mothers and 36.7% of delinquents' mothers comprise the unskilled labor sector (X^2=1.57, df=4, p=.81), whereas 45% of nondelinquents and 44.7% of delinquents have fathers coming from professional occupations (X^2=3.83, df=4, p=.43). Of mothers who are unemployed, 7.9% are found in the nondelinquent group and 7.3% come from the delinquent group. Similarly, 10.1% include unemployed fathers of nondelinquent youth and 8.5% are unemployed fathers of delinquent youth.

Statistical differences in the area of developmental experiences between nondelinquent and delinquent youth did emerge (X^2=19.4, df=3, p<.01). More delinquent youth experienced prenatal complications (29.3%) than did nondelinquent youth (12.8%), with 22% of delinquents experiencing perinatal distress such as breech birth presentation, forceps delivery, and syndromes related to mothers' substance addictions. In terms of early childhood experiences, although more nondelinquents experienced medical problems than delinquents, delinquent youth reached their developmental milestones both earlier and later than nondelinquent youth (X^2=8.56, df=3, p<.04).

Comparisons on experiences of physical abuse indicate that more delinquents were physically abused than nondelinquents (X^2=8.24, df=1, p<.01). Approximately one third (33.5%) of nondelinquent adolescents and half (50.4%) of delinquent adolescents reported instances of physical abuse. Similarly, more delinquents reported being sexually abused than nondelinquents (X^2=22.6, df=9, p<.01). Nondelinquent youth, on the other hand, reported more repeated acts of intrafamilial sexual abuse (9%), in comparison to delinquents who reported more isolated acts of extrafamilial sexual abuse (12.4%).

Over 86% of both nondelinquent and delinquent youth reported some form of psychopathology in their family backgrounds (X^2=.13, df=1, p=.72). More specifically, more than 65% of both nondelinquent and delinquent youth reported the existence of maternal psychopathology (X^2=.40, df=1, p=.53). On the other hand, 60.6% of nondelinquents and 72.3% of delinquents reported some form of paternal psychopathology (X^2=4.28, df=1, p<.04). Finally, over 70% of both nondelinquent and delinquent (X^2=1.58, df=1, p=.21) adolescents indicated that they had at least one relative who experienced a pathology. Specifically, substance abuse, attention deficit, aggression and depression disorders made up almost three quarters of the pathologies reported by the youth in the sample. Anxiety disorders, eating disorders, and learning disabilities comprised a total of only 3% of the pathologies exhibited by mothers, fathers, and other relatives of the adolescents.

Differences were found in maternal attachment (X^2=3.91, df=1, p<.05), with more nondelinquents (57.8%) reporting positive and strong attachments than delinquents (45.3%). With regard to youth attachment to fathers, statistical significance was not reached on comparisons between nondelinquents and delinquents (X^2=.77, df=1, p=.38). Similarly, the results reveal no differences in perceived strength of attachment to peers between nondelinquents and delinquents (X^2=.03, df=1, p=.86).

School performance differences emerged, however, between nondelinquent and delinquent groups, as more delinquent youth performed poorly at school than nondelinquent youth (X^2=20.2, df=1, p<.01).

Finally, 19 different types of delinquent behaviors were reported by the female and male youth in the hospital program. The results indicate that 57% of the delinquent acts were engaged in by females, while 43% were performed by males. Although the five most frequently recorded delinquent behaviors in the youth files include truancy, substance abuse, self-mutilation, sexual activity, and running away from home, adolescent females and males engaged in these acts at different rates. For instance, 9% of females abused substances, and 8% were truant, whereas 6% of males were truant and 10% abused substances and self-mutilated. Only two of these top five delinquent behaviors were statistically different. Accordingly, females in this sample were more sexually active (X^2=4.40, df=1, p<.04), and abused more substances than males (X^2=4.64, df=1, p<.03).

In contrast to these more 'status type offenses', the most frequently engaged in forms of criminal acts by females were the use of street drugs such as cocaine and marijuana (5%), break and enters (4%), physical assaults against persons (2%), and drug trafficking (2%). Male delinquents on the other hand, engaged in break and enters (4%), sexual demeanours such as flashing or inappropriately touching other youth (3%), street drug crimes (2%), physical assaults against persons (2%), and shoplifting (2%). Interestingly, there were half as many female firesetters as male firesetters in the present sample, and double the number of females who violated traffic laws than males.

Discriminant analysis

A stepwise backward discriminant analysis was performed on the groups defined as delinquent and nondelinquent. Because complete data are required on each variable, only 124 subjects were used in these analyses involving 12 discriminating variables. Table 13.1 shows the stepwise discriminant function for the combination of variables for the whole group. Several discriminant analyses were performed before the final one was accepted. A single discriminant function was formed from the twelve variables and was found to separate the delinquent group from the nondelinquent group (Wilks' Lambda=.63, df=6, p<.01).

Compared to the nondelinquent group, more of the delinquent adolescents received a conduct disorder diagnosis, experienced prenatal complications, performed poorly in school, had mothers who experienced a greater number of psychopathologies, were physically abused, and had negative or weak attachments to their fathers. Furthermore, based on the discriminant analysis and resulting model, adolescents can be correctly classified as either delinquent or nondelinquent approximately 78% of the time. More specifically, one would be correct in predicting delinquency 84% of the time, and nondelinquency 68% of the time.

Discussion

The major findings of the present study may be summarized in two main points. First, compared to nondelinquents, more delinquent adolescents experienced prenatal problems, were proportionally advanced or delayed in reaching their developmental milestones, reported histories of physical as well as sexual abuse, described their attachments to their mothers more negatively, reported more instances of paternal psychopathology, and performed more poorly in school. Second, a stepwise backward discriminant analysis was performed on the whole sample of youth and six variables clearly differentiated between the nondelinquent and delinquent groups (78% correct classification). More of the delinquent than nondelinquent adolescents were diagnosed as conduct disordered, more described their mothers as having some type of psychopathology, more experienced prenatal complications, more reported instances of physical abuse, more were negatively and weakly attached to their fathers, and more performed poorly at school.

One heavily emphasized indicator of healthy development is that of a child's attachment(s) to significant others. Based on the attachment theory, happy and healthy children are said to feel connected to either one or both of their parents, and as a result are able to use their first attachments as models for entering into other intimate and positive relationships throughout their growing years (Rutter, 1990). However, the results of the present investigation revealed an inverse relationship of this attachment model for delinquent adolescents. While nondelinquents perceived themselves to be negatively and weakly attached to their fathers, they described their attachments to their mothers and peers as positive and strong. In contrast, delinquent adolescents reported being negatively and weakly attached to both their fathers *and* mothers, and perceived themselves as more positively and strongly attached to their peers.

Given that peers play a significant role during the adolescent developmental period, it was not surprising to find both nondelinquent and delinquent youth strongly and positively attached to their friends. However, precipitating causes and explanations for these strong peer attachments may differ among nondelinquent and delinquent youth. For instance, while nondelinquent youth may have used their strong maternal attachments as models for their peer attachments, delinquent youth may have reported positive peer attachments because it is in these relationships that they may have been more able to find support and fulfil their need to belong. Thus, not only may the attachments between delinquents and peers be based on convenience, but they may also be transient in nature.

Still, the attachment findings of the present investigation support both the social control theory and the attachment theory. These theories posit that adolescents with strong parental attachments are less prone than others to engage in delinquency for fear of parental disapproval and subsequent rejection (Warr, 1993; Wilkinson, 1982). While the nondelinquent youth in this sample may have been able to avoid delinquent activities because they experienced a positive maternal attachment and thus feared threatening this relationship, the delinquent youth had neither parent to serve as a barrier to delinquent conduct. Instead, coupled with a pathological home environment, the 'negative' insecure, anxious, or avoidant attachment styles of these youth may have exacerbated feelings of rejection and promoted youth involvement in delinquency.

One possible explanation for the negative attachments between mothers and delinquent youth may be in the high rate of psychopathology experienced by the mothers of the youth in the present study. Experiences of depression and suicidality, for example, may have made it more difficult for mothers to provide the reassurance, sensitivity, and care required by these youth as they were growing up. A second explanation involves the possibility that in not approving of their children's delinquent conduct, mothers may be viewed by delinquent youth as more difficult and oppositional. Researchers have indicated that families of delinquents tend to have more conflict and frequent disagreements (Tolan et al., 1986). Although more information on parenting styles of the delinquents in the present sample would have been beneficial, based on Henggeler's (1989) findings, delinquency is associated with high rates of conflict and low levels of parental acceptance. If dad is typically away from home and mom does not agree with what the adolescent is doing, the parent typically at home (i.e., mom) tends to become enmeshed in escalations of conflict with the youth. From this perspective, it would be less likely that youth acting against their mother's wishes would be able to retain a positive attachment to her, especially, if they interpret maternal disciplining as a form of rejection.

Whether a child will develop secure and positive attachments to others has also been found to depend on whether or not (s)he has been personally violated. Researchers of childhood abuse have found that children who are abused are typically insecurely attached to their caregivers as well as other persons they interact with (Cicchetti & Olsen, 1990; Perry, Perry, & Boldizar, 1990). Moreover, adolescent delinquents have been associated with parents or guardians who employ lax, erratic, or overly strict physical punishment (Loeber & Stouthamer-Loeber, 1986; Tolan et al., 1986). In contrast to the results of Brown (1984) who found that physical abuse was not positively correlated with any form of delinquency, the present investigation showed that more youth who were classified as delinquent rather than nondelinquent, had previously experienced both physical and sexual abuse. Specific distinctions within the category of sexual abuse showed that while abused nondelinquents experienced more repeated instances of intrafamilial sexual abuse (i.e., incest), the majority of delinquents tended to be sexually abused extrafamilially, both in isolated and repeated instances.

Although incest has been considered one of the more devastating forms of abuse inflicted on a child, in this sample, the uncertainty of being sexually abused by anyone, at anytime, and anywhere could be equally destructive and painful. In constantly looking for the next perpetrator, it not surprising that these youth may be unable to trust anyone long enough to form any type of bond or attachment. Moreover, it may well be that with this 'hyper-vigilance' operating, adolescents are more prone to finding opportunities to act out delinquently, and seek revenge on real and potential perpetrators. Esbensen and Huizinga (1991) argued that crime and victimization have traditionally been studied as separate domains. Yet, based on the findings of the present investigation, a plausible argument could be that adolescent involvement in delinquent activities may be associated with an increased risk of victimization, both in the past and future. It may be that victimized youth are more likely to retaliate against society through delinquent conduct.

Given the kind of problems in the personal lives of delinquent adolescents (i.e., negative attachments to both parents and greater instances of physical and sexual abuse), it is no wonder that the school delinquency correlate was supported in the present study.   Specifically, more delinquents than nondelinquents performed poorly at school. This finding replicates previous studies which have similarly found that school competency is negatively correlated with delinquent behaviour (Ellis, 1987; Gottfredson, McNeil III, & Gottfredson, 1991). One possible explanation for this finding may be that in being mentally overtaxed with their own personal problems, these adolescents are unable to concentrate on meeting homework deadlines or master subject content. When this problem overload is manifested in ways such as absences, late arrivals, or uncompleted projects, school personnel may judge the youth as mentally slow, unmotivated, apathetic, or delinquent. With an abundance of negative judgments to choose from, adolescents may lose interest in school, drop out, or begin acting out. According to Violato and Travis (1994), the consistent association of delinquency with poor school performance may be a result of over-supervising and monitoring of delinquent youth by school personnel, as well as weak, inconsistent, and ineffective reactions to delinquents by teachers and principals.

It has been argued that family influences are apt to be multidirectional or reciprocally influential between parents and youth (Bartol & Bartol, 1989; Rutter & Giller, 1984), and that family factors "never operate in a vacuum but take place against a backdrop of other influences such as those exercised by children's peers, their school, and society in general" (Loeber & Stouthamer-Loeber, 1986, p.128). The findings of the present study demonstrate that as the number of familial handicaps increase, so too do the chances that youth will become delinquent. Thus, given the backdrop of other conditions, it may be that certain families are at a greater risk of producing delinquent youth than others.

Table 13.1 Stepwise discriminant analysis for the whole sample in the young adult program (N=285)

Variables	Correlation with the Discriminant Function
Diagnosis	.88
Prenatal Problems	.40
School Performance	.40
Physical Abuse	.33
Maternal Psychopathology	.32
Paternal Attachment	-.21

Canonical Discriminant Function

Eigenvalue	Canonical Correlation	Wilks' Lambda	Chi-square	df	p
.5897	.6091	.6290	55.163	6	<.001

Classification Results

Membership Actual Group	No. of Cases	Predicted Group	
		Delinquent	Nondelinquent
Delinquent	96	81 84.4%	15 15.6%
Nondelinquent	62	20 32.3%	42 67.7%

Percent of cases correctly classified: 77.85%

References

Bartol, C.R. & Bartol, A.M. (1989). *Juvenile Delinquency: A Systems Approach.* Prentice Hall: New Jersey.

Brown, S.E. (1984). Social Class, Child Maltreatment, and Delinquent Behaviour. *Criminology,* 22, 259-526.

Cicchetti, D. & Olsen, K. (1990). The developmental psychopathology of child maltreatment. In *Handbook of Developmental Psychopathology.* M. Lewis & S.M. Miller (Eds.), (pp.261-280). New York: Plenum Press.

Elliott, D.S. (1982). Delinquency, school attendance and dropout. In R. Giallombardo (Ed.), *Juvenile Delinquency: A Book of Readings.* Fourth Edition (pp.226-232). New York: John Wiley and Sons Inc.

Elliott, D.S., Ageton, S.S., & Canter, R.J. (1979). An Integrated Theoretical Perspective on Delinquent Behavior. *Journal of Research in Crime and Delinquency,* 16, 3-27.

Ellis, D. (1987). *The Wrong Stuff.* Collier Canada: Macmillan.

Ellis, L. (1987). Neurohormonal Bases of Varying Tendencies to Learn Delinquent and Criminal Behavior. In E.K. Morris & C.J. Baukmann (Eds.), *Behavioral Approaches to Crime and Delinquency: A Handbook of Application, Research, and Concepts,* (pp.499-514).

Esbensen, F.A. & Huizinga, D. (1991). Juvenile Victimization and Delinquency, *Youth and Society,* 23, 202-227.

Giallombardo, R. (1982). *Juvenile Delinquency: A Book of Readings,* Fourth Edition. New York: John Wiley and Sons, Inc.

Gibbons, D.C. (1976). *Delinquent Behavior. Second Edition.* Englewood Cliffs, New Jersey: Prentice-Hall, Inc.

Gottfredson, D.C., McNeil III, R.J. & Gottfredson, G.D. (1991). Social Area Influences on Delinquency: A Multilevel Analysis. *Journal of Research in Crime and Delinquency,* 28, 197-226.

Henggeler, S.W. (1989). *Delinquency in Adolescence.* Developmental Clinical Psychology and Psychiatry. London: Sage Publications.

Hirschi, T. & Gottfredson, M. (1988). Towards a General Theory of Crime. *Explaining Criminal Behavior.* In Buikhuisen, W. & Mednick, S.A. (Eds.). E.J. Brill, Leiden, the Netherlands; (pp.8-26).

Hurrelmann, K. & Engel, U. (1991). Delinquency as a Symptom of Adolescents' Orientation Toward Status and Success. *Journal of Youth and Adolescence,* 21, 119-138.

Jensen, P.S., Koretz, D., Locke, B.Z., Schneider, S., Radke-Yarrow, M., Richters, J.E., & Rumsey, J.M. (1993). Child and Adolescent Psychopathology Research: Problems and Prospects for the 1990s. *Journal of Abnormal Child Psychology,* 21, 551-580.

LeBlanc, M. (1992). Family Dynamics, Adolescent Delinquency, and Adult Criminality. *Psychiatry,* 55, 336-353.

Letourneau, K.M. (1994). *An Examination of Sex-Role Correlates of Adolescent Male Sex Offenders*. Master of Science Thesis; Calgary, Alberta: University of Calgary.

Lewis, M. (1990). Models of Developmental Psychopathology. In M. Lewis & S.M. Miller (Eds.), *Handbook of Developmental Psychopathology* (pp.15-28). New York: Plenum Press.

Loeber, R. & Stouthamer-Loeber, M. (1986). Family Factors as Correlates and Predictors of Juvenile Conduct Problems and Delinquency. In M. Tonry & N. Morris (Eds.), *Crime and Justice: An Annual Review of Research, 7,* 29-150.

Mussen, P.H., Conger, J.J., Kagan, J. & Huston, A.C. (1990). *Child Development and Personality* (pp.653-688). Seventh Edition. New York: Harper & Row Publishers.

Palenski, J.E. & Launer, H.M. (1987). The 'Process' of Running Away: A Redefinition. *Adolescence*, Vol.22, 347-362.

Perry, D.G., Perry, L.C., & Boldizar, J.P. (1990). Learning of Aggression. In M. Lewis & S.M. Miller (Eds.), *Handbook of Developmental Psychopathology* (pp.135-146). New York: Plenum Press.

Roberts, J.V. & Hudson, J. (1993). Evaluating Justice in Canada: An Overview. *Evaluating Justice: Canadian Policies and Programs*. Thompson Educational Publishing, Inc., 3-18.

Rutter, M. (1990). Psychosocial Resilience and Protective Mechanisms. In J. Roff, A.S. Masten, D. Cicchetti, K.H. Neuchterlein, & S. Weintraub (Eds.), *Risk and Protective Factors in the Development of Psychopathology* (pp.181-212). New York: Cambridge University Press.

Rutter, M. & Giller, H. (1984). *Juvenile Delinquency: Trends and Perspectives*. New York: The Guilford Press.

Santrock, J.W. (1990). *Adolescence*. Fourth Edition. Wm. C. Brown Publishers: USA.

Schafer, S. & Knudten, R.D. (1970). *Juvenile Delinquency: An Introduction*. New York: Random House.

Scudder, R.G., Blount, W.R., Heide, K.M., & Silverman, I.J. (1993). Important Links Between Child Abuse, Neglect, and Delinquency. *International Journal of Offender Therapy and Comparative Criminology, 37,* 315-323.

Simons, R.L., Robertson, J.F. & Downs, W.R. (1989). The Nature of the Association Between Parental Rejection and Delinquent Behavior. *Journal of Youth and Adolescence, 18,* 297-310.

Smith, R.B., Bertrand, L.D., Arnold, B.L., & Hornick, J.P. (1995). *A Study of the Level and Nature Of Youth Crime and Violence in Calgary*. Prepared for the Calgary Police Service by the Canadian Research Institute for Law and the Family. Solicitor General Canada.

Tappan, P. (1982). The Nature of Delinquency. *In* R. Giallombardo (Ed.), *Juvenile Delinquency: A Book of Readings*. Fourth Edition (pp.4-21). New York: John Wiley and Sons, Inc.

Thompson, G.R. (1986). Offender Groups and Correctional Services in Canada. In J.C. Turner & F.J. Turner (Eds.), *Canadian Social Welfare*. Second Edition (pp.219-239). Collier Macmillan Canada, Inc.

Tolan, P.H., Cromwell, R.E., & Brasswell, M. (1986). Family Therapy with Delinquents: A Critical Review of the Literature. *Family Process, 25,* 619-650.

Violato, C. & Travis, L.D. (1994). *Advances in Adolescent Psychology.* Calgary: Detselig (in press).

Warr, M. (1993). Parents, Peers, and Delinquency. *Social Forces, 72,* 247-264.

Wilkinson, K. (1982). The Broken Family and Juvenile Delinquency: Scientific Explanation or Ideology? In R. Giallombardo (Ed.), *Juvenile Delinquency: A Book of Readings.* Fourth Edition (pp.233-244). New York: John Wiley and Sons, Inc.

14 Origins of Psychopathology: A Developmental Model

CLAUDIO VIOLATO AND MARK GENUIS

Abstract

The main purpose of the present study was to test a latent variable path model of the influence of childhood attachment on psychological adaptation in adolescence. A total of 138 adolescents (mean age = 14.54 years; 64 males and 74 females) along with their mothers and fathers, when available, formed the present sample. Approximately 40% of the adolescents were drawn from a clinical sample and the remainder were from the community. Data were collected on the adolescents and their mothers and fathers on affective, cognitive, life history and demographic variables. The latent variable path model which specified that childhood attachment is central to the development of psychological adaptation in adolescence was fit to the data. Two latent variables, Abuse and Social/Emotional Isolation, were posited to have mutually reciprocal and dynamic effects on a third latent variable, Childhood Attachment which is directly linked to psychological adaptation. Using an Arbitrary Distribution Least Squares (ALS) method, the model resulted in a good fit to the data (Comparative Fit Index = .984), and all three latent variables were significantly ($p < .05$) intercorrelated as expected. Moreover, a single path from Childhood Attachment to psychological adaptation (Psychopathology) was confirmed by a significant path coefficient (.48, $p < .01$). Stepwise discriminant analyses revealed that the specific experiences in childhood did not discriminate among the types of pathology demonstrated in adolescence. The significance of the findings for a general theory of developmental psychopathology are discussed.

Introduction

Human infants, like many other vertebrates, form special affiliative bonds with their caregivers called attachments. In the first 6-9 months of life human infants

191

express no preference for particular caregivers though they can distinguish among them. By nine months and beyond, however, infants demonstrate a clear preference for a few caregivers with whom they interact regularly (Bowlby, 1969). Separation protest and stranger wariness develops coincidentally with preferred attachment as do a number of other cognitive, social and emotional changes. Infants use their attachment figures as secure bases from which to explore the world.

Recently, psychologists have observed that attachment patterns vary among children and that these patterns co-vary with behavior and psychological adjustment (Suess, Grossman & Sroufe, 1992). Moreover, it has been observed that these attachment patterns can remain stable throughout childhood into adolescence. It has been suggested that these attachments either potentiate or are correlated with psychological adjustment and psychopathology (Waters, Posada, Cromwell & Keng-Ling, 1993). In this article, we report results from a study designed to address questions about the relevance of attachment to psychological adjustment and psychopathology. Our basic premise is that psychological adjustment in adolescence (including psychopathology) can be directly linked to early childhood attachments. We propose that much of the variation of adolescent psychological adjustment can be accounted for by the variations in childhood attachment patterns. Accordingly, much of psychopathology in adolescence and beyond may have its origins in early childhood.

Infant attachments are thought to have high survival value because they result in closeness between the relatively helpless infant and its principal caregivers that provide comfort, shelter and protection. These attachments, moreover, result in proximity seeking behavior from the infant particularly in times of distress, fear, illness and hunger. In response to nurturing, responsive and dedicated caregiving, infants and children develop secure attachments. These children appear confident that their caregivers are available, responsive and helpful should they encounter adverse or frightening situations. Because of this assurance, securely attached children explore the world confidently and effectively. Although they show distress upon separation from the principal caregiver, they are quickly soothed and comforted upon reunion.

The Strange Situation Procedure (SSP), which was invented by Ainsworth and her colleagues (Ainsworth, 1991), is designed to assess a child's attachment classification in a standardized way by separating a child from its principal caregiver and then reuniting the two. When general community samples are assessed in the SSP for attachment classification, approximately 70% of children are classified as securely attached to their principal caregivers such as their mother and father (Ainsworth, 1991).

Children who receive inconsistent care, are neglected, or otherwise maltreated, develop insecure attachments. Three types of insecure attachment patterns have been identified: disorganized, ambivalent and avoidant (Ainsworth, 1991). Children who have ambivalent insecure attachment appear uncertain whether their primary caregiver will be available or responsive when needed. These children oscillate between seeking proximity and contact with their primary caregiver, and resisting such contact. Ambivalently attached children have difficulty using their caregivers as a secure base for exploration and appear to experience considerable emotional conflict. While showing distress at separation from the principal caregiver, insecure ambivalent children are not easily soothed or comforted by the return of the caregiver.

Insecure avoidant children, while distressed upon separation from the caregiver, avoid the caregiver upon reunion. They appear to expect rejection or negative consequences from the caregiver when exhibiting attachment behaviors. Children with disorganized attachments show distress upon separation from the caregiver but demonstrate fearful backing away from the caregiver upon reunion. When the caregiver approaches, these children avert their gaze, show hypervigilance, and aimless wandering rather than proximity seeking (Bentler, 1995). Their behavior suggests a fragmented, poorly developed strategy for handling the stress of separation, and abnormalities in their strategies for obtaining comfort. As assessed in the SSP, approximately 30% of community sample children demonstrate insecure attachments (Ainsworth, 1991).

The importance of early childhood attachment in humans for psychological adaptation and development has recently begun to be recognized and has led to the development of a comprehensive theory of attachment (Cicchetti, 1993). Modern attachment theory draws upon several disciplines -- cognitive development (e.g., developmental changes in the working cognitive models of the attachment relationships), psychoanalysis (e.g., object relations), ethology (e.g., imprinting and bonding), information processing (e.g., narrative scripts of attachment history) – as a focus on human emotional development. Attachment theorists are particularly concerned with the development of emotions from a life span perspective (Freud, 1896; Lamb, 1984), hypothesizing that human affiliative behaviors and emotional responses towards others is a function of attachment. Attachment theorists have thus focused on the long-term implications of childhood attachments (e.g., lasting into the teenage and adult years). It is thought that emotional stability, affiliative behaviors and level of psychological adaptation are rooted in childhood attachments. Insecure and disorganized attachment patterns in infancy and early childhood may be predictors of psychological adaptation and behavior, as well as psychopathology in adolescence and adulthood (Bowlby, 1969; Lamb, 1984). Other researchers have cautioned that early childhood attachments may be superseded by maturation and subsequent events so that attachments may not necessarily be related to long-term psychological adaptation but are unique to the periods of infancy and early childhood (Shaw, Vondra, Hommerding, Keenan, & Dunn, 1994; Shaw, & Vondra, 1993). Nevertheless, it has long been suspected if not yet compellingly demonstrated that early childhood experiences are central to subsequent psychological adaptation (Greenberg, Speltz, Deklyen, & Endriga, 1991; Speltz, Greenberg, & Deklyen,1990).

Greenberg, Speltz & Deklyen (Lyons-Ruth, Alpern, & Repacholi, 1993), in a comprehensive review of the role of attachment in the development of early disruptive behaviors, proposed that four factors interact to produce a risk of psychological disturbances in children: 1) insecure attachment relationships (particularly disorganized), 2) family ecology and adversity (e.g., socioeconomic conditions), 3) intrinsic child characteristics (e.g., temperament), and 4) parenting strategies and socialization practices (e.g., coercive discipline). Shaw and colleagues (Kobak & Sceery, 1988) employing longitudinal studies provided empirical support for such a model in boys. Similarly, Waters, et al. (4) in a theoretically based review of the role of attachment in the development of psychopathological behaviors provided two possible theoretical models: 1) attachment problems potentiate disruptive behavior, or 2) that attachment disturbances and disruptive behavior patterns may arise from an interactive complex of family, situational and biological variables.

A number of studies have directly investigated the relationship between insecure and disorganized attachments and psychopathology in preschoolers. Using groups of clinically referred preschoolers who had been diagnosed with Oppositional Defiant Disorder, Greenberg and his colleagues (Kwakman, Zuiker, Schippers & Wuffel, 1988) reported that about 80% of the sample were classified as insecurely attached. In a comparison group matched for age, social class and family composition, about 30% were insecurely attached (significantly less than the clinical group). In a longitudinal study, Lyons-Ruth, Alpern & Repacholi (Kenny, 1990; 1988) found that 71% of their sample of preschoolers who were insecurely attached were later identified as having abnormally high levels of hostility in the classroom. Mother psychosocial problems during the preschool period independently predicted hostile and aggressive behavior. These factors (mother psychosocial problems and children's attachments) were additive in predicting hostile aggressive behavior.

Some studies have focused on adolescent adaptation and attachment. In a retrospective study, Kobak & Sceery (Ryan & Lynch, 1989) assessed university students (i.e., late adolescents) and found that those who had been securely attached to a primary caregiver in early childhood were more ego-resilient, less anxious and less hostile but reported more social support than their insecurely attached peers. Focusing on concurrent adolescent attachment and adaptation, Kwakan, Zuiker, Schippers and de Wuffel, 1988 (Armstrong & Roth, 1989) found that both male and female high school students (mean age = 13.4 years) who were insecurely attached to parents tended to use alcohol consumption as a means of facilitating social contact more frequently than did the securely attached adolescents. In similar concurrent studies, Kenny, 1990 (Resnik, Bearman, Blum, Bauman, Harris, Jones, Tabor et al., 1998) found relationships between assertiveness, dating competence, maturity in career planning and attachments. Compared to insecurely attached adolescents, both males and females who were securely attached to their parents were more assertive, more competent in dating, and more mature in their career planning. In a similar vein, Ryan and Lynch, 1989 & Achenbach, 1991 found that emotional detachment and isolation in adolescents were related to insecure attachments to their parents.

In a study utilizing a clinical sample of 27 women with eating disorders (modal age = 20 years), Armstrong and Roth, 1989 & Achenbach, 1991 found that 96% showed insecure attachments compared to 27% of a matched comparison group. Finally, in a large scale study (n = 12, 118) of American adolescents involved in the National Longitudinal Study of Adolescent Health, Resnik and colleagues (Parker, Tupling & Brown, 1979) found that "parent-family connectedness and perceived school connectedness" were protective factors against seven of the eight health risk behaviors measured: emotional distress, suicidal thoughts and behavior, violence, cigarette use, alcohol use, marijuana use, and age of sexual debut. Pregnancy history was the exception. Parent-family connectedness was defined as "closeness to mother and/or father, perceived caring by mother and/or father, satisfaction with relationship to mother and/or father, feeling wanted by family members". School connectedness included feeling "that teachers treat students fairly, close to people at school, and part of the school" (p. 825).

The foregoing review suggests that attachment relationships are either co-occurrences with psychological adaptation or causal factors in its development including the outcome of psychopathology. The main question addressed in the present study was "To what extent can a latent variable path analysis explicate a direct link between early attachment patterns and adolescent psychological adaptation?" Specifically, this study was designed to assess a sample of both community and clinical adolescents on demographic, life history, and psychological variables. We wished to investigate the link between early attachments and psychopathology in adolescence. Employing structural equation modeling (SEM) as well as descriptive and other multivariate analyses, the intention was to fit a latent variable path model to the data. The latent variable path model allows both the identification of latent variables as well as their interrelationships so as to identify the link between childhood attachments and adolescent psychological adaptation.

Within this model secure attachment results in emotional stability and positive psychological outcomes, while insecure attachments results in psychological disturbances and pathology. As we have seen, attachments in childhood is affected by the relationships between the child and principal caregiver. If the child is emotionally isolated form the caregivers (e.g., caregiver fails to provide touching, contact comfort, eye contact, verbal responses, and facial expressions indicating positive emotions) or experiences overt abusiveness due to physical beatings, sexual abuse, overt neglect, threats of abandonment or punishment and so on, insecure attachment between the child and caregiver will result. Conversely, emotional responsiveness and systematic care promotes secure attachment. Insecure attachment leads to further isolation and increases further the risk of abuse which both, in turn, further affect attachment patterns. Accordingly it is posited in this model that attachment, abuse and isolation are mutually influential and interdependent. Over time (i.e., developmentally), isolation and abuse (which are distinct but correlated latent variables) lead to insecure attachment which, in turn, reciprocally affects abuse and isolation which in turn further affect attachment and so on.

Measurement and structural model

A schematic summarizing the measurement and structural latent variable path model is depicted in Figure 14.1. By adolescence, this developmental pattern leads to disturbed psychological processes and pathology. In Figure 14.1, the latent variable of Abuse is indicated by a number of observed variables, as is Childhood Attachment and Social/Emotional isolation. The double headed arrows between the latent variables indicate correlation or reciprocal influence. The outcome of pathology is indicated by a square since this can be measured directly. This model was tested by fitting it to data employing SEM techniques. The measurement model is the identification of the latent variables (depicted as circles) by the indicator variables (the squares). The structural model refers to the relationships between the latent variables.

Method

Participants

A total of 138 adolescents (mean age = 14.54; 64 (46.4%) males and 74 (53.6%) females) along with their mothers and fathers, when available, formed the sample for the present study. Approximately 40% of the adolescents were from a clinical sample and the remainder were from the community. The main features of the sample are summarized in Table 14.1. Data were collected from the adolescents and their mothers and fathers on affective, cognitive, life history and demographic variables.

Instruments and procedures

Adolescents completed the Adolescent Attachment Survey (AAS) along with the Parental Bonding Instrument (PBI) and the Youth Self Report (YSR), while the parents were administered the Child Behavior Checklist (CBCL).

The YSR is a self-report measure which contains 118 behavior problem items and a social competence scale (Genuis & Violato, 1998). It was used in the present study to assess psychological adaptation and psychopathology of the adolescents. The YSR has several individual scales (withdrawn, somatic complaints, anxious/depressed, social problems, thought problems, attention problems, delinquent behavior, aggressive behavior, self-destructive identity problems) as well as composite scale scores including externalizing and internalizing and an overall total problem score. Numerous studies have provided reliability and validity evidence for the YSR (Genuis & Violato, 1998). Test-retest and internal consistency reliability (Cronbach's alpha coefficient) ranged from .59 to .90 on individual scales, .89 for internalizing, .89 for externalizing, and .95 for the total problem scale. Research provided evidence for content, criterion-related and some construct validity for the YSR (Genuis & Violato, 1998).

The CBCL is a checklist that is completed by parents on the same scales as the YSR. Numerous reports have documented the evidence for both reliability and aspects of validity of this instrument (Genuis & Violato, 1998; Bentler, 1995; Kendall-Tackett, Myer & Finkelhor, 1993). Reliability coefficients including test-retest, inter-interviewer and internal consistency (Cronbach's alpha coefficient) range from .68 to .96 in numerous studies (Genuis & Violato, 1998). Several empirical studies have provided content, criterion-related and some construct validity evidence for the CBCL (Genuis & Violato, 1998).

The PBI, a 25 Likert-type item scale, is intended to assess two components of childhood attachments (parental care and overprotection). Parker, Tupling and Brown, 1979 (Sameroff, Seifer, Zax & Barocas, 1987) found substantial test-retest reliability (.70 on a six month interval) and substantial split half reliability for the PBI as well as some evidence of validity.

The AAS made up of 177 items consists of 8 subscales (attachment, separation, neglect, parental involvement, blame, threats, physical abuse and sexual abuse) intended to measure childhood attachments and experiences as well as demographic variables. Internal consistency reliability coefficients (Cronbach's alpha) for the 8 subscales range from .82 to .94 and the research has provided evidence of validity (Oddone-Paolucci, Genuis, & Violato, 1998).

Adolescent participants and their parents (where available) were individually assessed on all of the instruments.

Results

Testing the latent variable path model

Fitting the latent variable path model involves minimizing the difference between the sample covariances and the covariances predicted by the model. Formally this is represented as:

$$\Sigma = \Sigma(\theta) \tag{1}$$

where Σ is the population covariance matrix of observed variables, θ is a vector that contains the model parameters, and $\Sigma(\theta)$ is the covariance matrix written as a functions of θ. This simple equation allows the implementation of a general mathematical and statistical approach to the analysis of linear structural equation system through the estimation of parameters and the fitting of models. Estimation can be classified by type of distribution (multinormal, elliptical, arbitrary) assumed of the data and weight matrix used during the computations. The function to be minimized is given by:

$$Q = [s - \sigma(\theta)]' \, W[s - \sigma(\theta)] \tag{2}$$

where s is the vector of data to be modeled -- the variances and covariances of the observed variables -- and σ is a model for the data. The model vector σ is a function of more basic parameters θ that are to be estimated so as to minimize Q. W is the weight matrix that can be specified in several ways to yield a number of different estimators that depend on the distribution assumed (27).

To test the model summarized in Figure 14.1, nine variables were included as identifying the three latent variables (Abuse, Childhood Attachment, and Social-Emotional). The nine measured variables (Other Close Adults from the

AAS, Bonding/Attachment from the Parental Bonding Instrument, Psychopathology from clinician diagnosis, and Attachment, Parental Involvement, Moves, Physical Abuse, Neglect, Threats all from the AAS) were intercorrelated. The intercorrelation matrix and standard deviations of all nine measured variables is summarized in Table 14.2. In order to fit the model, this intercorrelation matrix was converted to a variance-covariance matrix. As **W** in this analysis will yield estimators based on arbitrary distributions, the model was fit using arbitrary distribution least squares (ALS) estimation.

The overall fit of the model to the data was good producing a Comparative Fit Index (CFI) = .984 and $X2$, = 115.1, df =24, $p < .001$. The minimizing of the Q function (Eq. 2) proceeded smoothly requiring 15 iterations. A CFI = .984 indicates that 98.4% of the variance and covariance in the data is accounted for by the proposed model. Further evidence of the model's fit comes from the average standardized residuals of .25 from the residual population matrix, $\Sigma - \Sigma(\theta)$, as estimated by its sample counterpart, $S - \Sigma$. The path coefficients and other parameters are summarized in Figure 14.1.

All three latent variables in Figure 14.1 are clearly identified. Abuse has loadings (ranging from .24 to .69) from five variables (Threats, Neglect, Physical Abuse, Parental Involvement, Attachment to Both Parents) which are all theoretically relevant to an Abuse construct. The loadings on Childhood Attachment range from .22 to .70 (Attachment to Both Parents, Changes in Residence, Parental Involvement, Physical Abuse). With the possible exception of Neglect (.95), none of theta-delta coefficients (residuals) on these variables are very large. Three of the above measured variables (Parental Involvement, Physical Abuse, Attachment to Both Parents) also serve to identify Childhood Attachment as they have split loadings. Changes in Residence is the fourth measured variable loading on Childhood Attachments (residual = .70).

There are three measured variables (Changes in Residence, Parental Bonding Instrument, Other Close Adults) which load on Social/Emotional Isolation with a particularly large loading (.84) from Changes in Residence. The Parental Bonding Instrument has a weak loading on Childhood Attachments (-.04) but a large residual (.99) and Other Close Adults has a moderate loading on Childhood Attachments (.35) and a large residual (.94). The overall model as well as the pattern of coefficients, therefore, fits the data very well although this last feature of it is problematic.

All of the latent variables are intercorrelated (see Figure 14.1) as predicted, and the crucial path coefficient from Childhood Attachments to Diagnosis of Psychopathology is significant (path coefficient = -.48; $p<.001$). The intercorrelations among Childhood Attachments, Social/Emotional Isolation, and Abuse are all significant (-.29, -.33, .24, $p < .05$ – see Figure 14.1). The negative correlations and path coefficient reflect the inverted scales of Social Isolation relative to Attachment and Abuse. These results support the role of childhood attachments in developmental psychopathology specifically. Overall, they also support the role of childhood attachments in the development of psychological adaptation generally. The data support the overall model and the particulars of the predicted relationships as well.

Secondary analysis: Non-specificity of psychopathology diagnosis and attachment

In order to evaluate the validity of the diagnosis of psychopathology of the participants, and the specificity of the diagnostic category relative to childhood attachment classifications, stepwise discriminant analyses were employed. Both the YSR and CBCL provide assessments of adolescent psychopathology. The intention in the present analyses was to determine the degree of correspondence of a classification of psychopathology rendered by the YSR, CBCL and independent clinical diagnosis.

Nine variables (Internalizing, Externalizing and Total Problem score from the YSR and CBCL for each parent) were selected and entered into the discriminant analysis (the total number of subjects for this analysis was 370 - adolescents, mothers, fathers). Four of the variables 1) internalizing from the CBCL from fathers, 2) problem score from the YSR, 3) total problem score from the CBCL from fathers, and 4) total problem score from the CBCL from mother, produced one significant discriminant function (Function one: $X2 = 342.42$, df =4, $p < .001$) producing an eigenvalue = 5.15 and a canonical correlation = .92. Using the derived discriminant function, 97.1% of the adolescents were classified correctly as belonging to the clinical or community samples. These results provide evidence of convergent validity for the clinical diagnoses.

An important research question that can be addressed in the present data is "Are there particular pathologies in adolescence that are significantly related to specific childhood experiences?". This question has to do with the specificity-nonspecificity of childhood experiences in the development of psychopathology. It appears that risk factors in childhood and later developmental outcomes are not specifically linked (Freud, 1896). Rather, the number of risk factors may be more predictive of outcomes than any particular combination of them. In order to address the specificity-nonspecificity question, the present data were further explored through univariate analyses to identify variables related to developmental outcomes: 1) moves between cities or towns, 2) regular separation from parents, 3) long-term separation, 4) permanent separation, 5) felt rejection, 6) threats of abandonment, 7) blaming child for parental illness, 8) parent threatening to harm self, 9) parent threatening to harm child, 10) physical abuse, and 11) sexual abuse. These variables were entered into a stepwise discriminant analysis with Withdrawn, Internalizing, Externalizing and Total Problem Score on the YSR as classification variables. Two non-significant discriminant functions were derived (Function one: $X^2 = 11.19$, df = 6, $p < .10$, eigenvalue = .09, canonical correlation = .29; Function two: $X^2 = 4.20$, df = 2, $p < .12$, eigenvalue = .05). The resulting group classification was not better than chance. These results support the nonspecificity of developmental outcomes for early childhood experiences.

Discussion

The main results in the present study are 1) that we were able to identify a latent variable path model with three latent variables (Abuse, Childhood Attachment, Social/Emotional Isolation), 2) the latent variable path model fit the data very well and indicates that there is a direct link from childhood attachment to adolescent psychological adaptation, 3) clinician diagnosis for the adolescent clinical subjects was cross-validated with the CBCL and YSR, and 4) the type of outcome was not related to any specific risk factor in childhood.

In total, the present findings provide support for the developmental nature of psychopathology. Specifically, they indicate that childhood attachments play a central role in subsequent psychological adaptation in adolescence. The reciprocal effects between behavioral experiences in childhood and the security of emotional attachment is evidenced by both the loadings of observed variables on to the latent variable, and the significant correlations found between attachment and the other two latent variables, Abuse and Isolation. Although various childhood experiences affect attachment security and the development of attachments type affects both the experiential and interpretive components of subsequent experiences, Childhood Attachment was the link leading to adolescent psychopathology.

As Waters (1993) and his colleagues have suggested (Zeanah, Boris & Scheering, 1997), one hypothesis is that attachments potentiate psychological adjustment and psychopathology. The present results favor this interpretation as indicted by the direct significant link between Childhood Attachments and psychopathology in adolescence. The alternative hypothesis that insecure attachment and disruptive behavior patterns may arise from a common underlying interactive complex of family, situational and biological variables was not supported in the present study. This hypothesis requires that the link should be indirect, and that it should be correlated with psychopathology in adolescence as one of a complex system of correlated interacting variables. It appears that the interacting complex of family, situational and biological variables function on attachment patterns which in turn determines psychological adaptation in adolescence.

The reciprocal influence between behavioral experiences in childhood and the security of emotional attachment is evidenced by both the significant loadings of observed variables on to the latent attachment variable, and the significant correlations between Childhood Attachment and the other two latent variables, Abuse and Social/Emotional Isolation. The directional influence of Childhood Attachment to adolescent psychopathology is supported in the present study. Attachment was assessed based on experiences prior to the age of 10 years, while psychopathology was diagnosed in adolescence with subject ranging in age from 12 to 17 years. The existence of attachment type before age 10 and its association with psychopathology in adolescence supports the contention for the direction of effect from childhood attachment to adolescent psychopathology.

Several features of the latent path model require clarification. Two of the indicator variables on Social/Emotional Isolation had small loadings (Other Close Adults, Parental Bonding Instrument) and large residuals. The variable Changes in Residence is a clear indicator of this latent variable with a large loading and small residual. Further study to examine the place of Social/Emotional Isolation in the model will be beneficial.

The effect of sexual abuse was not clear in the model even though much previous research has shown the many detrimental effects of sexual abuse in child development. It may be that the other forms of abuse assessed in the present study (e.g., physical) may have rendered the effects of sexual abuse redundant. Alternatively, the effects of sexual abuse may be so pervasive that they are dissipated throughout the model. Further research should be designed to clarify this relationship.

Our findings that there is a lack of specificity in type of risk factor (e.g., physical abuse, sexual abuse, felt rejection, etc.) and psychopathological outcome (e.g., withdrawn, internalizing, externalizing) confirms the findings of many others (Kobak & Sceery, 1988). It appears that the number of risk factors may be more predictive of outcome than any particular combination of them (Freud, 1896). Their lack of specificity may also be due to the potentiating and mediating effects of attachment.

Our current results indicate that future research should focus on extending and replicating the following model. First, a prospective longitudinal research design should be employed in further work (as opposed to a retrospective longitudinal design as in the present case). Second, the various forms of insecure attachment (ambivalent, avoidant, disorganized) should be assessed so that any differential effect of different types of insecure attachment can be assessed. Third, any subsequent work would benefit by examining how the variables within the present model work interactively and dynamically over time, and how this interaction affects the model as a whole.

The main finding in the present study suggests that childhood attachment plays a central and direct role in the development of adolescent adaptation and psychopathology. While such a role for attachment has long been suspected, it has been demonstrated in the present study. While more research is required to work out the particulars (e.g., specific experiences that lead to secure/insecure attachment; the reciprocal dynamic of the latent variables over time), the latent variable path model in the present study provides a simple and parsimonious model of developmental psychopathology.

Figure 14.1   Latent variable path model of adolescent psychopathology

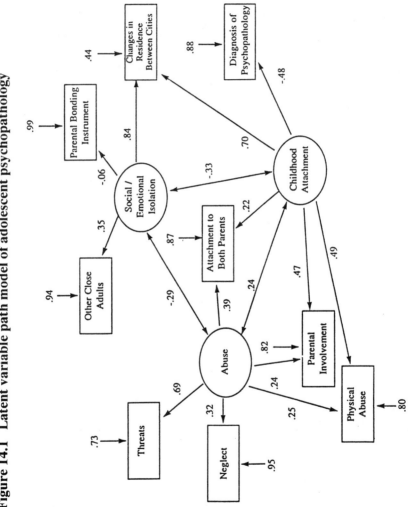

Table 14.1   Descriptive characteristics of the sample

Variable	Clinical Group n[a]	(%)[b]	Community Group n[a]	(%)[b]	Total n[a]	(%)[b]
Gender: Adolescents						
Male	25	(39.1)	39	(60.9)	64	(100)
Female	30	(40.1)	44	(59.9)	74	(100)
Family Constellation						
Family triads	21	(20.2)	83	(79.8)	104	(100)
Adolescent-mother dyads	19	(100)	0	(0)	19	(100)
Adolescent-father dyads	8	(100)	0	(0)	8	(100)
Adolescent only	7	(100)	0	(0)	7	(100)
Repeated Grades						
Zero	33	(28.9)	81	(71.1)	114	(100)
One	20	(90.1)	2	(9.9)	22	(100)
Two or more	2	(100)	0	(0)	2	(100)
Ethnicity						
Caucasian	40	(34.8)	75	(65.2)	115	(100)
Metis	8	(66.7)	4	(33.3)	12	(100)
Asian	2	(66.7)	1	(33.3)	3	(100)
Black	1	(100)	0	(0)	1	(100)
East Indian	0	(0)	1	(100)	1	(100)
Aboriginal	1	(100)	0	(0)	1	(100)
Mixed	1	(100)	0	(0)	1	(100)
Other	2	(50.0)	2	(50.0)	4	(100)
Socioeconomic Status						
Entrepreneurial or professional	18	(36.0)	32	(64.0)	50	(100)
Skilled labor	8	(15.1)	45	(84.9)	53	(100)
Unskilled labor/ unemployed	4	(80.0)	1	(20.0)	5	(100)

[a] Number of subjects within this category
[b] Percentage of subjects within this category
* Ages for the clinical group ranged from 12 to 17 years, mean age = 14.32, standard deviation = 1.40. For the community group, the ages also ranged from 12 to 17 years, mean age = 14.54, standard deviation = 1.68 years.

Table 14.2   Pearson product moment correlations among nine variables

	Attachment	Parental Bonding Ins	Diagnosis	Other Adults	Parental Involvement	Neglect	Threats	Physical Abuse	Changes in Residence
Attachment	1.00								
Parental Bonding Ins	.03	1.00							
Diagnosis	.49	.18	1.00						
Other Adults	-.51	-.13	-.32	1.00					
Parental Involvement	.85	.12	.46	-.46	1.00				
Neglect	.11	-.18	-.15	.08	.15	1.00			
Threats	.13	.00	-.14	-.03	.20	.60	1.00		
Physical Abuse	-.40	-.09	-.51	.30	-.26	.34	.24	1.00	
Changes in Residence	-.35	-.13	-.45	.42	-.29	.15	.05	.42	1.00
Standard Deviations	5.8	6.4	6.9	4.9	7.9	4.1	1.6	4.4	2.7

References

Achenbach, T. (1991). *Manual for the youth self report.* University of Vermont: Vermont, VT.

Achenbach, T. (1991). *Manual for the child behavior checklist/4-18 and 1991 profile.* University of Vermont: Vermont, VT.

Ainsworth, M. (1991). Attachments and other affectional bonds across the life cycle. In C. Parks, J. Stevenson-Hide & P. Marris (Eds.), *Attachment across the life cycle.* Routledge: London.

Armstrong, J. & Roth, D. (1989). Attachment and separation difficulties in eating disorders: A preliminary investigation. *International Journal of Eating Disorders, 8,* 141-155.

Bentler, P. (1995). EQS program manual. BMDP: Los Angeles.

Bretherton, I. (1992). Origins of attachment theory: John Bowlby to Mary Ainsworth. *Developmental Psychology, 28,* 283-297.

Bowlby, J. (1969). *Attachment and loss: Vol. 1* (1st ed.). Basic Books: New York.

Cicchetti, D. (1993). Developmental psychopathology: Reactions, reflections, projections. *Dev. Rev. 13,* 471-502. In D. Cicchetti & D. Cohen (Eds.). (1995). *Developmental psychopathology.* Wiley: New York.

Freud, S. (1896). *Aetiology of neuroses.* In P. Gay (Ed.), The Freud reader. Norton & Company: New York.

Genuis, M. & Violato, C. (1998). The adolescent attachment survey: Psychometric properties. *NFFRE Journal, 2,* 3-26.

Greenberg, M., Speltz, M. & Deklyen, M. (1993). The role of attachment in the early development of disruptive behavior problems. *Developmental & Psychopathology. 5,* 191-213.

Greenberg, M., Speltz, M., Deklyen, M. & Endriga, M. (1991). Attachment security in preschoolers with and without externalizing problems: A replication. *Developmental & Psychopathology, 3,* 413-430.

Kendall-Tackett, K., Myer, L. & Finkelhor, D. (1993). Impact of sexual abuse on children: A review and synthesis of recent empirical studies. *Psychological Bulletin,* 113, 164-180.

Kenny, M. (1990). College senior's perceptions of parental attachments: The value and stability of family ties. *Journal College Studies and Development, 31,* 39-46.

Kenny, M. (1988). The extent and function of parental attachments among first-year college students. *Journal of Youth and Adolescence, 16,* 17-29.

Kobak, R. & Sceery, A. (1988). Attachment in late adolescence: Working models, affect regulation, and representations of self and others. *Child Development, 59,* 135-146.

Kwakan, A., Zuiker, F., Schippers, G. & Wuffel, F. (1988). Drinking behavior, drinking attitudes and attachment relationship of adolescents. *Journal of Youth and Adolescence, 17,* 247-53.

Lamb, M. (1984). Fathers, mothers and childcare in the 1980's: Family influence on child development. In K. Borman, D. Quarm & S. Gideones (Eds.). (1984), *Women in the workplace: Effect on families* (pp. 61-88). Ablex: Norwood, NJ.

Lyons-Ruth, K., Alpern, L. & Repacholi, B. (1993). Disorganized infant attachment classification and maternal psychosocial problems as predictors of hostile-aggressive behavior in the preschool classroom. *Child Development, 64*, 572-585.

Oddone-Paolucci, E., Genuis, M. & Violato, C. (1998). The effects of childhood sexual abuse on child development. A meta-analysis of the published research. *Paper submitted for publication,* August.

Parker, G., Tupling, H. & Brown, L. (1979). A parental bonding instrument. *British Journal of Psychiatry, 52*, 1-10.

Resnik, M., Bearman, P., Blum, W., Bauman, K., Harris, K., Jones, J., Tabor, J., et al. (1998). Protecting adolescence from harm: Findings from the national longitudinal study on adolescent health. *Journal of the American Medical Association, 278*, 823-832.

Ryan, R. & Lynch, J. (1989). Emotional autonomy versus detachment: Revisiting the vicissitudes of adolescence and young adulthood. *Child Development, 60*, 340-356.

Sameroff, A., Seifer, R., Zax, M. & Barocas, R. (1987). Early indicators of developmental risk: Rochester longitudinal study. *Schizophrenia Bulletin, 13*, 383-394.

Shaw, D., Vondra, J., Hommerding, D., Keenan, K. & Dunn, M. (1994). Chronic family adversity and early child behavior problems: A longitudinal study of low income families. *Journal of Child Psychology and Psychiatry, 35*, 1109-1122.

Shaw, D. & Vondra, J. (1993). Chronic family adversity and infant attachment. *Journal of Child Psychology and Psychiatry, 34*, 1205-1215.

Speltz, M., Greenberg, M. & Deklyen, M. (1990). Attachments in preschoolers with disruptive behavior: A comparison of clinic referred and nonproblem children. *Development & Psychopathology, 2*, 31-46.

Suess, G., Grossman, K. & Sroufe, L. (1992). Effects of infant attachment to mother and father on quality adaptation in preschool: From dyadic to individual organization of self. *International Journal of Behaviour Development, 15*, 43-65.

Waters, E., Posada, G., Cromwell, J. & Keng-Ling, L. (1993). Is attachment theory ready to contribute to our understanding of behavior problems? *Development & Psychopathology, 5*, 215-224.

Zeanah, C., Boris, N. & Scheering, M. (1997). Psychopathology in infancy. *Journal of Child Psychology and Psychiatry, 38*, 81-99.

15   Parallels Between Dyadic Interactions: Parent-Child and Child-Peer

LEIGH A. MOORE, DARLA J. MACLEAN, AND
THOMAS P. KEENAN

Abstract

The present study set out to draw parallels between two dyadic interactions. The first, a parent and child interaction and the second, interactions between the child and a peer of their choice. Three minute segments were coded from a video for each interaction. The task presented on the video was a Lego design. In the parent-child interaction, the parent scaffolded the child's abilities; the child then went on to scaffold his or her peer on the identical task. Three measures were obtained from the video: (1) a sensitivity measure, (2) a global scaffolding measure, and (3) a measure of positive verbal reinforcement. Measures of warmth and control were also taken from portions of the NLSC questionnaire. In total there were 44 children, with equal representation across gender. The overall mean age of the subjects was 5 years 6 months. Results showed a strong parallel between the two dyads through the reinforcement measure. A higher frequency of positive verbal reinforcement in the parent-child dyad was related to higher frequencies of reinforcement in the child-peer dyad. Verbally reinforcing parents were good scaffolders and very sensitive teachers. Verbally reinforcing children were also good scaffolders. Measures of warmth and control were weakly correlated with the three main measures from the video tapes. Within this study, evidence of modeling behaviors was clearly revealed. However, interestingly, it seemed that within this young sample there was an interaction between age and gender on the control scale. As the age of the female subjects increased, so did the scores of control; however, the findings for the males was opposite. As the boys got older, the control scores decreased. In conclusion, consistent with previous research, it appears that parents are undoubtedly highly influential in the lives of their children.

Introduction

One of the goals of parenthood is to raise a competent child who will one day have the ability to contribute something meaningful to society. The question which arises time and time again is how one can raise such a child in a single trial, one child, one lifetime. Although researchers have examined this question for several decades, parents still question their parenting abilities. The present paper may not provide the answers to all of these questions, but rather will provide one more piece of information which may shed light on the tunnel of questions which meets the tunnel of answers.

The purpose of the present paper was to examine how a child's interactions with his or her parent may influence the child's interactions with a peer. A child or any other human being is not an isolated creature; thus, human development can not be meaningfully studied in the absence of an interaction. Hence, dyadic interactions were structured for the present study. The majority of people do not function in a world devoid of social interaction. Of course, there are a few individuals who choose to live a life of isolation, but even those few individuals must have had early social and physical interactions as infants.

Society's social norms assist in regulating behaviors of individuals, and help keep many individuals within the realm of "normalcy" (Minuchin, 1985). Each individual is the product of several interactions which occur between her or himself and several others (Mead, 1934). Children are one of the many parts making up a large systems model developed by Bronfenbrenner (1979), in which the development of each person is viewed as the result of numerous interactions within the family, various institutions, and society. In reality, when studying people, we are dealing with what Ricci and Selvini-Palazzoli (1984) would refer to as an "N-adic" model, depicting the idea of having an infinite number of interactions within a single lifetime. Humans are social creatures; thus, in order to be accurately examined, one should observe people within a naturalistic setting (i.e., interacting with others).

The choice was made to study preschoolers because researchers have viewed this age as one involving several dramatic transitions. In North American culture the preschool child is bombarded by interactions with numerous new situations and people, thus, making this a critical age at which to study the development of social interactions. When the child begins school it is a key developmental transition and a time of reorganization for the child, as well as the entire family (Higgins & Parsons, 1983; Minuchin, 1985). The child will experience changes that she or he has never been confronted with in the past, such as a change in social roles. The child shifts from the monorole of being a family member to a more complex interplay among the various roles of classmate, student, and friend. Adjusting to new faces, such as those of teachers who will act as socializing agents, depends on the child's abilities to regulate himself or herself in novel contexts. The entire family must also make necessary adjustments to the new friends, and parents of these friends who now play an active role in the life of their child. With many new faces, the need for accommodation to overall adjustments is apparent. The transition made by the preschool child, moving from having a very intimate, nurturing parent-child interaction to becoming a social butterfly, interacting with several peers and adults (Higgins & Parsons, 1983) is developmentally intriguing.

It is important to observe children interacting with their parents because parents are highly influential in their lives in so many areas (Belsky, 1984; Denham, Renwick, & Holt, 1991). Baumrind (1967) maintained that parenting style is an important factor to consider when examining interactions between children and their parents. Conclusions drawn from Baumrind's (1967) research provide a framework for classifying parenting styles. Her investigations were the first to drive home the idea of three distinctly different methods of parenting.

Baumrind (1967) examined a large group of parents interacting with their children, and was able to identify three distinct groups of parents. Within the large group there were parents who seemed to be quite uninvolved with their child and they were referred to as the permissive group of parents. Another group was observed as being highly controlling yet showed little nurturing in their interactions and they were labeled as authoritarian. The last group was moderately controlling and highly nurturing. This group was titled authoritative. A fourth parenting style was found in later research (Baumrind, 1971). These parents were classified as harmonious. When children of these parents were further studied, their daughters were found to be outstandingly competent, while the opposite was true for the sons of these parents; an interesting finding from a group labeled with such a positive term.

In addition to observing parent-child interactions, Baumrind also used warmth and control scales to classify parental styles. Using a simple warmth and control scale in conjunction with parent style ratings, she found that authoritative parents tended to be characterized as scoring high on a warmth scale and moderate on a control scale (Baumrind, 1971). Authoritarian parents rated low on the warmth scale and high on the control scale, while permissive parents rated low on warmth and on control. In keeping with Baumrind's idea of authoritative parents being highly warm and moderately controlling, Carter and Welch (1981) described authoritative parents as being helpful as they encouraged activities while also giving their children reasons behind their decisions. Examination of the participants in this study showed that, married males were either authoritarian or permissive while females and single parents in general tended to be authoritative. As the age of the parents increased, they tended to be less authoritative and when the number of children in the family increased, the parents shifted from being authoritative to being more authoritarian.

When warmth and control was combined with measures of the parent's attachment, Cohn, Cowan, Cowan, and Pearson (1992) found that those parents who were insecure as children were less warm than parents who were secure. Further findings showed that parents with an insecure attachment provided an environment with very little structure and showed very little warmth toward their children. Additionally, children of insecure parents were significantly less warm toward their parents. In conclusion, parent's attachment formation in childhood appears to affect their own methods of parenting.

Another point of view on parenting style comes from Belsky (1984), who proposed a process model of parenting that has been used to help determine individual differences in parental functioning. The model presumed that parental functioning was multi-fold so that external factors such as stress, a common experience during parenthood, could influence the functioning of the parent. Sources of stress can influence parenting both directly or indirectly and may be detrimental to the psychological well-being of the parent. In turn, the psychological well-being of the parent greatly influences the parent-child relationship. A depressed, stressed, or psychologically ill parent does not have the mind set required for nurturing a child; hence, both parent and child suffer.

The interactions a child has with his or her parents will influence his or her interactions with peers (child-peer interactions). From their parents, young children learn social skills. These learned skills are partially reflected in the child's interactions with his or her peers. For example, positive emotion within the parent-child dyad tends to predict developmentally appropriate emotional and behavioral competence with peers (Denham, Renwick, & Holt, 1991) and thus, possibly provides evidence of the learned skills.

In addition to influencing a child's interactions with his or her peers, parent-child interactions are also associated with the child's interactions with other adults and, in turn, the ways in which others interact with the child. Hinde, Tamplin, and Barrett (1991) drew several conclusions concerning these associations. Preschool girls who were hostile toward their mothers, were also hostile toward their peers and other adults. This group of girls also experienced more hostile behaviors from peers. Boys who experienced hostility from their peers tended to have very controlling mothers. Therefore, it is not only within the family that parental influence is evident, but also within other interactions.

The preschool stage is a critical age for encouraging positive peer interactions. The opportunity for peer interactions at this age is mainly regulated by mothers. Mothers who promote a secure relationship tend to be responsive to their child's growing interest in peers (Leiberman, 1977). The idea of learning through peer interaction was examined by Lewis and Rosenblum (1975) who believed that peers provide the opportunity for expanding and elaborating communicative, aggressive, defensive and cooperative skills. Peer experience is considered to promote peer competence through a direct social learning process. Those children who had extensive peer experience tended to interact more verbally with others (Leiberman, 1977). Large amounts of new responsibilities became those of the mother. In addition to being the regulator of the when and where of the child's social time, mothers need to understand their child enough to place him or her in comfortable situations. They must also allow the child enough space to experience novel situations and be concerned for their child's health and safety, since the child's social system is growing at a rapid pace and new interactions with new people are constantly occurring.

It is through the natural formation of internal working models that children learn to interpret their world (Bowlby, 1969). Therefore within the parent-child relationship, a child with a developing internal working model perceives the behaviors of his or her parent, accepts the behaviors, internalizes the behaviors, and interprets the behaviors of the parent as appropriate. As mentioned earlier, there is a chance when the child becomes a parent he or she may then model these behaviors to her or his own children.

Mead (1934) believed that social skills develop through the opportunities for role playing which are provided by peer interactions. A psychological term for role playing is modeling. Many skills and abilities that one acquires throughout life are learned through the process of modeling or imitating others' behaviors. This concept, suggested years ago by Mead (1934), ties together several aforementioned ideas. In many instances, behaviors emitted by parents are later reflected in the child's interactions with their peers. According to Mead, the child is seen as imitating the parent who plays the part of a role model.

The idea of imitation within interactions is part of Bandura's Social Learning Theory which holds that one learns through example. From the Social Learning perspective, Bandura (1977) explained psychological functioning in terms of the continuous reciprocal relationship that exists between personal and environmental determinants. This process of reciprocal interactions acts to regulate the individual. To understand this reciprocal relationship it is important for one to take a close look at the social roles played by each of the individuals. The ability to distinguish between the "modeler" (who behaves first), and the "modelee" (who imitates the observed behavior) is critical for understanding the direction of the learning behavior. A mother's belief that her child acquires skills through observation tends to increase when the child is between 4 and 6 years old (Mills and Rubin, 1992). Therefore, it is expected that the mothers of preschool age children will make great efforts to model appropriate behavior in the presence of their preschool age children. It is important, with many changes occurring in the life of a preschool child, for the caregiver to understand the functions and importance of a model. Most parents, in the hope that their children will imitate the behaviors that they observe, want their children to be around, "modelers" who have strong morals, a strong self-esteem, and a desire to contribute to the world. If parents are instructed about modeling, it may increase the likelihood that their child or children will be exposed to positive models.

There is a difference between interactions with peer-acquaintances and interactions with peer-friends that appears in children as early as the preschool years. At this age a child's concept of friendship is changing. The frequency of a play session and the type of association the child has with other children is the most popular means used to define a friend (Berndt, 1981). Children are more interactive (Brachfeld-Child & Schiavo, 1984; Matsumoto, Haan, Yabrove, Theodorou, & Carney, 1986;), are more likely to share their favorite foods (Birch & Billman, 1986), and use more fantasy play when playing with a friend as opposed to a peer acquaintance (Roopnarine & Field, 1984). In a modified prisoner's dilemma game Matsumoto et al. (1986) found that 4- and 5-year-old children interacting with a good friend were more likely to work towards a mutually satisfying solution and solve the conflict in a morally sensitive way. When playing, friends also tended to be more competitive than they were when playing with acquaintances (Berndt, 1981; Brachfeld-Child & Schiavo, 1984).

Sibling interactions are unique and very different in comparison to peer interactions. Researchers have shown that children with older siblings perform better on role-taking measures than children with younger siblings (Light, 1979). Parents play a significant role in sibling interactions. Mothers who intervene in a sibling conflict and who tend to control the older child more often than the younger child, produce more aggression and conflict between the siblings (Volling & Belsky, 1992). This finding would be unlikely in a friendship interaction because the parent has control of only half of the situation - her own child. There are several differences found when comparing sibling-child interactions and friendship-child interactions. These differences may arise from the uniqueness of the sibling relationship.

Family size is another variable to consider when investigating relationships between children and their siblings. The more children there are in a family, the greater the chances of success on a particular task for any one single child from that family (Perner, Ruffman, & Leekman, 1994). This finding suggests that those children with numerous siblings may have somewhat of a cognitive advantage.

Siblings, both younger and older play a very important role in the development of the family. Older siblings may act as a communication system which lies between the parent and the younger child. The older child understands both the younger sibling and the parent. This allows for clear communication of the younger child's needs to the parents, hence increasing the likelihood that there is a mutual understanding and that the needs of the younger child are being understood and met. Older siblings have had the opportunity to experience the world to a greater extent than the younger siblings. The valuable knowledge which they have obtained as a result can be shared with the younger siblings, thus placing the younger child at an advantage in comparison with the children who do not have older siblings. Older siblings also act as a model from whom younger siblings can learn and benefit. Children with younger siblings play the role of a teacher while interacting with their younger brother or sister, thus assisting the older child in the development of social competence (Denham, 1986). All who are involved in an interaction may benefit in some way. It is not only the learner who takes knowledge from the invested time spent with the teacher, but the individual who plays the teacher role may also benefit. Therefore those with the opportunity to interact should do so with the sense that they will obtain something of value from the interaction.

Parent-child interactions and peer, friend, sibling-child interactions provide important opportunities for learning many skills and acquiring various abilities. Teaching and learning opportunities occur within these interactions. As Vygotsky stressed, intellectual progress is a result of social interaction (Vygotsky, 1978, as cited in Perner, Ruffman, & Leekam, 1994, and Pratt, Green, MacVicar, & Bountrogianni, 1992). Vygotsky theorized the idea of the zone of proximal development (ZPD). It is within the 'zone' that those aspects of task functioning exist which a person can perform with support and guidance, but not yet on their own space (Bruner, 1984; Pratt et. al., 1992).

Wood (1980) extended the idea of ZPD and substituted the term 'scaffolding'. Scaffolding is the process by which an adult expert assists a child in performing a task. Optimally the teacher obey's the 'contingent shift rule' (CSR), another term developed by Wood (1980). This rule specifies that the teacher should provide either more or less support, depending on the success or failure of the learner on the task. Pratt, Kerig, Cowan, and Cowan (1988) found that teaching within the region of sensitivity (RSI), the region in which the abilities of the child are best matched with the instructions of the teacher, was associated with more success by children during the tutoring. In addition, Pratt et. al. (1988) found that children were more successful when tutors obeyed the contingent shift rule.

Parent styles seem to influence a parent's ability to assist or scaffold their child on a task. There is an association between the use of the RSI and CSR and authoritative parenting styles. Authoritative parents are more likely to focus interventions contingent on success or failure. As Baumrind found, it is the authoritative parent who is moderately controlling and very warm and nurturing.

Authoritative parenting styles are linked to high academic achievement in school (Pratt et. al, 1992). It appears that these parents use just enough power to engender compliance in the child who, in turn, internalizes parent-induced rules and standards. Yet these parents avoid the over use of power that would make the child attribute his actions to external factors (Lepper, 1982 as cited in Pratt et. al., 1992). This trend results in children who have a high self concept. Authoritative parents are more likely to be rated as good teachers and have children with high achievement scores in math (Pratt et. al. 1992). More authoritative parent-child dyads are successful at completing a task and show appropriate scaffolding skills (Pratt, Kerig, Cowan & Cowan, 1988). Clearly, parenting style is a critical variable when discussing successful scaffolding abilities within the parent-child dyad.

An area of increasing popularity is the study of peer teachers. Peer teachers are of interest because peer communication seems to be as effective, if not more so than adult communication with children. Both adults and children are able to teach children small games and skills. When compared to adult teachers, children use more non-verbal skills and make reference to specific items as they teach a peer of the same age (Ellis & Rogoff, 1982). There is a difference between friends and acquaintances on peer-peer teaching tasks. Learners taught by friends are rated as more playful and friendly than those taught by acquaintances. Furthermore, older children give more comprehensive instructions than younger children. When peer-teachers are compared to learners, learners take the first turn, issue commands, and change the rules (Brachfeld-Child & Schiavo, 1984). It is obvious that there is an abundance of information that remains undisclosed, keeping one from fully understanding the teaching abilities of a child. However, there is evidence showing the great potential of peer-teachers, and it is important that new research takes us into the world of the child.

Humans are social creatures, continually developing from birth to death. It is within our social interactions that we learn and develop into contributing individuals. It is important to explore these social interactions and link them to the developing individual in order to allow for a better understanding of one's developmental trajectory.

Hypotheses

The purpose of the present study was to uncover some of the existing relationships between parent-child interactions and child-peer interactions. In general, the observed behaviors in the child-peer interactions were expected to be a mirror image of the parent-child interactions. It was expected that there would also be some relationships between variables within each dyadic interaction. There were four specific hypotheses:

1. Parent scaffolding behavior and parent sensitivity was to predict their child's scaffolding behavior and sensitivity on the task in the child-peer interaction. Specifically, parent global scaffolding rating and parent average sensitivity were hypothesized to be positively correlated with global scaffolding rating and average sensitivity of their child.

2. Positive verbal reinforcement emitted by the parent was expected to predict whether their child used positive verbal reinforcement. It was predicted that the frequency of positive verbal reinforcement observed in the parent-child dyad would be positively correlated with the frequency of positive verbal reinforcement observed in the child-child dyad. Highly reinforcing parents were expected to be good scaffolders and more task sensitive. Parental positive verbal reinforcement was expected to be positively correlated with the global scaffolding rating assigned to the parent and parental sensitivity.

3. Children who have high positive verbal reinforcement scores were believed to be better scaffolders and more sensitive. Like their parents, it was anticipated that there would be a high positive correlation between the children's positive verbal reinforcement scores, and both their child's global scaffolding and average sensitivity ratings.

4. Measures of parental warmth and control are important indicators of parent style. An authoritarian style is associated with scores revealing high control and low warmth. An authoritative parenting style reveals high warmth and moderate control. A permissive parenting style exhibits low control and moderate warmth.

It is these parenting styles which are evident during a parent-child dyadic interaction. It was predicted that the measures of warmth and control would be significantly correlated with global scaffolding rating, average parent sensitivity, and frequency of verbal reinforcement.

Method

Participants

Participants in the present study were 44 English speaking preschool children from middle class families. All of the children were presently participating in a longitudinal laboratory study based in Southern Ontario. The mean age of the participants was 5.568 years.

Procedures and measures

In a three minute segment the child was instructed by the researcher to duplicate a Lego design which had been placed in front of the child. The Lego model was designed on the basis of pretesting which was difficult enough to pose a challenge to some children, but also within the capacity of most children. Once a short period of time had lapsed and the child had the opportunity to examine and attempt the task on his or her own, the parent was instructed to enter the room and give assistance to the child as needed. The segment was cut off at a three minute time limit because many of the subjects completed the task and at this point there was no further parent-child interactions occurring.

Coding of the parent-child and peer-child interactions

The parent-child and peer-child interactions were coded by using a scale consisting of seven levels of interaction. The first level, rated as 0 involved an interaction that was not oriented toward the completion of the task and was titled "no intervention". For example, the greeting given when the teacher entered the room or any reinforcing remarks made by the teacher. A level rating 1 was a "general verbal start". Here the teacher would get the learner started on the task, for example "you do one". Level rating 2 was "verbal hints" in which the teacher would say something like "what about another block". Level 3 was reached when the teacher gave the learner "specific verbal instructions". Level 4 was more specific where the teacher "identified the materials OR placement" of the block to be used next. Level 5 was similar to the previous level, but the "person specified BOTH material and placement" of the next move. Level 6 was the highest level possible in which the teacher "demonstrated" the next progression. The original scale constructed by Wood (1975) consisted of six levels. Pratt, Kerig, Cowan, and Cowan (1988) revised the scale by inserting an additional level of level 2 (verbal hints).

An example of an interaction and explanation to illustrate the procedure may be useful. When the teacher made a comment such as "you need a green block", the child would or would not proceed to comply with the suggestion of the teacher. A response of some sort would end the coding of that particular interaction. According to the coding scheme, the comments given by the teacher in this interaction would be coded as a "3".

The success "1" or failure "0" on the task was also accounted for and coded after each interaction was scored. If the child responded accordingly, thus choosing the green block, this was considered a "success". If the child did not choose a green block, but responded in a different manner illustrating that he or she did not understand the instructions of the teacher, did not hear the teacher, or possibly choose to ignore the teacher, the interaction was considered a "failure".

Sensitivity rating

A sensitivity rating was assigned to each interaction. The sensitivity rating tended to bridge the gap between one interaction and the subsequent interaction. To calculate a sensitivity rating, each single interaction was compared to the previous single interaction. Using the illustration from above, optimally the child would choose the green block; this would be considered a success and coded with a "1". The teacher would than be expected to interact at a lower, less invasive level during the next interaction; a level less than a "3" to allow the child to apply the abilities that were supported by the teacher in the previous interactions. The sensitivity rating could range from -1 to 1. If the teacher did not move up or down the scale of the levels of interaction in the theoretically correct direction, their sensitivity was rated as -1. A teacher who remained at the same level regardless of the response of the child, was given a sensitivity rating of 0. A teacher who moved according to the success or failure of the task by the child, one who was "sensitive", was be given a rating of 1. The sensitivity rating created a bridge between each pair of interactions, however pairs were not bridged; each pair was considered a separate entity, a clean start.

Coding positive verbal reinforcement

The number of positive, encouraging comments given by the teacher following each interaction was recorded in a tally style. These comments were considered positive verbal reinforcement throughout the 3 minute segment. Each positive comment was given a single tally point.

Coding global scaffolding rating (GSR)

At the end of the observation of each participant, a global scaffolding rating (GSR) was given to each child-teacher dyad. This rating consisted of the average of three scores which were each out of 5. The rates answered the following statements: (1) the teachers ability to instruct; (2) the teachers ability to keep the subject focused on the task at hand; and (3) the amount of the Lego design that was replicated.

Warmth and control ratings (parent-child dyads only)

The National Longitudinal Survey of Child (NLSC) was administered to the parents through mail as a portion of another study. It is an extensive paper-and-pencil questionnaire that asks several questions about many aspects of family life. Twelve questions were taken from the NLSC questionnaire to be used as a warmth and control rating for the parents. The idea behind this rating was to get a sense of parenting style for each participant.

Results

Three raters independently coded 40% of the sample. The ratings of the three observers' global scaffolding rating was assigned for both dyadic interactions (e.g., parent-child and child-child). The ratings were positively correlated ($r = .89$), and thus accounted for 79% of the variability. This is an acceptable level of reliability. An alpha level of .05 was used for all statistical tests.

Hypothesis #1

Recall that hypothesis one stated the expectation that the two parent-child measures (global scaffolding and sensitivity) would predict the same child-child measures (global scaffolding and sensitivity). As seen in Table 15.1, the expected relationship was not found. Parent-child global scaffolding was very weakly correlated with child-child global scaffolding, $r = .12$, $p<.05$. Interestingly sensitivity revealed a negative relationship, $r = -.29$, $p< .05$. It seems that the more sensitive parents had less sensitive children. Since, the expected outcome was not found hypothesis one was not supported.

Hypothesis #2

The initial component of hypothesis 2 predicted a strong positive relationship between the frequency of positive verbal reinforcement emitted from the parent-teacher and the frequency of positive verbal reinforcement directed at the peer-learner from the child-teacher. The relationship between these two variables can be seen in Table 15.1, r = .36, p < .05. Those children who were more frequently positively verbally reinforced used more positive verbal reinforcement as teachers in this particular interaction. This finding was significant and thus provided support for hypothesis 2.

The second part of hypothesis 2 predicted that parents who were users of positive verbal reinforcement would also be good scaffolders and more task sensitive. As Table 15.1 shows, the relationship between these variables was strong. The correlation between verbal reinforcement and global scaffolding was both positive and significant, r = .34, p< .05. A second correlation indicated that there was a strong positive relationship between parental verbal reinforcement and parent sensitivity, r = .40, p<.05. The data provided support for this second part of hypothesis 2. Those parents who are highly reinforcing tended to be better scaffolders and were also more sensitive.

Hypothesis #3

The third hypothesis predicted that highly reinforcing children, like their parents, would be better scaffolders and would also be highly sensitive. This hypothesis was not entirely supported. As seen in Table 15.1, child verbal reinforcement showed a strong positive relationship with child global scaffolding, r = .31, p<.05. However, we failed to find any strength in the relationship between child verbal reinforcement and average child sensitivity. The children who emitted high frequencies of verbal reinforcement were good scaffolders revealing a general success. Sensitivity, which was more of a unit to unit measure, did not seem to be related to the frequency of the reinforcement in the child-child interaction. Highly reinforcing children were good scaffolders, but were not highly sensitive.

Hypothesis #4

It is possible that the use of the NLSC questionnaire was not a suitable measure for this variable. In Table 15.2, it is evident that the warmth and control measure did not correlate with scaffolding, sensitivity, or verbal reinforcement. However, the scales did reveal an interesting interaction. Although there was no main effect, 2 (age) by 2 (gender) ANOVA revealed a significant interaction, $F(1,34) = 4.436$, $p < .05$. It seems as the age of female participants increased, parental control also increased. Although not as extreme a change, the opposite was true for the males in the sample. As their age increased, the parents amount of control slightly decreased.

Discussion

The purpose of the present study was to compare two dyadic interactions. The first was as children interacted with their parents, and then the second was as the same preschoolers interacted with a peer whom they had chosen to bring to the laboratory. The importance of studying such interactions simply rests in the frequency with which interactions occur and the lifelong influence these interactions can have on an individual. Humans are social creatures with the ability to communicate and learn. In the eyes of many theorists, these interactions make up the person (Bandura, 1977; Bronfenbrenner, 1979).

When the observed interactions (parent-child and child-peer) are illustrated as two separate chains, one can say it is possible that the links between the chains are of interest to the author. Of the number of hypothesized links, the results show a single significant principal link between the two chains. Although there was no link between the parent-child interaction and child-peer interaction on global scaffolding and sensitivity, there was a prominent link, as predicted, on the reinforcement measure. Further analysis revealed an interesting finding about the two chains.

It seems that the parent reinforces the child for behaviors on the Lego task; then, this reinforcing behavior is modeled by the child in the child-peer interaction where the child plays the role of the teacher. This finding clearly illustrates what a Piagetian would refer to as deferred imitation, or the ability to act and imitate something one has observed at a later time.

Within the linkages of the child-peer interaction, reinforcement was found to be related to the child-peer global scaffolding rating. This finding was also found in the parent-child interaction. Parent-child reinforcement was related to the parent-child global scaffolding rating.

Parent-child reinforcement was related to parent-child sensitivity, showing that parents who remained within the region of sensitivity were also highly reinforcing. Parent-child reinforcement was also related to the global scaffolding rating. This finding was similar to that of Pratt, Kerig, Cowan, and Cowan (1988), who found a positive relationship between CSR and task success in their participants.

When parenting style was measured by the warmth and control ratings of the parent, as the age of the child increased, the parents became increasingly controlling with their daughters. In contrast, they became just slightly more lenient with their sons. However, there was no other relationships between warmth and control and any other variables. It is possible that using the NLSC questionnaire was not an accurate report of warmth and control.

Some results revealed relationships in the child-peer interaction which were almost identical to those in the parent-child interactions, while other findings were very different or opposite. Like the parent-child interaction, child-peer reinforcement and child-peer scaffolding were related, thus showing that those children who displayed extensive amounts of reinforcement tended to have higher global scaffolding scores.

There was no relationship between child-peer reinforcement and child-peer sensitivity. Although not all participants were insensitive, those who were may have been showing their egocentric personality. According to Piaget, preschoolers are unable to understand how another person feels and therefore they fail to adjust their degree of sensitivity as the needs of their friends change. However, there seems to be a determining variable for the level of sensitivity. This variable is length of friendship between the child and the peer. Longer friendships tended to result in lower sensitivity ratings. Possibly egocentrism is more prominent when the child is familiar with those around him or her.

Similar to the Wood and Middleton (1975) finding, child-peer sensitivity was related to success of the task. Those few children who remained within the region of sensitivity were teachers to peers who experienced more success on the task. Also having a longer friendship and playing with their best friend both resulted in higher task success. In conclusion, if long term friends are highly successful on the given task but are not 'taught' by a 'sensitive' friend, then the peer-teacher's sensitivity is not as crucial as his or her familiarity with the learner. This is an important idea to consider, especially at a time when peer tutoring is being studied and implemented in the education system.

There are some drawbacks of this study that need to be mentioned for future reference. First and foremost, a larger sample would increase the power of the research. It would be interesting to test the hypotheses with a parent pool of both mothers and fathers. As the study stands, it holds only two fathers and 44 mothers in the sample. Finally, it would have been beneficial to have a preschool measure of attachment to relate to the present data on parenting styles and parent-child interactions. Because the literature on attachment is so extensive, it would be an interesting variable to include in the area of parent styles and parent-child interaction.

Table 15.1   Correlations of three dominant measures in this study

	p-ch global scaffolding	ch-ch global scaffolding	p-ch average sensitivity	ch-ch average sensitivity	p-ch positive verbal reinforcement	ch-ch positive verbal reinforcement
p-ch global scaffolding	1					
ch-ch global scaffolding	.12	1				
p-ch average sensitivity	.11	.08	1			
ch-ch average sensitivity	-.00	.38	-.30	1		
p-ch positive verbal reinforcement	.34	.08	.40	-.03	1	
ch-ch positive verbal reinforcement	.17	.31	-.03	.03	.36	1

Table 15.2   Correlations between parental warmth and control scores and the three major measures (parents only)

	parent global scaffolding rating	parent average sensitivity	parental positive verbal reinforcement
warmth	.08	.06	.16
control	-.01	-.16	-.12

References

Bandura, A. (1977). Analysis of self-efficacy theory of behavioral development. *Cognitive Therapy and Research, 1,* 287-310.

Baumrind, D. (1971). Harmonious parents and their preschool children. *Developmental Psychology, 4,* 99-102.

Baumrind, D. (1967). Child care practices anteceding three patterns of preschool behavior. *Genetic Psychology Monographs, 75,* 43-88.

Belsky, J. (1984). The determinants of parenting: A process model. *Child Development, 55,* 83-96.

Berndt, T.J. (1981). The effects of friendship on prosocial intentions and behavior. *Child Development, 52,* 636-643.

Birch, L.L. & Billman, J. (1986). Preschool children's food sharing with friends and acquaintances. *Child Development, 57,* 387-395.

Brachfeld-Child, S. & Schiavo, R.S. (1984). Interactions of preschool and kindergarten friends and acquaintances. *The Journal of Genetic Psychology, 15,* 45-57.

Bronfenbrenner, U. (1979). Contexts of child rearing: Problems and prospects. *American Psychologist, 34,* 844-850.

Bruner, J. (1984). Vygotsky's zone of proximal development: The hidden agenda. *New Direction for Child Development, 23,* 93-97.

Carter, D. & Welch, D. (1981). Parenting styles and children's behavior. *Family Relations, 30,* 191-195.

Cohn, D.A., Cowan, P.A., Cowan, C.P., & Pearson, J. (1992). Mothers' and fathers' working models of childhood attachment relationships, parenting styles, and child behavior. *Development and Psychopathology, 4,* 417-431.

Denham, S.A. (1986). Social, cognitive, prosocial behavior, and emotion in preschoolers: Contextual validation. *Child Development, 57,* 194-201.

Denham, S.A., Renwick, S.M., & Holt, R.W. (1991). Working and playing together: Prediction of preschool social-emotional competence from mother-child interaction. *Child Development. 62,* 242-249.

Ellis, S. & Rogoff, B. (1982). The strategies and efficacy of child versus adult teachers. *Child Development, 53,* 730-735.

Higgins, E.T. & Parsons, J.E., (1983). Social cognitions and the social life of the child: Stages as subcultures. In E. T. Higgins, D.N. Ruble, & W.W. Hartup (Eds.), *Social Cognition and Social Development* (pp. 15-62). New York, NY: Cambridge University Press.

Hinde, R.A., Tamplin, A., & Barrett, J. (1991). Home correlates of aggression in preschool. *Aggressive Behaviour, 19,* 85-105.

Lepper, M.R. (1982). Social control processes, attributions of motivation and the internalization of social values. In E.T. Higgins, D.N. Ruble, & W.W. Hartup, (Eds.), *Social Cognition and Social Behaviour: Developmental Perspectives* (pp.294-332). Cambridge: Cambridge University Press.

Lewis, M. & Rosenblum, L.A. (1975) Introduction. In M. Lewis & L.A. Rosenblum (Eds.), *Friendship and Peer Relations.* New York: Wiley.

Lieberman, A.F. (1977). Preschoolers' competence with a peer: relations with attachment and peer experience. *Child Development, 48,* 1277-1287.

Light, P. (1979). *The development of social sensitivity.* Cambridge: Cambridge University Press.

Maccoby, E. & Martin, J.(1983). Socialization in the context of the family: Parent-child interaction. In P.H. Mussen (Ed.), *Handbook of Child-Psychology: Vol. IV.* New York: John Wiley & Sons.

Matsumoto, D., Haan, N., Yabrove, G., Theodorou, P., & Carney, C.C. (1986). Preschooler's moral actions and emotions in prisoner's dilemmas. *Developmental Psychology, 22,* 663-670.

Mead, G.H. (1934). *Mind, self, and society.* Chicago: University of Chicago Press.

Mills, R. & Rubin, K. (1992). A longitudinal study of maternal beliefs about children's social behaviors. *Merrill-Palmer Quarterly, 38,* 494-512.

Minuchin, P. (1985). Families and individual development: Provocations from the field of family therapy. *Child Development, 56,* 289-302.

Perner, J., Ruffman, T., & Leekman, S.R. (1994). Theory of mind is contagious: You catch it from your sibs. *Child Development, 65,* 1228-1238.

Pratt, M.W., Green, D., MacVicar, D. & Bountrogianni, M. (1992). The mathematical parent: Parental scaffolding, parenting style, and learning outcomes in long-division mathematics homework. *Journal of Applied Developmental Psychology, 13,* 17-34.

Pratt, M.W., Kerig, P.K., Cowan, P.A., & Cowan, C.P. (1992). Family worlds: Couple satisfaction, parenting style, and mothers' and fathers' speech to young child. *Merrill-Palmer Quarterly, 38,* 245-262.

Pratt, M.W., Kerig, P., Cowan, P.A., & Cowan, C.P. (1988). Mothers and fathers teaching 3-year-olds: Authoritative parenting and adult scaffolding of young children's learning. *Developmental Psychology, 24,* 832-839.

Ricci, C. & Selvini-Palazzoli, M. (1984). Interaction complexity and communication. *Family Process, 23,* 169-176.

Roopnarine, J.L. & Field, T.M. (1984). Play interactions in nursery school. In T.M. Field, J.L. Roopnarine, & M. Siegel (Eds.), *Friendships in normal and handicapped children* (pp. 89-98). Norwood, NJ: Ablex.

Volling, B.L. & Belsky, J. (1992). The contribution of mother-child and father-child relationships to the quality of sibling interaction: A longitudinal study. *Child Development, 63,* 1209-1222.

Vygotsky, L. (1978). *Mind in society: The development of higher psychological processes.* Cambridge, Mass.: Harvard University Press.

Wood, D. & Middleton, D. (1978). A study of assisted problem-solving. *British Journal of Psychology, 66,* 181-191.

16 Modern Approaches to Children's Cognitive Development

CAROL MILES

Introduction

Perhaps the most highly disputed general concept in the field of psychology is that of intelligence. This problem stems, in part, from intelligence's role as both a scientific, and a lay concept. Popular public opinion holds that intelligence refers to the capacity of an individual, and carries the interpretation that intelligence is an inherited, unchangeable characteristic. These ideas have lead to the expectation that a test of "real intelligence" should measure this unalterable capacity. None of the tests designed so far have been able to meet this ideal.

In contrast to this idealistic view of intelligence as a finite, measurable, unified quantity, intelligence has alternatively been defined as a family resemblance concept, meaning that it is a concept with no defining attributes but with prototypical instances, a hierarchical organization, and a stable correlational structure (Neisser, 1979). This implies that intelligence at different points in life may be conceptualized by different prototypes, hierarchical organization, and correlational structures (Siegler & Richards, 1982; Miles, 1998). This suggests, then, that the study of how children develop in areas of cognition commonly associated with intelligence is a primary endeavor for those interested in the explication of childhood development.

In pursuit of theorizing a framework from which to conceptualize and eventually measure the development of intelligence, the scientific community has created a variety of approaches to the study of intellectual development, and of the development of specific thought processes. Three of the most widely accepted, and rigorously promoted approaches to children's cognitive, or intellectual, development are described as the psychometric, Piagetian, and information processing approaches.

The psychometric approach provides a quantitative perspective on the growth of intellect, while Piagetian psychologists provide a qualitative perspective on these same phenomena. The information processing approach instead focuses on specific thought processes construed as components of intelligence: memory strategies, processing speed, transitive inference, analogical reasoning, counting, and a variety of problem-solving processes.

The definitions of these approaches indicate a current tension between the conceptualization of intelligence either as a consistent trait, or as a collection of loosely-related skills—theories which appear, on the surface, in distinct opposition to one another. The psychometric and Piagetian approaches emphasize unity among intellectual skills, whereas information processing tends to emphasize individual skills in isolation These differences are perhaps best illustrated by the primary factors which each of these approaches identify as comprising intelligence, and the models by which they construct these factors into an overall definition of intellectual ability and a blueprint with which one can follow a child's development.

A detailed description and evaluation of these three approaches could be, and indeed, has been, the topic of many lengthy volumes. Therefore, the current paper will focus on briefly defining each approach and outlining some of the research which has followed it, considering some of the instruments applied to individual assessment, and a comparison of the primary factors of intelligence as identified by the approach. A discussion of the similarities and differences within the approaches will then attempt to show that in many areas, the theories converge, joining to offer a more comprehensive model of intelligence than that offered by any individual approach.

The psychometric approach

The psychometric approach to intellectual development has as its goal the definition and quantification of dimensions of intelligence through the construction of valid and reliable measurement scales, and the collection of data aimed at defining individual differences. That is, this approach utilizes standardized instruments such as the Wechsler Intelligence Scales, or the Stanford-Binet scales, as well as many others, in order to quantify and study human intellectual capabilities and development.

Violato (1996) described the psychometric approach to intelligence as a product-oriented view, because the focus is on the scores obtained on intelligence tests intended to measure specific mental abilities. As psychologists are thereby attempting to assign a metric, or score, to psychological properties, the term psychometric is applied to the approach.

This perspective is based upon three underlying assumptions: (a) that the nature of intelligence can be effectively studied by examining individual differences, and that these differences are independent of the growth of the average level of intellectual functioning (McCall, 1981); (b) that mathematical techniques, such as factor analysis, can elucidate the structure of mental abilities; and, (c) that the development of assessment instruments which effectively measure intellectual abilities is as important a goal as building the theories themselves. This final assumption points to the pragmatic side of psychometrics, which has been useful when theoretical notions of intelligence become bogged down in rhetoric, as psychometricians have been able to continue on in the development of reliable, valid, predictive tests of intellectual ability (Gardner & Clark, 1992).

Theoretical considerations of the psychometric approach

Historically, two camps have formed among psychometric theorists: those who promoted a general-factor ("g") theory of intelligence (Spearman, 1927) and those who espoused a multiple-factor theory (Guilford, 1967 and 1985; Kaufman, 1975; Wechsler, 1939). Another point of contention which has been debated since the beginning of the field of psychometrics has been the nature of the tests which best measure intelligence. Some original theorists, such as Galton (1883) and Cattell (1890) believed that this could be most effectively accomplished by analyzing only simple components, testing physical abilities, and simple sensory discriminations—combining these to yield an index of overall intelligence. Others, however, such as Binet (Binet & Simon, 1916) and Thurstone (1938) believed that a more direct approach was appropriate (Violato, 1996). These theorists argued that in order to properly assess intellectual abilities, complex processes such as judgment and reasoning should be measured. While the physical, sensory approach quickly lost favor to the more popular higher-level processes approach, especially with the advent and subsequent popularity of the Binet scales (Binet & Simon, 1916), study of these sensory components has recently been taken up with considerable interest by information processing theorists (Kranzler, 1997; Riccio, Cohen, Hall & Ross, 1997; Tiholov, Zawallich & Janzen, 1996) .

The study of the psychometric properties of intelligence has been facilitated primarily through the statistical technique of factor analysis originally developed by Spearman in 1904 (Spearman, 1927). Factor analysis utilizes any of several methods of analysis that enable large numbers of variables to be reduced to a smaller number, or "factors" or "latent variables" (Vogt, 1993). The development of factor analytic techniques provided a way of generating and testing theories of mental ability, through the calculation of intercorrelations between specific test scores, and the subsequent identification of an underlying set of unobserved factors which are fewer in number than the tests themselves. Factor analytic theories have become more sophisticated and diverse, especially with the advent of computer programs to perform complex statistical analyses, causing few theorists to doubt the existence of some form of general intelligence, or, at least, a set of interrelated group factors. Nevertheless, theorists continue to differ on which level the analysis is most important. Gardner and Clark (1992) warned that caution is advised in interpreting factor analytic studies, as it is sometimes difficult to separate the portions of a factor analytic theory which is dictated by the data from the mathematics, and its inherent limitations. In recent years, however, new factor analytic techniques such as confirmatory factor analysis and structural equation modeling have reduced these problems considerably (Bentler, 1995; Byrne, 1996; Joreskog & Sorbom, 1989).

Regardless of the statistical methods employed, results of factor analysis are strongly dependent on decisions made by the researcher while conducting the analysis, on the tests chosen to be analyzed, the subject bases, and many other situation-specific factors. As well, when factors are identified, indicating clusters of tests loading on the same factor, it is up to the researcher to give the factor a label, and this process is purely arbitrary. Models to be factor analyzed should, therefore, be well grounded in theoretical construct prior to initial factor analysis (Bollen, 1989).

Psychometric models of the structure of intelligence

One of the earliest models of intelligence heralded by the popularization of factor analysis was that of Thurstone (1938), whose theories are considered the beginning of modern intellectual research (Violato, 1996). Thurstone expanded on Spearman's (1927) more limited conception of a single general intelligence factor labeled *g*, and developed an instrument intended to assess seven primary mental abilities: verbal comprehension, verbal fluency, number, spatial visualization, memory, reasoning, and perceptual speed. Thurstone saw each of these capabilities as equal and independent of one another—not related to any general intelligence factor.

J. P. Guilford (1967, 1985) proposed a more complex model of intelligence incorporating many more factors than that proposed by Thurstone. His three-dimensional structure of intellect model (SOI) classified mental activity in three dimensional space: (1) mental operation, (2) contents, and (3) products of operations on content. Each of these classifications then had several subclassifications (five contents subclassifications: visual, auditory, symbolic, semantic and behavioral; six products subclassifications: units, classes, relations, systems, transformations, and implications; and five operations subclassifications: cognition, memory, divergent production, convergent production, and evaluation). By this structure, Guilford's (1967) model proposed a total of 150 mental abilities. Because of the detailed specificity of the mental abilities proposed by Guilford's SOI model, challenges have been directed toward the theory by several authorities in the field of psychometrics (Carroll, 1993; Cronbach & Snow, 1977; Eysenck, 1967; Vernon, 1961). Several of these authors have questioned the model's applicability and testability as it related to human intellect, specifically because of its complex nature. While Guilford's SOI has been generally rejected overall as a plausible model of the structure of human intelligence, certain constructs have been further explored and incorporated into other areas of psychological research. An example of this is the application of Guilford's concept of "divergent thinking" to research on creativity (Violato, 1996).

The theory of fluid and crystallized intelligence was proposed by Raymond Cattell in 1943. Cattell (1943) posited two separate types of mental abilities. Fluid intelligence was interpreted as an individual's basic, biological capacity, whereas crystallized intelligence represented the products of acquired knowledge, and acculturation. Fluid intelligence, therefore, was seen to be primarily genetically determined—the capacity of the individual to note complex relationships, synthesize information, and solve problems. Crystallized intelligence was defined as more culturally determined, and represented knowledge and content collected by an individual from the environment through life experience and education (Horn & Cattell, 1966).

Kaufman (1975) conducted an extensive factor analysis of those factors measured by the Wechsler Intelligence Scale for Children—Revised, concluding that the structure of intelligence, as measured by this instrument, consisted of a Verbal factor, a Performance factor, and a Freedom-from-Distractibility factor. The factor structure of this scale has since been subjected to perhaps the most widespread series of analyses of any scale in the history of intelligence testing (Kaufman, 1993). In its newest iteration, the Psychological Corporation, publishers of the WISC-Third Edition, contend that factor analytic study has yielded a four factor structure for this newest version of the world's most administered intelligence test (Wechsler, 1991). These factors are reported, and interpreted, to be Verbal, Performance, Freedom-from-Distractibility, and Processing Speed. Many authors, however, have challenged both the existence and the labeling of the third and fourth factors, contending that they are neither grounded in empirical theory nor statistical justification (Kamphaus, Benson,

Hutchinson, & Platt, 1994; Keith & Witta, 1997; Miles, 1998; Riccio, et al., 1997). The structure of intelligence, then, as measured by the Wechsler scales, remains controversial. Most authors, however, concede the existence of a Verbal factor and a Performance factor, and several contend that the structure is hierarchical, with general intelligence, or "g" as a second factor on which the other, more specific factors depend (Keith & Witta, 1997; Miles, 1998).

John Carroll (1993), through an extensive re-analysis of an almost exhaustive collection of all factor analytic studies ever published in the field of human intellect (incorporating, in total, over 10,000 individual studies), proposed a hierarchical model of intelligence incorporating specific factors at three strata. His three strata were labeled narrow (stratum I: a general intelligence, or g factor), broad (stratum II: fluid and crystallized intelligence, memory ability, auditory ability, and cognitive speediness), and general (stratum III: a number of factors including general sequential reasoning, lexical knowledge, free recall, spatial scanning, sound lateralization, numerical facility, mental comparison speed, as well as many others). In this theory, a culmination of research of some of the best known psychologists (Spearman, Thurstone, Cattell, Guilford) is presented in one comprehensive theory resulting from a synthesis of thousands of previous factor analytic studies (Carroll, 1993; Violato, 1996).

Howard Gardner's (1983 and 1993) theory of multiple intelligences is in direct opposition to models containing a single factor or g. Gardner identified seven distinct intelligences which he described as being totally independent from each other. These distinct intelligences were labeled linguistic, logical-mathematical, spatial, musical, bodily-kinesthetic, interpersonal and intrapersonal. Gardner's theory is substantively different than those of Spearman, or Carroll, who proposed that abilities are organized hierarchically, or function together to produce an overall intellectual effect. Instead, Gardner's theory proposed that different modules of intelligence are governed by distinct portions or modules of the brain, requiring the individual identification of each location in the brain governing each module. Gardner allowed that it may be possible that some higher order control may govern these modules but, unlike the factorial theories, maintains that each module functions totally independently of the others. Gardner's theory differed from others previously outlined in that it was not based on any form of factor analytic or other statistically advanced study. It was also based only on the study of exceptionally talented individuals, not on sampling of normal populations, and due to this theory's lack of specificity, it is seen as difficult, or impossible, to disconfirm (Kline, 1991).

As is apparent from the above-described models, factorial models have been the focus of the majority of psychometric research in the area of human intelligence. As both computer technologies and statistical techniques become more sophisticated, it can be expected that these and other models may become more precise, and often more complex, offering increasingly detailed theories regarding the relationships among the factors of human intellect. An example of this is the current research indicating a hierarchical structure of intelligence, with three or more first order factors, all influenced by a general intelligence factor ("g") (Carroll, 1993; Keith & Witta, 1997; Miles, 1998: Siegler & Richards, 1982).

Integral to the psychometric approaches to intellectual development are the test instruments on which these approaches are based. This approach involves the administration of standardized tests, and the analysis of the results to determine, through complex statistical analysis, the factor structure inherent in the development of human intellect. Many hundreds of different standardized tests, along with a few very widely-administered ones, The Wechsler Intelligence Scale for Children—Third Edition (WISC-III) (Wechsler, 1991), The Stanford-Binet: Fourth Edition (SB:FE) (Sattler, 1988), The Kaufman Assessment Battery for Children (K-ABC) (Kaufman & Kaufman, 1983) and the Bayley Scales of Infant Development (Bayley, 1969) are employed every day by researchers, as well as practitioners in the fields of counseling as well as educational psychology. The results of these tests provide the data from which much can be learned regarding the development of human intelligence. The statistical analysis of the psychometricians, however, only yields information regarding the individual tests or abilities that can be said to be statistically related. Identifying the constructs which underlie these factors (e.g., Verbal Intelligence, Perceptual Organization, Crystallized Intelligence, Sequential Processing), requires considerable interpretation, applying what is currently accepted and published regarding the theory of human development. It is only in the combination of the statistical findings and theoretical frameworks that cohesive, accurate factor structures can emerge.

The Piagetian approach to intellectual development

One of the most widely-accepted and rigorously-researched and adapted cognitive developmental theories was that of Jean Piaget (1950, 1971, 1974), who was one of the first researchers to describe and popularize behavioral evidence for a theory of development characterized by several distinctly different stages from early childhood through adolescence. Underlying Piaget's conception of cognitive development as a series of qualitatively different stages, was that these stages were paralleled by the physical development of the human brain. The four decades of research into Piaget's theories that ensued resulted in some corroborating, some challenging and yet other researchers' revising Piaget's original model. Bjorklund and Harnishfeger (1990), Case (1985), Nelson (1991), Pascual-Leone (1970) and Spelke (1991) were just a few of the researchers offering revised versions of this seminal model of stage-related cognitive development. Most theories of cognitive development proffered since Piaget's publications indicate a paradigm of gradual cognitive development characterized by several more or less distinct, qualitatively different stages of intellectual development which predict increasing capacities for attention, memory, language manipulation, and complex reasoning (Hallett & Proctor, 1996; Peterson, 1994).

While psychometric approaches seek to quantify intellectual skills, and identify individual differences, the Piagetian approach is more concerned with qualitative aspects of intelligence, and the establishment of universal, invariant patterns of major transitions. Perhaps the most distinct difference between the two approaches can be seen through the types of data collected and analyzed in each. While psychometricians generally focus on the number of correct answers achieved by the subject, Piagetians are more interested in the number, and types, of errors made during test completion.

According to Piaget (1950; 1971), the development of cognitive processes is neither a direct function of biological development, nor a direct function of learning. Rather, it represents a reorganization of psychological structures which results from the interaction of the individual as he/she interacts with the environment.

Piaget proposed that two inherent tendencies mediate interactions with the environment: Organization is the combination of two or more separate schemes into one higher-order, integrated scheme. Schemes are individual structures that produce changes in cognitive development—such as those involved in comprehending the concept of time. Adaptation contains two complementary processes: assimilation and accommodation. Assimilation is a process of taking in information and experiences and allowing them to fit into schemes or concepts already mastered. Accommodation is the process whereby existing cognitive behaviors and structures are modified to take into account new information and experiences.

Piagetian theory is hierarchical, covering an age group from infancy through adolescence. Concepts are seen to evolve from elementary forms in infancy, to more and more complex ones through childhood and into adolescence. Essential to Piaget's theory is the assumption that age-related consistencies in types of reasoning exist across these concepts, and these consistencies are indicative of qualitatively distinct developmental stages. Piaget's theory argues for the existence of four developmental stages or periods. Each stage is characterized by substages, and as development proceeds, different types of organization and adaptation occur.

At first, (sensorimotor period) children's mental ability is seen as being dominated by their perceptions. By about age 2, (preoperational period) the development of language has begun, and memory concerning actions and prior responses is available, although the child's thinking is still egocentric. By the age of 7 (concrete operations period), children's thought processes become more systematic, and concrete problem-solving skills are developing. Finally, by 11 years (formal operations period) of age, the child can construct theories and make logical deductions without having had direct experience with the concept.

Transitions from stage to stage are seen as being mediated by the accommodation and assimilation processes, which are seen as continuous, as well as by equilibration—the primary mechanism of stage transition. This developmental model sees mental organization operating as a unified set of structures, which include rules of transformation, is self-regulating, and changes with age, producing new, higher levels of organization, and increasing in complexity as levels increase.

While the intention of conventional Piagetian study has not been, traditionally, to identify or predict any form of general factor of intelligence, Carroll's (1993) work has shown the possible utility of some of the reasoning tasks in this area. The relation of these factors to Inductive, Sequential, and Quantitative Reasoning factors, as previously established, is unclear, but Carroll posited that there is sufficient evidence to suggest that Piagetian reasoning factors load substantially on one or more higher level factors (Fluid, Crystallized, or General Intelligence). Reasoning tasks are said to load on the second- or third-order (higher) factors due to the factorial complexity of these tasks, which generally involve many elements.

Proponents of the Piagetian approach have generally not worked within a quantitative/factor analytic framework, choosing instead to pursue study of the qualitative features of human development with theories of concrete stages. Some limited factor analytic work has however, allowed many of the Piagetian tasks to be included with the framework of several psychometric theories of intellectual development.

The information processing approach

Most cognitive researchers agree that general intelligence (g) reflects not only a person's knowledge of the world, but also more basic skills for processing information which do not depend on the knowledge of content (Carroll, 1993; Hallett & Proctor, 1996; Kranzler, 1997). In recent years, a great deal of research in the field of intellectual development has been directed toward the isolation of these basic skills, and to determining the extent of their relationship with traditional psychometric measures, and Piagetian theory (Blanco & Alvarez, 1994; Case, 1985; Miles, 1998; Peterson, 1994).

Perhaps the greatest weakness of the Piagetian and psychometric approaches is that they do not address the specific processes involved in intellectual performance. This is where the information processing approaches make their major contribution (Siegler & Richards, 1982). At present, the information processing perspective appears to be dominating the study of cognitive development. The majority of researchers are using at least some concepts, methods, and interpretations that are drawn from an information processing perspective (Kail & Bisanz, 1992; Matarazzo, 1992; Violato, 1996).

Information processing conceptions of intelligence concentrate on the way that an individual mentally represents and processes information. These models categorize mental processes in terms of the different operations performed on this information. Human cognition is conceived of as occurring in a series of discrete stages, with information received being operated on at one stage, and then passed on as input to the next stage for further processing. Mental processes are described as being comprised of specific covert cognitive behaviors that transform and manipulate information between the time it enters as some form of stimulus and the time a response is selected by the individual. (Torgesen, 1979).

While the current interest in pursuing the study of cognitive development from an information processing perspective has led to a diverse "family" of theories (Kail & Bisanz, 1992), most theories do encompass of common framework, which was described by Swanson (1985) as:

> The information processing framework assumes that a number of component operations or processing stages occur between a stimulus and a response. It is assumed that all behavior of a human information processing system is the result of combinations of these various processing stages. Typically, two theoretical components are postulated in information processing analysis: a structural component, which defines the constraints of a particular processing stage (e.g. sensory storage, short-term memory, long-term memory), and a functional component, which describes the operations of the various stages. Of particular

interest in the area of intelligence are functional components or strategies that must be performed if a task is to be successfully completed (p. 257).

Kail and Bisanz (1992) list four core assumptions that they contend are common to all current theories of information processing. A brief description of these assumptions will delineate the basic theory underlying information processing approaches.

The first of these assumptions is that cognitive phenomena can be explained and described by way of mental processes and representations that intervene between observable stimuli and responses. That is, information processing theorists assume that information is internally represented in symbolic form, and manipulated by real-time mental processes. Researchers, then, seek to identify what types of information are represented and how information is coded and organized. As well, they attempt to identify specific processes and how they are organized in a coherent, functional system. These processes have been likened to those of the information processing components of computers—interpreting symbolic information, performing operations on this interpreted information, and emitting a response—and the analogy has prevailed throughout the language and models describing information processing (Kail & Bisanz, 1992).

The second core assumption is that a relatively small number of elementary processes underlie all human cognitive activity. Acts of knowing can be decomposed into distinct, component processes, which themselves can be decomposed even further. Cognitive activities can, therefore, be studied on many different levels, and lend themselves well to the statistical techniques of factor analysis. While there is still little agreement on the actual number of these most basic underlying processes, or even their exact nature, it is the goal of information processing research to identify them (Kail & Bisanz, 1992).

That individual processes operate "in concert," is the third core assumption (Kail & Bisanz, 1992). It is a primary goal of research to understand how fundamental processes are combined and organized to produce performance on various tasks. It is also generally assumed that higher levels of organization may have properties that are qualitatively different from those of the lower-level operations. To fully understand cognitive performance, then, information processing theorists strive to first identify the most basic components of the cognitive system, and then identify their various interactions.

Kail and Bisanz's (1992) last core assumption is that cognitive development occurs by means of self-modification. Information processing theories are comprised of descriptions of how a system of processes and coded information interact, to account for observed performance. In contrast to the emphasis on environmental intervention in Piagetian theory, the primary focus in information processing is placed on internal factors, rather than external ones. When growth and development occur within these structures, information processing theorists again look to internal factors. This approach does not deny the importance of environmental events, but sees the information processing system as having to eventually encode, store, index, and process information from the environment.

While the preceding assumptions are shared by most information processing theories, the theories themselves vary greatly in the phenomena investigated, the level of analysis used, and the properties of cognition postulated and studied. At the simplest level, however, all information processing theorists seek to explain relations between observable stimuli (input) and observable responses (output), by describing mechanisms enabling activities intervening between input and output. Complete models incorporate specific mechanisms for all cognitive activities, including perceptual mechanisms for encoding information, processes for manipulating and storing information, processes for selecting and retrieving stored information, and processes that decide among alternative actions. As well, complete models specify how information is organized, sequenced, and represented internally. Models which incorporate learning and development have the additional components of describing how information processing changes over time, and identifying characteristics of the system and its environment that could alternatively enable or constrain change.

Assessment of information processing abilities

Information processing researchers use a variety of analytic methods to test theories of how the human cognitive system functions. Emphasis is placed on analytically decomposing tasks into their components, and trying to infer how the cognitive system must operate in order to deal with each component.

Patterns of response latencies or reaction times can give evidence about the sequential timing of information processing. Verbal reports, as is used in Piagetian research, may reveal conscious plans and strategies used during problem solving. Eye-movement data can offer information about the subject's attentional patterns, and inferences about functioning can be made from what the subject remembers and forgets about information presented. As in Piagetian research, analysis of patterns of correct answers and errors over a set of tasks is used to assess the nature and development of a child's knowledge and reasoning (Flavell, 1985).

Neuropsychological test batteries have been employed by information processing researchers, in order to assess cognitive and perceptual-motor abilities. The most common of these batteries are the Halstead-Reitan Neuropsychological Test Batteries and the Reitan-Indiana Neuropsychological Tests Batteries (Reitan & Wolfson, 1985), and the Luria-Nebraska Neuropsychological Batteries (Golden, 1987). While predominantly testing a variety of perceptual-motor tasks, these tests are not independent of intellectual functioning, but include reasoning and other cognitive tasks which have been shown to be significantly correlated with other measures of intelligence (Sattler, 1988).

Neurophysiological measures of development

There is accumulating evidence of a statistically significant correlation between differences in individual's scores on traditional measures of Spearman's such as the Binet scales, Wechsler scales, and Raven's matrices (Raven, Court & Raven, 1986) and direct and indirect measures of biological indices theoretically related to speed of information processing (such as Inspection Time, Reaction Time, Average Evoked Potentials, Glucose Metabolism, Myelination, Dendritic Branching, Nerve Conduction Velocity). Matarazzo (1992) predicted that with rapidly advancing technologies, some of these biological indicators will become valid, acceptable measures of what has been measured by the traditional IQ tests. He predicted that along with the traditional IQ test items, primarily measuring verbal and performance capabilities, other new types of test items, tapping reaction time, and other physiological measures of mental processing speed as measures of "g", will emerge. These measures, in conjunction with neurophysiological development, may add considerably to the explication of developmental changes in children's cognition, and serve well in the illustration of the compatibility of psychometric and information processing theories of intellectual development.

Thatcher, Walker, and Guidice (1987) reported significant correlations between brain growth spurts, and the emergence of new Piagetian stages of cognitive development. This research was interpreted by neuroscientists as indicating that the brain develops in an extremely regular fashion, and that bursts of maturation in its physical structure as well as higher cognitive functioning are the outcome of closely-related and well-synchronized neurophysiological processes (Peterson, 1994).

Reported correlations between cognitive development and rate of brain growth (Hallett & Proctor, 1996; Thatcher, et al., 1987) are consistent with a resources perspective of cognitive development. Speed of mental processing, for example, is a common index of mental efficiency (Tiholov, Zawallich & Janzen, 1996). This measure is based on the assumption that the speed at which children can process information affects the amount of information they can process within a given period of time.

Case (1985) suggested that regular increases in processing speed may be interpreted as reflecting developmental differences in the mental resources available for cognitive processing, which are a function of maturational changes in the central nervous system.   Several authors have proposed that these mediating changes in speed of processing may be caused by the formation of myelin (Bjorklund & Harnishfeger, 1990; Case, 1985; Dempster, 1985; Hallett & Proctor, 1996; Matarazzo, 1992).

Produced by glial cells, myelin is the fatty sheath surrounding nerve cells, which eventually covers and insulates the axon, and facilitates rapid impulse transmission from neuron to neuron. Myelinated axons fire more rapidly and efficiently than unmyelinated fibers.   Churchland and Sejnowski (1992) reported that generally the transmission velocity for myelinated axons is 10 to 100 meters per second, compared with a speed of about 1 meter per second for unmyelinated axons. True maturity of the central nervous system cannot be considered complete until the myelination process has fully developed, usually by the mid-teens (Hallett & Proctor, 1996).

Other physical maturation functions of the brain have also been linked with cognitive development. Hallett and Proctor (1996) presented a comparison of brain growth, brain metabolism of glucose, myelination, increasingly complex dendritic branching patterns, communication milestones, and cognitive development (from a Piagetian perspective), indicating that certain Piagetian stages were associated with certain events in neurophysiological development.

How the psychometric, Piagetian, and information processing approaches relate to each other

In contemplation of the previous descriptions of the theories, measures, and proposed factors inherent in each of the three approaches, critical relationships among all become apparent. Rather than attempting to define, or compare, the approaches in terms of differences, the following section will attempt to delineate the ways in which all of the approaches can fit together and contribute to a more thorough understanding of the development of children's intelligence.

The relationship between the Psychometric and Piagetian approaches

While the goal of Piagetian assessment is to discover the nature of mental organization at successive age levels, and provide information regarding concrete stages, psychometric assessment aims to define and quantify the distinctive dimensions of intelligence which may assist in quantifying individual differences. The two approaches are not in direct opposition, but share several similarities, and complement each other in several ways.

Both approaches accept that intelligence is determined to some extent by genetic influences, and both accept that there is a significant maturational influence on intellectual development. As well, both Piagetian and psychometric research employs primarily non-experimental, often correlational methodology in attempting to measure mental functions that children or adults are expected to have developed by certain ages. Both theories contend that the majority of intellectual development has occurred by late adolescence (Sattler, 1988). The results of the non-experimental analyses from both approaches are used to predict intellectual behavior outside of the test situation.

The approaches do differ significantly, however, in several distinct ways. Whereas psychometric theorists assume that tested intelligence is randomly distributed in a given population, with the distribution following a normal curve, Piagetian theorists assume that there are factors which give development a definite, non-random direction. Piagetian theorists assume that mental growth is qualitative, presupposing significant differences in younger children's compared with older children's thinking. As well, Piagetians are concerned with intra-individual changes occurring throughout development, while psychometricians concern themselves with inter-individual differences.

The two approaches also differ on their perceptions of the course of mental growth. Piagetian theorists view mental growth as the formation of new mental structures and the emergence of new mental abilities, while psychometric theorists view this growth as a curve, from which the amount of intelligence at any age can be predicted by the intelligence at any preceding age.

Lastly, Piagetian researchers view genetic and environmental factors as interacting in a functional and dynamic manner in order to produce regulatory control over mental activity. Conversely, psychometricians assume that genetic and environmental contributions to intelligence can be statistically separated, and thus measured (Sattler, 1988).

Psychometricians generally agree that the general intelligence factor that is present in all tests of mental ability appears in its purest forms on tests of generalization and abstraction. For Piagetians as well, the essence of intelligence lies in the individual's reasoning capacities. Piagetians have been more specific in their descriptions of these abilities, and define them in terms of mental operations which have the general properties of mathematical groupings, and the specific properties of reversibility (Elkind, 1974). Nevertheless, both approaches could be described as sharing the common view of intelligence through the rational nature of mental ability.

Studies have found correlational evidence of relationships between Piagetian and psychometric scales of intelligence in infant, pre-school, and school-age populations (Carroll, 1993). There appears to be a general factor common to Piagetian tasks and standard intelligence tests, although there is an element of uniqueness to these tasks which leads to inconsistent results from these studies of an underlying factor between Piagetian and psychometric measures of intelligence. In concert, the two methods allow the study of both the quantitative developmental changes that individuals experience, and the qualitative differences described by these quantitative changes.

The information processing approach's relationship to the other two

The information processing approach is fundamentally different in that it is not phenomenological in nature, and because it does not rely on the principles of conscious experience for explanation (Kail & Bisanz, 1992). The approach can be characterized as an effort to map relations between input (stimulus) and output (response). Unlike the earlier, rudimentary stimulus-response theories, however, it is the primary goal of information processing to describe in detail (albeit through a vast number of differing models) the interactions between the components of information processing between the original input and final output. Psychometric theories attempt to identify abilities that vary among individuals and that determine how individuals respond differently to input. Piagetian theorists attempt to describe relations between input and output in terms of logical, mathematical formulations. From an information processing perspective, these approaches fail to specify how the mapping function between input and output is carried out in real time (Kail & Bisanz, 1992), and these theorists attempt to specify how stimuli are manipulated and transformed, in sequence, to produce a particular response.

The other two approaches are not irrelevant to information processing. Insights, findings, and concepts can be generated within these approaches and can be incorporated at different levels into information processing theories. Hunt (1980) described how psychometric theories and findings have contributed significantly to information processing research on individual differences. Hunt concluded that these individual differences could be identified as: Basic Functions, Choice of Strategy, and Attentional Resource Allocation. All of these factors are, to a greater or lesser extent, implicit in the factors previously identified in psychometric theories. As well, the choice of strategy factor, very specifically, relates to Piagetian concepts. Hunt indicated that an exploration of studies employing models such as the fluid and crystallized intelligence theory, which examine the information processing correlates of psychometric tests should aid in advancing our understanding of the relationship between psychometric and information processing theories.

Information processing cannot be defined as a unified approach, but rather a diverse group of theories which have in common the interest in discovering the mental processes involved in cognitive behavior and functioning. Some theorists follow a route similar to that of the Piagetian tradition, most notably the neo-Piagetians (Case, 1985; Pascual-Leone, 1978), who have sought more detailed explanations of the cognitive processes involved in the developmental concepts unfolding within the stages. Established psychometricians (Carroll, 1993), have attempted, often through factor analysis, to identify and quantify the mental processes which underlie the identified factors of general intelligence, and to assess the contribution of these processes to general intelligence. In this pursuit, Carroll identified a three strata theory of cognitive abilities that recognizes abilities classified as narrow, broad, and general strata. This theory provides a framework through which correlations between psychometric variables and information-processing variables, and even some Piagetian variables, can be interpreted.

Conclusion

The psychometric, Piagetian, and information processing approaches have each yielded useful findings in the search for explication of children's cognitive development. None of these approaches has proven to be a panacea, perhaps because the optimal integration of these approaches has not yet been discovered. The relative fragmentation of the approaches may not be undesirable, however, just as there is often no single exemplar of a concept, there may be no single approach that is ideal for studying all aspects of the complex factors of human cognitive development. Each approach has developed procedures for selecting which aspects of intellect on which to focus, which analytical procedures to employ, and which representational languages are most appropriate. Each approach may be said to be optimal for the study of certain aspects of cognitive development.

As has been demonstrated here, however, the approaches converge in their addressing the development of intelligence more often than they diverge. With the current emphasis on the measurement of specific neurophysiological functioning, the information processing approach is lending new insight into the physiological as well as cognitive bases underlying the other two approaches. The Piagetian approach offers a more qualitative framework from which to view and assess the products of children's intellectual development from a holistic perspective. Psychometric evaluation strives to create and improve testing instruments which allow for the valid and reliable measurement of individual differences in intellectual capabilities, as well as attempting to provide an overall definition and measurement of general intelligence. It is, then, not within any one of these individual approaches that the developmental psychologist should seek to find the "answer" to the structure of children's cognitive development, but rather by the appreciation of, and application of all three approaches. It is only in this way that a more complete explication of the intricacies of a child's intellectual development can be sought.

References

Bayley, N. (1969). *Bayley scales of infant development: Birth to Two Years*. San Antonio, TX: Psychological Corporation.

Bentler, P. M. (1995). *EQS: Structural equations program manual*. Los Angeles, CA: BMDP Statistical Software.

Binet, A. & Simon, T. (1916). *The development of intelligence in children*. Baltimore, Maryland: Williams and Wilkins.

Bjorklund, D. & Harnishfeger, K. (1990). The resources construct in cognitive development: Diverse sources of evidence and a theory of inefficient inhibition. *Developmental Review, 10*, 48-71.

Blanco, M.J. & Alvarez, A.A. (1994). Psychometric intelligence and visual focused attention: Relationships in nonsearch tasks. *Intelligence, 18*, 77-106.

Bollen, K. A. (1989). *Structural equations with latent variables*. New York, NY: John Wiley & Sons.

Byrne, B.M. (1994). *Structural equation modeling with EQS and EQS/Windows: Basic concepts, applications, and programming*. Thousand Oaks, CA: Sage.

Carroll, J.B. (1993). *Human cognitive abilities*. Cambridge, England: Cambridge University Press.

Carroll, J. B. (1997). Commentary on Keith and Witta's hierarchical and cross-age confirmatory factor analysis of the WISC-III. *School Psychology Quarterly, 12*(2), 108-109.

Case, R.(1985). *Intellectual development: Birth to adulthood*. New York: Academic Press Inc.

Cattell, J. M. (1890). Mental tests and measurements. *Mind, 15*, 373-380.

Cattell, R. B. (1943). *The measurement of adult intelligence.* Psychological Bulletin, 40, 153-193.

Churchland, P. S. & Sejnowski, T. J. (1992). *The computational brain.* Cambridge, Massachusetts: Bradford Books.

Cohen, J. (1959). The factorial structure of the WISC at ages 7-6, 10-6, and 13-6. *Journal of Consulting Psychology, 23*, 285-299.

Cronbach, L. J. & Snow, R. E. (1977). *Aptitudes and instructional methods: A handbook for research on interactions.* New York, NY: Irvington.

Dempster, F. N. (1985). Short-term memory development in childhood and adolescence. In C. J. Brainerd and M. Pressley (Eds.), *Basic processes in memory development: Progress in cognitive development research.* New York, NY: Springer.

Elkind, D. (1961). Children's discovery of the conservation of mass, weight, and volume: Piaget replications. *Journal of Genetic Psychology, 98*, 219-227.

Elkind, D. (1974). Piagetian and psychometric conceptions of intelligence. In R. Landrum & D. Kuhn (Eds.), *Stage theories of cognitive and moral development: Criticisms and application.* Cambridge, Mass.: Harvard University Press.

Eysenck, H. (1967). Intellectual assessment: A theoretical and experimental approach. *British Journal of Educational Psychology, 37*, 81-98.

Flavell, J.H. (1985). *Cognitive development.* Englewood Cliffs, NJ: Prentice-Hall.

Frank, G. (1983). *The Wechsler Enterprise: An assessment of the development, structure and use of the Wechsler tests of intelligence.* New York, NY: Pergamon.

Galton, F. (1883). *Inquiry into human faculty and its development.* London: Macmillan.

Gardner, H. (1983). *Frames of mind: The theory of multiple intelligences.* New York: Basic Books.

Gardner, H. (1993). *Multiple intelligence: The theory in practice.* New York, NY: Basic Books.

Gardner, M.K. & Clark, E. (1992). Psychometrics and childhood. In R.J. Sternberg & C.A. Berg (Eds.), *Intellectual development.* Cambridge, England: Cambridge University Press.

Glutting, J.J., McGrath, E.A., Kamphaus, R.W., & McDermott, P.A. (1992). Taxonomy and validity of subtest profiles on the Kaufman assessment battery for children. *The Journal of Special Education, 26*, 85-115.

Golden, C. J. (1987). *Luria-Nebraska Neuropsychological Battery: Children's Revision.* Los Angeles, CA: Western Psychological Services.

Guilford, J. P. (1967). *The nature of human intelligence.* New York: McGraw Hill.

Guilford, J. P. (1985). The structure-of-intellect model. In B. B. Wolman (Ed.), *Handbook of intelligence.* New York: Wiley.

Gutkin, T. B. & Reynolds, C. R. (1981). Factorial similarity of the WISC-R for white and black children from the standardization sample. *Journal of Educational Psychology, 73*(2), 227-231.

Hallett, T. & Proctor, A. (1996). Maturation of the central nervous system as related to communication and cognitive development. *Infants and Young Children, 8,* 1-15.

Horn, J. & Cattell, R. B. (1966). Refinement and test of the theory of fluid and crystallized intelligence. *Journal of Educational Psychology, 57,* 253-270.

Hunt, E. (1980). Intelligence as an information processing concept. *British Journal of Psychology, 71,* 449-474.

Joreskog, K.G. & Sorbom, D. (1989). *LISREL 7 Users Reference Guide.* Mooresville, IN: Scientific Software.

Kail, R., & Bisanz, J. (1992). Information processing. In R.J. Sternberg & C.A. Berg (Eds.), *Intellectual development.* Cambridge, England: Cambridge University Press.

Kamphaus, R. W., Benson, J., Hutchinson, S. & Platt, L. O. (1994). Identification of factor models for the WISC-III. *Educational and Psychological Measurement, 54,* 174-186.

Kaufman, A. S. (1975). Factor analysis of the WISC-R at 11 age levels between 6 ½ and 16 ½ years. *Journal of Consulting and Clinical Psychology, 43,* 135-147.

Kaufman, A. S. (1978). WISC-R research: Implications for interpretation. *School Psychology Digest, 8,* 5-27.

Kaufman, A.S. (1993). King WISC the Third assumes the throne. *Journal of School Psychology, 31,* 345-354.

Kaufman, A.S. & Kaufman, N.L. (1983). *K-ABC: Kaufman assessment battery for children.* Circle Pines, MN: American Guidance Service.

Keith, T. Z. & Witta, E. L. (1997). Hierarchical and cross-age confirmatory factor analysis of the WISC-III: What does it measure? *School Psychology Quarterly, 12*(2), 89-107.

Kline, P. (1991). *Intelligence: The psychometric view.* London: Routledge.

Kranzler, J. H. (1997). What does the WISC-III measure? Comments on the relationship between intelligence, working memory capacity, and information processing speed and efficiency. *School Psychology Quarterly, 12*(2), 110-116.

LoBello & Gulgoz (1991). Factor analysis of the Wechsler Preschool and Primary Scale of Intelligence—Revised. *Psychological Assessment. 3* (1), 130-132.

Matarazzo, J. D. (1992). Psychological testing and assessment in the 21st century. *American Psychologist, 47,* 1007-1018.

McCall, R.B. (1981). Nature-nurture and the two realms of development: A proposed integration with respect to mental development. *Child Development, 52,* 1-12.

Miles, C. A. (1998). *Structural Equation Modeling of the WISC:III: A developmental approach.* Doctoral dissertation, University of Calgary: Calgary, Alberta, Canada.

Neisser, V. (1979). The concept of intelligence. *Intelligence, 3,* 217-227.

Nelson, C. A. (1991). Pioneering research challenges accepted notions concerning the cognitive abilities of infants. In C. Raymond, *The chronicle of higher education,* Jan. 23.

Pascual-Leone, J. (1970). A mathematical model for the transition rule in Piaget's developmental stages. *Acta Psychologica, 32*, 301-345.

Pascual-Leone, J. (1978). Compounds, confounds, and models in developmental psychology: A reply to Trabasso and Foellinger. *Journal of Experimental Child Psychology, 26*, 18-40.

Peterson, R. W. (1994). School readiness considered from a neuro-cognitive perspective. *Early Education and Development, 5*, 120-139.

Piaget, J. (1950). *The psychology of intelligence.* London, England: Routledge & Kegan.

Piaget, J. (1971). *Biology and knowledge: An essay on the relations between organic regulations and the cognitive processes.* Chicago, Illinois: The University of Chicago Press.

Piaget, J. (1974). *The language and thought of the child.* New York, NY: The New American Library.

Posner, M. I., Inhoff, W. R., Friedrich, F. J. & Cohen, A. (1987). Isolating attentional systems: A cognitive-anatomical analysis. *Psychobiology, 15*, 107-121.

Post, K.R. & Mitchell, H.R. (1993). The WISC-III: A reality check. *Journal of School Psychology, 31*, 541-543.

Raven, J.C., Court, J.H. & Raven, J. (1986). *Manual for Raven's Progressive Matrices and Vocabulary Scales (1986 edition with US norms).* London, England: Lewis.

Reitan, R. M., & Wolfson., D. (1985). *The Halstead-Reitan Neuropsychological Test Battery.* Tucson, Arizona: Neuropsychology Press.

Riccio, C. A., Cohen, M. J., Hall, J., Ross, C. M. (1997). The third and fourth factors of the WISC-III: What they don't measure. *Journal of Psychoeducational Assessment, 15*, 27-39.

Sattler, J.M. (1988). *Assessment of Children.* San Diego, California: Jerome M. Sattler.

Siegler, R.S. & Richards, D.D. (1979). Development of time, speed, and distance concepts. *Developmental Psychology, 15*, 288-298.

Siegler, R.S. & Richards, D.D. (1982). The development of intelligence. In R.J. Sternberg (Ed.), *Handbook of human intelligence.* Cambridge, England: Cambridge University Press.

Spearman, C. (1904). General inte'ligence objectively determined and measured. *American Journal of Psychology, 15*, 201-293.

Spearman, C. (1927). *The abilities of man.* New York, NY: Macmillan.

Spelke, E. S. (1991). Pioneering research challenges accepted notions concerning the cognitive abilities of infants. In C. Raymond (Ed.), *The Chronicle of Higher Education*, Jan. 23.

Stankov, L., Roberts, R., & Spilsbury, G. (1994). Attention and speed of test-taking in intelligence and aging. *Personality and Individual Differences, 17* (2), 273-284.

Swanson, H.L. (1985). Assessing learning disabled children's intellectual performance: An information processing perspective. In K.D. Gasow (Ed.), *Advances in learning and behavioral disabilities.* Greenwich, CT.

Thurstone, L. L. (1938). Primary mental abilities. *Psychometric Monographs, 1.*

Tiholov, T. T., Zawallich, A. & Janzen, H. L. (1996). Diagnosis based on the WISC-III processing speed factor. *Canadian Journal of School Psychology, 12*(1), 23-34.

Torgesen, J.K. (1979). What shall we do with psychological processes? *Journal of Learning Disabilities, 12*, 514-521.

Vernon, P. A. (1961). *The structure of human abilities* (2nd Ed). London: Meuthen.

Vernon, P. A. (1983). Speed of information-processing and general intelligence. *Intelligence, 7*, 53-70.

Violato, C. (1996). Intelligence: the psychometric perspective. In C. Violato (Ed.), *Child Development*, Calgary, Alberta: Detselig.

Vogt, W. P. (1993). *Dictionary of statistics and methodology: a nontechnical guide for the social sciences.* Newbury Park, California: Sage.

Wechsler, D. (1939). *Measurement of adult intelligence.* Baltimore, Maryland: Williams and Wilkins.

Wechsler, D. (1991). *Manual for the Wechsler Intelligence Scale for Children - Third Edition.* San Antonio, Texas: Psychological Corporation.

Section IV:

Attachment

17 Attachment Security to Mother, Father, and the Parental Unit

MARK GENUIS AND CLAUDIO VIOLATO

Abstract

The purpose of the present study was to test for a relationship between security of childhood attachment (secure/insecure) to parents individually and parents as a unit. A total of 138 adolescent subjects (mean age = 14.54, 64 males and 74 females) participated in a retrospective-longitudinal study in which their childhood attachments (prior to 10 years of age) to each parent and the parental unit were assessed. Subjects reported the same attachment type (secure/insecure) to each parent individually as well as to the parental unit. That is, children who were insecurely attached to one parent were significantly more likely to be insecurely attached to the other parent as well as the parental unit. These findings are consistent with other empirical findings in this area of study.

Attachment security to mother, father, and the parental unit

This study was conducted within the context of attachment (Bowlby, 1982) which draws on several lines of thought to create an integrated body of knowledge about human emotional and behavioral development. Bowlby (1982) was primarily interested in real life experiences in childhood and their impact on child development (Ainsworth, 1991; Ainsworth & Bowlby, 1991). One of the claims of attachment theory is that attachment security is a reflection of the relationship between the child and her or his parents. It is further postulated that attachment security is an important determinant of childhood, adolescent, and adult behavior (Bowlby, 1982). Substantial evidence for these claims has accumulated (Genuis, 1995; Isabella, 1993) and attachment theory has attracted considerable attention within both the research and clinical communities. A recent focus of the development of attachment has been the comparative manner in which children attach to both of their parents (Fox, Kimmerly, & Schafer, 1991). That is, do children attach similarly (secure/ insecure) to mother and father or are the attachment patterns independent?

The present study was designed to assess a sample of both normal and clinical adolescents on demographic, life history, and psychological variables. The current analysis was conducted within the context of a larger empirical study (for details see Genuis & Violato, 1997). The Adolescent Attachment Survey (AAS) (Genuis & Violato, 1997) is a questionnaire designed to retrospectively assess childhood attachments from adolescent subjects. The AAS has demonstrated adequate psychometric properties and was therefore deemed appropriate for the present use. Within this instrument is a specific assessment of attachment to mother and father separately, as well as to both parents as a unit.

Method

Adolescents completed the AAS along with the Parental Bonding Instrument (Parker, Tupling, & Brown, 1979) and the Youth Self-Report (Achenbach, 1991). The measure of attachment was therefore based on a questionnaire administered to each adolescent individually. Furthermore, all questionnaires were completed in the home of the subjects, in a room of the participant's choice. The researcher was situated in an adjacent room for the time that the participants completed the questionnaires and was available in the event that the subject decided to discuss or disclose any personal or other information.

The AAS consists of eight scales that were developed to assess a unique developmental experience that affected or was associated in some way with childhood attachment. As well as assessing childhood attachment, the AAS included a number of questions about childhood experiences. The scales included attachment, child sexual abuse, child physical abuse, regular separation from parents prior to full-time school, long-term separation from parents (more than 6 months), and permanent separation from parents. The AAS is made up of a total of 177 questions, each loading on one of the scales, designed to obtain a description of each subject, information on variables identified in published research to be related to attachment, and to obtain a measure of attachment.

Cronbach alpha reliabilities of each subscale exceeded .80, indicating adequate internal consistency of the AAS subscales. Content validity was secured for the AAS by including variables based on a thorough search of the published literature on attachment, as well as consulting individually with developmental and clinical psychologists. Concurrent criterion-related validity is another form of validity evidence examined for the AAS. The attachment scale of the AAS has been found to be correlated with the care and overprotection scales of the PBI, and with each of the internalizing, externalizing and total problems scales of the YSR. Attachment as measured with the AAS is positively and significantly correlated with care as measured by the PBI (r=.21, p<.05), as well as negatively and significantly correlated with overprotection (r=-.25, p.01). Moreover, secure attachment has been found to be significantly related with each of the internalizing [x2(1)=10.30, p<.01], externalizing [x2 (1)=18.28, p<.001], and the total problem scores [x^2(1)=5.63, p<.05], thereby demonstrating a significant relationship between attachment type in childhood and clinically maladaptive behavior in adolescence. Significant findings between overall attachment and attachment to each parent separately, insecure attachment and clinically maladaptive behavior, and between each strand of attachment and overall attachment, care, and overprotection, therefore provide evidence for the concurrent criterion-related validity of the AAS.

Correlation coefficients (Pearson r) were calculated to examine relationships in the present study. Attachment to father was examined separately for any correlation with attachment to mother and the parental unit. Attachment to mother was likewise examined individually for any relationship with attachment to the parental unit. As six univariate tests were run, a significance level of p<.001 was employed to guard against Type I error.

Results

Analyses demonstrated that attachment to father was significantly related to attachment to mother (r=.36, p<.0001) and to the parental unit (r=.95, p<.0001). Attachment to mother was also significantly related to attachment to the parental unit (r=.43, p<.0001). An overall score of attachment was based on the addition of individual scores obtained from attachment to mother, father, and the parental unit. Analyses were conducted examining the relationship of attachment to each of mother and father with this overall attachment measure. Analyses demonstrated that attachment to father was significantly related to overall attachment (r=.97, p<.0001), attachment to mother was also significantly related to overall attachment (r=.54, p<.0001), and finally, attachment to the parental unit was significantly related to overall attachment (r=.98, p<.0001). The very high correlations (>.90) are, in part, a result of the individual parent attachment contributing to the overall attachment component. Even so, these are clearly significant correlations.

Discussion

The findings in the present study support those in previous investigations in that attachment to each parent was closely related to attachment with the other parent. Furthermore, the present information provides introductory evidence on the concept of the parental unit. It may be that children view their parents as a unit as well as or rather than two individuals. The present investigation is clearly exploratory in nature but provides a useful impetus for further empirical inquiry into the nature of attachment to both parents. Recent evidence explicating causal pathways of insecure attachment in childhood to psychopathology into adolescence (Genuis & Violato, 1994) demonstrates an urgent need for further understanding of the nature and development of secure and insecure attachment in childhood. Moreover, there is a need to conduct investigations aimed at more directly assessing the concordance of attachment classification to both mother and father, as well as to parental attachment classifications in various family structures.

References

Achenbach, T.M. (1991). *Manual for the Youth Self-Report and 1991 Profile.* Burlington, VT: University of Vermont, Department of Psychiatry.

Ainsworth, M.D.S. (1991). Attachments and other affectional bonds across the life cycle. In C.M. Parkes, J. Stevenson-Hinde, & P. Marris (Eds.), *Attachment across the life cycle.* London: Routledge.

Ainsworth, M.D.S. & Bowlby, J. (1991). An ethological approach to personality development. *American Psychologist, 46,* 333-341.

Bowlby, J. (1982). *Attachment and loss: Vol.1 Attachment.* (2nd Edition). London: Penguin Books.

Fox, N.A., Kimmerly, N.L., & Schafer, W.D. (1991). Attachment to mother/attachment to father: A meta-analysis. *Child Development, 62,* 210-225.

Genuis, M.L. (1995). Childhood attachment and adolescence. In C. Violato & L.D. Travis. (Eds.), *Advances in Adolescent Psychology.* Calgary: Detselig.

Genuis, M.L. & Violato, C. (1997). The adolescent attachment survey: The development and psychometric analyses of an instrument for assessing childhood attachment retrospectively from adolescence. Manuscript submitted for publication.

Genuis, M.L. & Violato, C. (1994). The role of childhood attachment in developmental psychopathology: A Latent variable path analysis. *Paper presented at the 55th Annual convention of the Canadian Psychological Association.* Penticton, British Columbia: Canada.

Isabella, R.A. (1993). Origins of attachment: Maternal interactive behavior across the first year. *Child Development, 64,* 605-621.

Parker, G., Tupling, H., & Brown, L.B. (1979). A parental bonding instrument. *British Journal of Psychiatry, 52,* 1-10.

18 Pilot Study of the Psychometric Properties of the Adolescent Attachment Survey (AAS)

MARK GENUIS, CLAUDIO VIOLATO,
ELIZABETH ODDONE-PAOLUCCI, STEPHANE ROBITAILLE,
AND DAWN MCBRIDE

Abstract

The purpose of the present pilot study was to determine the psychometric properties of the Adolescent Attachment Survey (AAS) and the Adolescent Attachment Survey - Parent Version (AAS-P). Attachment was defined as the desire for persons to seek and maintain proximity with their primary caregivers, both individually and together. Four measures were used in order to assess childhood attachment and current level and type of psychopathology. These measures included the AAS and AAS-P, the Parental Bonding Instrument, the Youth Self-Report Instrument, and the Child Behavior Checklist. Data was collected from a total of 53 male and female adolescents between the ages of 12 and 17 years, and each of their parents wherever possible. Adequate internal consistency, using Cronbach's Alpha was found for all of the variables used in the AAS. Criterion-related validity coefficients for the attachment scale in the AAS were also consistent and significant. The psychometric properties established for the AAS indicate that it is a valid and reliable instrument and can thus be used in the assessment of adolescent attachment patterns.

A pilot study of the psychometric properties of the Adolescent Attachment Survey (AAS)

Attachment theory is concerned with the development and organization of human emotions through the life span (Ainsworth, 1991). Based on the theory of natural selection, attachment theorists have posited that attachment behavior has survival value for the infant and/or child (Ainsworth, 1991). Within the first six months of life, infants are said to develop an intense affectional bond to their primary caregiver and experience varying levels of success in maintaining proximity to the primary caregiver. Attachment is defined as being strongly disposed to seek proximity to and contact with a specific figure, notably when frightened, tired, or ill (Bowlby, 1969). For a child to be securely attached to a caregiver that child must feel safe and secure in that caregiver's presence. Numerous variables have been identified as having an important influence on the development and maintenance of secure attachment relationships. One of the main elements is that of consistent, responsive, and appropriate care of infants and developing children by their caregivers.

A recent and essential focus for the development of attachment theory is that of the long-term (i.e., lasting into the teenage years) implications of attachment (Violato & Travis, 1995). Theorists and researchers have hypothesized that insecure attachment patterns in infancy and early childhood are strong predictors of maladaptive behavior and psychopathology in adolescence and adulthood (Ainsworth, 1991; Bowlby, 1969. Others, however, have proposed that early childhood attachments may be superseded by the effects of maturation and therefore are not central to long-term mental health (Lamb, 1984). This issue remains unresolved because, in part, there is currently a lack of instruments that allow for research examining the long-term effects of secure and insecure attachment. The present study was undertaken, therefore, to determine the psychometric properties of the Adolescent Attachment Survey (AAS) and the Adolescent Attachment Survey - Parent Version (AAS-P), thus enabling subsequent investigation into the substantive theoretical issues relevant to attachment theory.

Method

Participants

The present pilot study collected data from male and female adolescents between the ages of 12 and 17 years, and each of their parents wherever possible. The total sample of 53 volunteer participants were families living within one western Canadian (n=31) and one eastern Canadian (n=22) city. Permission was granted by the Roman Catholic Separate School Board to randomly select students who met the inclusion criteria for the study from four junior high and three senior high schools located in each of four quadrants of the western city. The randomly selected adolescents and their parents were then invited to participate in the present study via a letter, and a convenient interview time and place was arranged with those who agreed to participate.

Instruments

A brief discussion of each of the measures used to assess childhood attachment and current level and type of psychopathology follows. These measures included the AAS and AAS-P (Genuis, 1994), the Parental Bonding Instrument (PBI) (Parker, Tupling, & Brown, 1979), the Youth Self-Report Instrument, and the Child Behavior Checklist (CBCL) (Achenbach, 1991a).

Adolescent Attachment Survey (AAS) and Adolescent Attachment Survey-Parent Version (AAS-P). There are two versions of the Adolescent Attachment Survey (AAS); one for the adolescent interviews and one for the adolescent's parents. The version for each parent is identical but separate for the mother and father. The AAS consists of 377 items, while the AAS-P is comprised of 242 items. The questions are designed to obtain a description of each participant, information on variables revealed in the literature to be related to attachment, and to obtain a measure of attachment.

A total of 66 items comprised the *attachment scale*, with each of 22 items measuring attachment to mother, father, and the parental unit together. Words were selected from descriptions of relationships found throughout the literature and the choices were divided into two main segments: secure and insecure. The first eight words on the list were used to signify security; the remaining 13 words denoted insecurity. The responses provided by each adolescent were coded (two for each secure word chosen and one for each insecure word chosen) and then summed across mother, father, and both parents. These total scores were then compared and a cut off score was established to differentiate between secure and insecure attachment. The cut off score was arrived at as follows. The range of the total scores was from 99 (if participants selected only insecure words) to 330 (if participants selected only secure words). Several exploratory chi-square analyses were conducted to determine the optimum score which empirically maximized group separation (secure versus insecure). These results indicated that the majority of lower score attachment assessments were in the clinical range of the Youth Self Report (YSR), while a fifty-fifty split was found for the higher score attachment assessments. This finding was consistent between various cutoffs of 300 to 328.

As well as assessing childhood attachment, the AAS includes other scales assessing a variety of childhood experiences. Eight items comprised the *proximity seeking* scale, measured by items such as pride in success and accomplishments and expression of emotions. The *parental involvement* scale includes 26 questions about number of days the adolescent spends with his/her mother, father, and parents together, as well as the participant's perception of whether this amount of time is adequate or inappropriate. The *socioeconomic* scale is the final AAS scale, consists of 12 items, and includes questions about education and occupation level of parents, as well as whether the non-custodial parent financially contributes to the upbringing of the adolescent.

The AAS-P contains the same items as the AAS, excluding those from the proximity seeking scale.

The Parental Bonding Instrument (PBI). The second instrument used to assess childhood attachment was the PBI. The purpose of using the PBI was to evaluate the criterion-related validity of the attachment subscale of the AAS. The PBI, which contains 25 items rated on a 4-point Likert type scale was designed to measure self-reported care and overprotection given by parents as perceived by the adolescent. The PBI focuses on two principal underlying dimensions of parental characteristics: care versus indifference/rejection and overprotection versus encouragement of autonomy and independence. As discussed in previous papers (Genuis & Violato, 1997; Genuis, 1994), the PBI has evidence for reliability and some evidence of validity and was thought to be adequate for the present purposes.

Youth Self-Report (YSR). The YSR is a self-report measure which contains 118 behavior problem items and a social competence scale (Achenbach, 1991b). Originally developed by Achenbach and Edelbrock (1983) and later revised by Achenbach (1991b), the YSR, along with the CBCL was used in the present study for the purpose of assessing current levels and type of psychopathology demonstrated by adolescent subjects. Individual scale scores (withdrawn, somatic complaints, anxious/depressed, social problems, thought problems, attention problems, delinquent behavior, aggressive behavior, and for boys, self-destructive identity problems), externalizing and internalizing scores, and an overall total problem score are produced. Scores based on age and sex appropriate norms for externalizing, internalizing, total problems, and each of the specific behaviors are available. The YSR has adequate reliability and validity evidence (refer to Genuis & Violato, 1997).

Child Behavior Checklist (CBCL). The CBCL was used to cross-validate the information gathered from the subjects through the YSR. It is designed to obtain parents' reports of children's competencies and problems in a standardized format (Achenbach, 1991a). Numerous reports have documented adequate reliability and validity for the CBCL.

Procedure

Computers have been used effectively to gather data and conduct interviews in areas such as childhood sexual abuse, suicide risk, substance use disorders, mental status examination, and sexual dysfunction (Baskin, 1990; Violato & Genuis, 1992; Mezzich & Mezzich, 1988), and thus the AAS was programmed onto a Macintosh computer for the purposes of the present study. The use of computers to collect data was based on the design of Violato and Genuis (1992) where the questionnaire was programmed on to a computer and the participants interacted with the computer in order to complete one of the questionnaires. As in the Violato and Genuis (1992) study, sheets of paper were placed beside the computer for the participants to write more about particular questions or at any time they wished while they were completing the questionnaire. The average length of time of meeting per family was 90 minutes. Adolescents completed the AAS along with the PBI and the YSR, while the parents were administered the AAS-P and CBCL. These adolescents along with their parents completed the questionnaires at their residence, with each available participant working alone in a private room. The researcher was situated in an adjacent room for the time that the participant completed the questionnaire and was available in the event that the participant or parents decided to discuss or disclose any personal or other information.

Results

The results of the pilot study are reported in three subsections: (1) description of the sample, (2) instrument reliability, and (3) instrument validity.

Description of the sample

The description of the total sample is summarized in Table 18.1. The pilot study included 53 adolescent participants and the parents they had contact with. The adolescents ranged in age from 12 to 17 years. The mean age was 14.8 with a standard deviation of 1.5 years. Seventeen of the adolescents were male and 36 were female. The most common family structure type among the 53 participants was having parents married and living together (85%), followed by single parent family as a result of paternal death (6%), and having divorced parents (4%). Of the 53 adolescents, the majority were in grade 9 or 10 (25% and 23% respectively) and were Caucasian (93%).

Socioeconomic status was determined by using both mother and father's education and occupation level. This was divided into three categories: 1) entrepreneurial or professional, defined as a parent having his/her own business or working in a professional field such as law, medicine, teaching, and so on; 2) skilled labor, defined as electricians, plumbers, carpenters, and so on; and 3) unskilled labor or unemployed. The majority of adolescents had mothers who completed senior high school (21%) and who reported their occupation as managing their family (42%). Forty-three percent of the fathers reported having attended college or university and 49% were employed as skilled laborers.

Instrument reliability

The internal consistency of various sub-scales of the AAS listed in Table 18.2 was determined using Cronbach's alpha (1951). Cronbach's alpha was selected because of the presence of both dichotomous and non-dichotomous items within the AAS. Table 18.2 contains the values found for each subscale together with the corresponding number of items and participants analyzed. As can be noted, the internal consistency of each subscale exceeded .83. These high alpha values are an indication of the adequate internal consistency of the AAS subscales.

Instrument content and empirical validity

The variables included in the AAS were generated from a thorough search of the published literature on attachment. The variables were selected from the literature if they were demonstrated to have an empirical relationship with attachment. Variables were also included if they were reported in the literature as being theoretically associated with attachment with the relationship not yet being tested. The researchers also consulted individually with two developmental and two clinical psychologists. Each of these professionals had a Ph.D. and held a full-time academic position at the time of the study. All of these professionals agreed that the selected variables were appropriate for the purpose of the AAS.

Concurrent criterion-related validity was another form of validity evidence for the AAS. The attachment scale of the AAS was correlated with the care and overprotection scales of the PBI, and with each of the internalizing, externalizing, and total problems scales of the YSR. In the present pilot study, attachment as measured with the AAS was significantly and positively correlated with care as measured by the PBI (r=.73, p<.001). Attachment was significantly but negatively correlated with overprotection (r=-.57, p=.001). These findings support the criterion-related validity of the attachment scale in the AAS as it is meant to positively correlate with parental care as measured by the PBI and negatively with overprotection.

The internalizing scale of the YSR combines measures of withdrawn behavior, somatic complaints, and anxious/depressed feelings. The externalizing scale combines measures of delinquent behavior and aggressive behavior. Achenbach (1991b) reported that these groupings of scales reflected a distinction that had been detected through multivariate analyses. The total problem score is an amalgamation of each of the behavior scales on the instrument.

Attachment was negatively correlated with each of the internalizing ($r=-.18$, $p=.21$), externalizing ($r=-.50$, $p<.001$), and the total problem scores ($r=-.29$, $p<.05$) attained by participants. This finding demonstrates a significant relationship between attachment type in childhood (secure versus insecure) and clinically maladaptive behavior in adolescence. The pattern of results does converge and suggests further evidence for the criterion-related validity of the AAS as a measure of attachment. The pattern of findings from this pilot study indicates evidence for the validity of the attachment scale of the AAS.

Discussion

As little work has been done to assess the long-term effects of childhood attachment, and no adequate instrument had yet been developed, it was necessary to develop and pilot test an instrument aimed at assessing and examining the long-term effects of secure and insecure childhood attachment. The present pilot study was conducted to establish the psychometric properties of the AAS.

Adequate internal consistency, using Cronbach's Alpha, was found for all of the variables used in the AAS. Criterion-related validity coefficients for the attachment scale in the AAS were consistent and significant. The psychometric properties established for the AAS indicate that it is a valid and reliable instrument and can thus be used in the assessment of adolescent attachment patterns.

The results of the present research highlight the difficulty in determining an optimum score to empirically maximize group separation between insecurely and securely attached adolescents. While this may reflect a sampling bias given that none of the participants were recruited from a clinical facility, it may also point to an important underlying theoretical issue. It may be hypothesized that a nonlinear relationship exists between scores on the attachment scale and scores on the YSR. That is, it may be possible that those at the extreme low and high ends of the attachment scale are demonstrating insecure attachments (possibly indicative of "A" and "C" attachment types), whereas those at the mid-range scores are denoting secure attachments. This question should be addressed as the sample size and representativeness of the sample increases at various levels of the scores.

Table 18.1   Descriptive characteristics of the pilot study sample

Variable	n (%)
Gender Male	17 (32%)
Female	36 (68%)
Age 12	3 (6%)
13	10 (19%)
14	10 (19%)
15	9 (17%)
16	14 (26%)
17	7 (13%)
Family Constellation	
Parents married & living together	45 (85%)
Parents married & not living together	1 (2%)
Parents divorced	2 (4%)
Parents not married & living apart	1 (2%)
Father deceased	3 (6%)
Other	1 (2%)
Present School Grade	
Seven	10 (19%)
Eight	6 (11%)
Nine	13 (25%)
Ten	12 (23%)
Eleven	8 (15%)
Twelve	4 (8%)
Ethnicity	
Caucasian	49 (93%)
Asian	1 (2%)
East Indian	1 (2%)
Other	2 (4%)
Father's Occupation	
Entrepreneur	2 (4%)
Professional/Business	24 (45%)
Unskilled Labour	1 (2%)
Skilled Labour	8 (15%)
Unemployed	2 (4%)

Table 18.2   Cronbach alpha reliabilities of the AAS subscales for the pilot study

Scale	# of Items	# of Participants	Alpha Values
Attachment to Mother	22	53	.97
Attachment to Father	22	49	.97
Attachment to Parental Unit	22	49	.96
Total Attachment	66	49	.84
Proximity Seeking	8	53	.75
Parental Involvement	26	49	.85

References

Achenbach, T.M. (1991a). *Manual for the Child Behavior Checklist/4-18 and 1991 Profile*. Burlington, VT: University of Vermont, Department of Psychiatry.

Achenbach, T.M. (1991b). *Manual for the Youth Self-Report and 1991 Profile*. Burlington, VT: University of Vermont, Department of Psychiatry.

Achenbach, T.M. (1966). The classification of children's psychiatric symptoms: A factor-analytic study. *Psychological Monographs, 80, No.615*.

Achenbach, T.M. & Edelbrock, C. (1983). *Manual for the Child Behavior Checklist and Revised Child Behavior Profile*. Burlington, VT: University of Vermont, Department of Psychiatry.

Ainsworth, M. (1991). Attachments and other affectional bonds across the life cycle. In C. Parks, J. Stevenson-Hinde, & P. Marris (Eds.). *Attachment across the life cycle*, Routledge: London.

Armsden, G.C. & Greenberg, M.T. (1987). The inventory of parent and peer attachment: Individual differences and their relationship to psychological well-being in adolescence. *Journal of Youth and Adolescence, 16*, 427-454.

Bagley, C. & Genuis, M.L. (1991). Sexual abuse recalled: Evaluation of a computerized questionnaire in a population of young adult males. *Perceptual and Motor Skills, 72*, 287-288.

Baskin, D. (1990). *Computer applications in psychiatry and psychology*. New York: Brunner-Mazel.

Conners, C.K. (1973). Rating scales for use in drug studies with children. *Psychopharmacology Bulletin: Pharmacotherapy with children*. Washington, D.C.: U.S. Government Printing Offices.

Cronbach, L.J. (1951). Coefficient alpha and the internal structure of tests. *Psychometrica, 16*, 297-334.

Fox, N.A., Kimmerly, N.L., & Schafer, W.D. (1991). Attachment to mother/attachment to father: A meta-analysis. *Child Development, 62*, 210-225.

Genuis, M.L. & Violato, C. (1997). *The adolescent attachment survey: The development and psychometric analyses of an instrument for assessing childhood attachment retrospectively from adolescence*. Submitted for publication.

Genuis, M.L. (1994). Childhood attachment and adolescence. In C. Violato & L.D. Travis (Eds.), *Advances in Adolescent Psychology*. Calgary: Detselig.

Kobak, R.R. & Sceery, A. (1988). Attachment in late adolescence: Working models, affect regulation, and representations of self and others. *Child Development, 59*, 461-474.

Lamb, M. (1984). Fathers, mothers and childcare in the 1980s: Family influence on child development. In K. Borman, D. Quarm, & D. Gideones (Eds.), *Women in the workplace: Effect on families*. Ablex: Norwood, N.J.

Mezzich, J. & Mezzich, A. (1988). The place of computers in psychiatry. In J. Howells (Ed.), *Modern Perspectives in Clinical Psychiatry*. New York: Brunner/Mazel.

Parker, G. (1979). Reported parental characteristics in relation to trait anxiety and depression in a non-clinical group. *Australian and New Zealand Psychiatric Journal, 13,* 260-264.

Parker, G., Tupling, H., & Brown, L.B. (1979). A parental bonding instrument. *British Journal of Psychiatry, 52,* 1-10.

Quay, H.C., & Peterson, D.R. (1983). *Interim manual for the revised behavior problem checklist.* Coral Gables, FL: University of Miami, Applied Social Sciences.

Serbin, L.A., Peters, P.L., McAffer, V.J., & Schwartzman, A.E. (1991). Childhood aggression and withdrawal as predictors of adolescent pregnancy, early parenthood, and environmental risk for the next generation. *Canadian Journal of Behavioral Science, 23,* 318-331.

Violato, C. & Genuis, M.L. (1992). A stepwise discriminant analysis of sexually abused males. *Paper presented at the 25th International Congress of Psychology.* Brussels: Belgium.

Violato, C. & Travis, L.D. (1995). *Advances in adolescent psychology.* Detselig: Calgary.

19 Effects of Nonmaternal Care on Child Development: A Meta-Analysis of Published Research

CLAUDIO VIOLATO AND CLARE RUSSELL

Abstract

A meta-analysis of published research on the effects of nonmaternal care on child development was undertaken. One hundred and one studies published between 1957 and 1995 involving 32,271 children met the inclusion criteria. Most of the children in these studies came from middle class homes (63 studies; 62.3%), were Caucasian (77 studies; 76.2%), and were American (78 studies; 77.2%). Dependent variables in four domains (attachment, social-emotional, behavioral, and cognitive) were coded and effect sizes (d) between maternal and nonmaternal care (independent variable) were computed for both unweighted and weighted effects size. Results of unweighted effect size analysis indicated that there was a small effect and negative effects of nonmaternal care in the cognitive ($d = .14$) and social-emotional ($d = .26$) domains, and larger negative consequences for nonmaternal care for behavioral outcomes ($d = .38$), and attachment to mother ($d = .39$). Weighted effects size analysis decreased the magnitude of effect sizes in the social-emotional ($d = .16$) and behavioral domains but not in the cognitive and attachment domains. Moreover, males tended to fare more poorly with nonmaternal care than did females in all domains. A number of potentially mediating family, quality of care, and study characteristic variables were assessed and analyzed. The results are discussed within the context of attachment theory. We conclude that extensive nonmaternal care of infants and children results in negative developmental outcomes for children's development.

Introduction

The effects on child development of nonmaternal care such as daycare continues to be controversial in both the popular (e.g., Gallagher, 1998) and scholarly press (e.g., NICHD Early Child Care Research Network, 1998; Scarr, 1998) despite substantial research efforts during the last three decades. Narrative attempts at integrating and reviewing the research on nonmaternal care generally results in confusing, contradictory, and equivocal results (e.g., Frye, 1982; Hennessy & Melhuish, 1991; McGurk, Caplan, Hennessy & Moss, 1993). Such reviews frequently end with a call for more research (Belsky & Rovine, 1988; Scarr, 1998; Scarr, Phillips & McCartney, 1990).

While further research is certainly required and to be encouraged, statistical integration of existing published data may provide at least some firmer conclusions about nonmaternal care than have previous reviews or empirical studies. Accordingly, the major purpose of the present study was to conduct a meta-analysis of the effects on child development of nonmaternal care. Outcomes in four domains were of particular interest: 1) cognitive, 2) social-emotional, 3) behavior, and 4) attachment to mother. The possible impact of a number of mediating variables (e.g., quality of care, family configuration, infant versus older day care) on outcomes in the four domains were also of particular interest.

Many commentators (Belsky & Steinberg, 1978; Clarke-Stewart, 1989; Gray, 1983; Hoffman, 1989; McGurk et al., 1993) have observed that early studies of nonmaternal care (i.e., pre mid-1980s) failed to show adverse effects on children's cognitive, social or emotional development. Indeed, a number of studies indicated positive effects for many children (Etaugh, 1980; Hoffman, 1984; Rutter, 1987). These studies, however, have since been criticized for having focused on high quality, university based day cares, employing very small samples which were highly biased (Clarke-Stewart, 1988; Gamble & Zigler, 1986). Studies that have been conducted since the mid-1980s and have focused on non-university day cares have frequently shown deleterious effects for children (Belsky & Rovine, 1988; Clarke-Stewart, 1989). These latter studies, like their earlier counterparts, have been criticized for the use of small, biased samples, frequently in cross-sectional comparisons rather than longitudinal studies (Fein & Fox, 1990; Richters & Zahn-Waxler, 1988; Scarr et al., 1990). Overall, there has been a paucity of good longitudinal studies that evaluate the long-term outcomes of early childhood nonmaternal care (McGurk et al., 1993).

Two longitudinal studies (Andersson, 1989, 1992; Vandell & Corasaniti, 1990), have focused on the long-term effects of day care. Andersson (1989,

1992) provided two reports of a prospective longitudinal study of a sample of Swedish children in high quality day care. He showed that subjects in the day care group had more positive developmental outcomes than a matched group who had been reared exclusively at home. At both ages 8 and 13 years, the day care children received higher school marks and had higher scores on socio-emotional ratings from their teachers, than did the exclusively maternal care group. By contrast, Vandell and Corasaniti (1990) in a retrospective longitudinal study, found that 8 year old children with extensive poor quality day care experience (in Texas) during infancy, compared unfavourably to children who had not experienced extensive day care during their early life. In comparison to children in part-time day care (< 30 hours/week) or exclusive maternal care, children with extensive experience were rated by teachers as having poorer peer relations, work habits, and emotional health, and as being more difficult to discipline. Extensive infant care was also associated with poor academic report cards and standardized test scores. In both the Andersson (1989, 1992) and the Vandell and Corasaniti (1990) studies, however, a variety of day care quality and family variables mediated social and cognitive outcomes in stepwise multiple regressions and path analyses. Moreover, there were no direct comparisons within the studies of differences in quality of care with maternal and nonmaternal care. Accordingly, the quality of care was confounded with family and socio-economic status as well as maternal versus nonmaternal care.

In a large scale study by McCartney, Scarr, Rochelau, Phillips, Eisenberg, Keefe, Rosenthal and Abbot-Smith (1997) employing 720 children ranging in age from 12 to 60 months enrolled in 120 child-care centers in three U.S. states, substantial effects of family and child characteristics of both teacher's and parents' ratings on children's adjustment and social behaviors were found. The effects of quality of child care on social adjustment were very small but statistically significant. In the recent NICHD study (1997) utilizing 1,153 infants, there were no differences in attachment security in children with extensive nonmaternal care compared to those with maternal care. The attachment of these infants was assessed at 15 months of age, however, and therefore it is too soon to draw conclusions about their attachment classifications. In a follow-up NICHD study, child care effects of young children's self-control, compliance, and problem behavior was evaluated (NICHD, 1998). At the 36 month assessment, there was little evidence that early and continued nonmaternal care was related to child functioning. But at 24 months, children who had spent more time in nonmaternal care were reported by their mothers to be less cooperative and by their caregivers to exhibit more behaviour problems than their counterparts who spent less time in nonmaternal care. It may be that there are "sleeper effects" of nonmaternal care such that problem behavior may emerge later in development (Broberg, Wessels, Lamb & Hwang, 1997). Conclusions about the lasting and long-term effects of nonmaternal care based on these results, therefore, can only be tentative at best.

Research on nonmaternal care in the last decade or so has focused on assessing and evaluating the quality of day care. Quality has been differentially defined across studies but some general variables have been utilized and studied. These include licensing of day care (Melhuish & Moss, 1991), ratio of children to care giver (Howes & Rubenstein, 1985; Vandell, Henderson & Wilson, 1988), group size (Howes, 1983; Kontos & Fiene, 1987), education and training of the staff (McCartney, Scarr, Phillips, Grajek & Schwartz, 1982; Vandell et al., 1988), university, public or employer day care (Melhuish & Moss, 1991), program quality such as whether or not there is a planned developmental curriculum (Finkelstein, 1982; McCartney et al., 1982), stability of the staff (Howes, 1990; Howes & Hamilton, 1992; Phillips, McCartney & Scarr, 1987; Raikes, 1993), and the nature of the physical facilities (Kontos & Fiene, 1987).

While the foregoing line of research has been, and continues to be, of heuristic value, it has failed to provide any conclusive results. This is due to the usual problems with representativeness (i.e., small, biased samples), but the most important flaw is the lack of standardized measures of "quality". Many studies mix important indicators of quality such as ratio or education of staff with relatively less meaningful measures such as the availability of toys. A number of attempts have been made to develop standardized instruments to assess quality of day care (e.g., Harms & Clifford, 1980; Tsiantis, Caldwell, Dragonas, Jegede, Lambidi, Banaag & Orley, 1991). While these attempts are quite promising, much more effort is required to unravel the impact of quality of day care on child development compared to nonmaternal care. In any case, the current conclusions on this issue are not clear and require further explication (NICHD, 1998).

Another set of factors that have been investigated as potentially affecting the developmental outcomes for children experiencing substantial nonmaternal care are family variables and structure. The effects of family structure (intact, single parent, reconstituted) has been studied extensively (Cherry & Eaton, 1977; Desai, Chase-Lansdale & Michael, 1989; Poteat, Snow, Ironsmith & Bjorkman, 1992; Vaughn, Gove & Egeland, 1980), as have mother's education (Altman & Mills, 1990; Belsky & Eggebeen, 1991; Hunter, 1972), socio-economic status (Baydar & Brooks-Gunn, 1991; Gottfried, Gottfried & Bathurst, 1988), number of children in the family (Cochran & Gunnarsson,

1985; Everson, Sarnat & Ambron, 1984), and maternal satisfaction with employment (Hock & DeMeiss, 1990; Stifter, Coulehan & Fish, 1993). As might be expected, the results from these studies are confused, confounded and equivocal. Most conclusions that have been derived from this work are tentative, highly qualified, and frequently contradictory. Thus there is an urgent need to clarify the impact of family factors as mediating variables on developmental outcomes due to nonmaternal care.

A number of researchers (Barglow, Vaughn & Molitar, 1987; Belsky, 1986, 1988; Belsky & Rovine, 1988; Gamble & Zigler, 1986) have expressed concern about infant day care in particular. Here it is believed that infants in day care are particularly at risk since it is at this time that attachment to a principal caregiver is being formed. If the principal caregiver (e.g., mother) is absent for long periods of time (e.g., due to employment commitments), the infant is at an increased risk for insecure attachment and subsequent developmental problems. There is by no means a consensus on this view and the controversy, conflicting and confusing conclusions continue (Belsky & Braungart, 1991; Clarke-Stewart, 1988; Scarr, 1998). Clearly, further work is required on the impact of infant day care as separate from older day care.

Notwithstanding substantial research efforts into the effects of nonmaternal care on subsequent child development, few firm conclusions have been offered as we have seen. Attempts at integrating the research findings of the last three or so decades with narrative reviews, have not produced any clarity (e.g., Gamble & Zigler, 1986; McGurk et al., 1993; Rubenstein, 1985, Scarr, 1998). On the contrary, confusion and contradictions reign. Accordingly, we set out to integrate the findings in this area with an empirical method - meta-analysis. Outcomes from studies comparing maternal versus nonmaternal care were of particular interest. Specifically, we wished to assess outcomes in four domains: 1) cognitive, 2) social-emotional, 3) behavioral, and 4) child-mother attachment. The possible impact of a number of mediating variables (quality of care, family configuration and background, infant day care versus older day care) on outcomes in the four domains were also of particular interest.

Method

Definition of terms

Hours of employment or day care were defined by the following categories: 1) part-time as less than 25 hours per week, and 2) full-time as greater than 25 hours per week. This definition was based on Belsky's and Rovine's (1988) cut-offs (20 hours/week) but were adjusted upwards (25 hours/week) since Belsky's and Rovine's (1988) definition is arbitrary and has been criticized (Clarke-Stewart, 1988). We, therefore, made the requirement for full-time nonmaternal care more stringent. Nonmaternal care was defined by "other than mother" not including father and relatives, but including baby-sitter in child's home, family day care home (child taken to baby sitter's home), and group care (child taken to a child care center). We made no attempt to distinguish between day care centers and other forms of nonmaternal care for two reasons. First, the large majority of studies in this area focus on institutional nonmaternal care. Second, considerable research has shown that type and stability of care experience irrespective of setting is not distinguishable in many outcomes (Barglow et al., 1987; Schwartz, 1983; Vaughn, Deane & Waters, 1985).

Literature search

The literature search focused on the following sources: manual journal searches, computer journal searches (CD-ROM), examination of reference lists from reviews and other studies, conference proceedings, contact with persons involved in relevant research, and computer and hand searches of abstracting and indexing data bases (*Psychological Abstracts, Sociological Abstracts, Dissertation Abstracts, Indicus Medicus, PsychLIT, Psychinfo, Sociofile*, and *MEDLINE*). The following key words were used in the search: day care, maternal employment, child care, and nonmaternal. This initial search yielded over 200 documents which included published articles, chapters and books, government reports, conference papers, and technical papers. Detailed screening of these documents revealed that the unpublished materials (e.g., government reports, conference papers) contained no or very sparse data, had been subsequently published (and therefore were redundant), were marginally or not at all relevant, or failed to meet our inclusion criteria (see below). They were thus eliminated from our analysis. Accordingly, we focused strictly on published materials.

Inclusion criteria

Our inclusion criteria required that the published studies had to have focused on the effects of maternal employment and day care on at least one of children's cognitive, social-emotional, and behavioral development, and the effects of maternal employment or day care on children's attachment to mother or father. One hundred and one studies met the following inclusion criteria: a) sample sizes greater than 12 subjects, b) data from at least one of cognitive, social-emotional, behavioral, and parental attachment, c) each study had to include a comparison between a maternal and nonmaternal care group or was required to report percent secure-insecure attachment within the nonmaternal care group, and d) only studies that used psychometric measures were included (i.e., standardized measurement instruments, observation techniques, checklists, attachment scales, strange situation technique, and so on). Our final data base included 101 published articles (see Appendix A).

Data coding

The effect sizes from the four domains (cognitive, social-emotional, behavioral, attachment) became the dependent variables. The cognitive domain included measures such as IQ, school grades, reading scores, scores on standardized achievement tests and so forth. Measures in the social-emotional domain included peer relations, daily living skills, and adjustment and personality measures. In the behavioral domain, measures such as aggression, motor activity and compliance were coded, while attachment was assessed as both secure and insecure (anxious, avoidant, resistant).

The independent variables consisted of 27 factors coded as the following: year of study publication, number of subjects, age of subjects, gender of subjects, socio-economic status of parent(s), ethnicity, country of study, type of care, hours of care, age of child when mother began work, sponsor of day care, education of care giver, adult-child ratio in care settings, license status of day care, program quality, mother's education, mother's age, percent primiparous, average number of children in the family, family structure, method of assessment, design of study, motive of study, type of study, type of sample, age assessed in retrospect, prospective study and/or prenatal recruitment, quality of care and quality of study. A summary of the coding results of some major characteristics of the studies and the effect sizes ($\underline{d}$) are presented in Table 19.1.

The effect size for each dependent variable was calculated from means and standard deviations, correlations, Chi-square, and $\underline{t}$ and $\underline{F}$ ratios as is conventional in meta-analysis of $\underline{d}$ values (Glass, McGaw & Smith, 1981). Effect sizes for percentages were computed from a table of probit transformations of differences in proportions to effect sizes (Glass et al., 1981). The baseline prevalence rate for insecure attachment was set at 30%, the approximate rate of insecure attachment in American samples (Ainsworth, Blehar, Waters & Wall, 1978; Lamb, Thompson, Gardner, Charnou & Estes, 1984).

Quality of care

The number of type of quality indicators were assessed for each study that reported the aspects of the quality of care. The criteria for the quality of care in each study was derived from 1) research that investigated differences between children in various types of nonmaternal care (e.g., Andersson, 1989), 2) research that compared groups of children in high versus low quality care (e.g., Peterson & Peterson, 1986; Winett et al, 1977), and 3) observations in daycare settings. A rating of high versus low was assigned to each study reporting quality of care indicators based on the number and type of quality indicators reported.

Quality of study

Each study was assigned a total score for quality derived from the following criteria: 1) clarity of stated purpose and/or hypothesis, 2) theoretical integrity (e.g., continuity of theoretical underpinnings across sampling procedures, study design, assessment instrumentation, and methodology, analyses, interpretation of results), 3) sampling procedures (e.g., prenatal recruitment, representative sampling, size, age appropriateness, etc.), 4) assessment procedures (e.g., between study, prospective, number of domains assessed, number of independent variables assessed), 5) dependent and independent variables assessed (e.g., clarity and diversity of operational definitions of constructs as indicated by validity and reliability criteria), 6) appropriateness of assessment procedures in context of subjects sampled (e.g., strange-situation valid for 12-18 month old children, need to have assessed duration of nonmaternal care prior to assessment, etc.), and 7) number and scope of potential mediating variables controlled for (e.g., maternal, infant, father, family, nonmaternal care variables). This rating scale resulted in a continuous variable.

Results

The results are presented in three main sections: 1) descriptive statistics for study characteristics, 2) effect size analysis, and 3) analysis of mediating variables on effect size.

Descriptive statistics for study characteristics

The 101 published articles involved 32,271 children (minimum = 23; maximum = 9,450). The range of publication dates of the studies was from 1957 to 1995 with almost half of the studies published after 1985 (n=47, 46.5%). These results as well as other descriptive data are summarized in Table 19.2.

The motive of the studies included the effects of day care on child development and attachment (n = 50; 49.5%), and the effects of maternal employment on child development and attachment (n = 51; 51.5%). Most of the children in these studies came from middle class homes (63 studies; 62.3%), were White (77 studies; 76.2%), and were American (78 studies; 77.2%). Other descriptive features of study characteristics are summarized in Table 19.2.

Day care variables and family variables are summarized in Table 19.3. A notable feature of these results is the large number of studies that are missing critical information such as education of caregiver (80.1%), day care program quality (56.4%), whether or not the day care was licensed (71.3%), and so on (Table 19.3).

The number and percentage of studies employing various methods of assessing subjects (both parents and children), are summarized in Table 19.4. Attachment was assessed by the Strange Situation Test in only 32 studies (31.7%). Other methods employed interviews (n = 44; 43.6%), questionnaires (n = 51; 50.5%), rating scales (n = 46; 44.6%), as well as other methods (see Table 19.4).

Effect size analysis

Both unweighted and weighted effect sizes were analyzed across all four domains (cognitive, social-emotional, behavioral, and attachment) and these results are summarized in Table 19.5. As can be seen from this table, males and females were analyzed separately for each domain.

The unweighted effect sizes across the four domains ranged from a minimum absolute value of 0.12 (social-emotional domain for females) to a maximum of 0.41 (behavioral domain for males). A positive effect size in this analysis indicates that the nonmaternal care group had deleterious or negative outcomes, while a negative $\underline{d}$ indicates that this group had positive consequences (no negative mean $\underline{d}$ emerged - see Table 19.5). The overall mean $\underline{d}$s for each of the domains were based on very large samples (cognitive n = 23, 986; social-emotional n = 7,795; behavioral n = 4,588; maternal attachment n = 2,678). The number of studies for the computation of each $\underline{d}$ varied from a minimum of 16 (behavioral domain separate analysis for males and females) to a maximum of 48 (social-emotional domain for males and females combined). Table 19.5 also contains a presentation of the 95% confidence intervals for the effect sizes.

The weighted effect size analysis was conducted in order to address the potential for small sample sizes to exert more influence on results than warranted. Compared to well designed studies with large samples, studies with small sample sizes may present unrepresentative samples of subjects. As in the unweighted effect size analysis, the weighted mean $\underline{d}$s and their confidence intervals are reported (Table 19.5). While the weighted ds are generally smaller in magnitude than the unweighted $\underline{d}$s, the pattern of results remain very similar. The 95% confidence intervals of the weighted $\underline{d}$s are quite narrow and none span 0. This indicates that all of the unweighted $\underline{d}$s have a non-zero value at a 95% level of confidence.

To further facilitate the interpretation of both weighted and unweighted $\underline{d}$s, Table 19.5 also contains a presentation of the percent increase of negative outcome for the nonmaternal care compared to the maternal care group across each domain. These percentages are based on Rosenthal's and Rubin's (1982) binomial effect size display (BESD). In BESD terms, the largest increase of negative outcomes is for attachment of the male and female combined analysis. There is a 19% increase of insecure attachments for children in nonmaternal care. Based on a baseline insecure attachment of 30% in the population as a whole (e.g., Ainsworth et al., 1978), this represents an increase of 63% (19/30 x 100) to the risk of insecure attachment as a consequence of nonmaternal care. Put another way, we would expect, on the average, a prevalence rate of insecure attachment of approximately 50% (30% + 19%) for nonmaternal care groups compared to the general prevalence rate of 30%.

The BESD results are quite variable across the different domains as can be seen in Table 19.5, but the overall pattern converges on a negative effect of nonmaternal care in all four domains. The smallest negative effect of nonmaternal care is in the cognitive domain (BESD = 7%). In the behavioral domain, the effect size (weighted $\underline{d}$ = .28; BESD = 14%) is larger than in the cognitive domain, but smaller than for attachment. The effect sizes for social-emotional outcomes (weighted $\underline{d}$ = .16; BESD = 8%) is quite similar to the cognitive domain. The pattern of $\underline{d}$s, whether weighted or unweighted, converge on the finding that extensive nonmaternal care has a negative overall effect in all four of the domains assessed.

Sex differences

As can be seen from Table 19.5, there are differences of both the weighted $\underline{d}$s and unweighted $\underline{d}$s between males and females in the cognitive and social-emotional domains, but not in the behavioral and attachment domains. In both of the domains where the differences exist, it is the males that fare more poorly than the females. These sex difference findings are consistent with other research (Jouriles & LeCompte, 1991; Hetherington, 1989).

Effect size analysis for Daycare and maternal employment studies

Some researchers (e.g., Clarke-Stewart, 1988, 1989) have criticized the meaning of results obtained from aggregating results of studies investigating the effects of maternal employment with those investigating the effects of daycare on the developing child directly (e.g., Belsky, 1988). The concern is that aggregating studies derived from different theoretical orientations creates significantly different data bases thereby confounding the results. Accordingly, to evaluate for these potentially confounding effects, effect size differences between the daycare studies and the maternal employment studies, a homogeneity of effect size analysis was conducted between the daycare studies (n = 50) and the maternal employment studies (n = 51).

The Levene statistic for homogeneity of variance of the effect sizes was computed for all domains. There were no significant differences in the cognitive domain (Levene = .002, $\underline{p}$ < .96), in the social-emotional domain (Levene = 1.624, $\underline{p}$ < .21), in the behavioral domain (Levene = 3.761, p < .067), and in the attachment domain (Levene = 1.064, $\underline{p}$ < .31). Even so, as a conservative approach, the effect sizes were computed separately for daycare and maternal employment research aggregates. The results are summarized in Table 19.6. As can be seen from these results, there were no significant differences between the daycare studies and the maternal care studies on either the unweighted or weighted $\underline{d}$s across all four domains.

Analysis of moderating variables

Ideally, a number of variables that are potentially moderating the effect sizes in the four domains assessed should be analyzed using hierarchical regression analyses with $\underline{d}$ as the criterion or dependent variable. Preliminary analyses, however, indicated that this was not possible in the present study because of missing data. No instances of independent variables had enough data points (at least 15) when combined with others to produce a meaningful regression analysis. Attempts at using either mean substitution or pairwise deletion of missing data produced impossible regression results as can frequently happen with such procedures. Accordingly, moderating variables were analyzed one at a time using univariate analyses.

Analysis of variance (ANOVA) were conducted for the 15 independent variables with both unweighted and weighted effect sizes as the dependent variables. Analyses of covariance (ANCOVA) were conducted for the same set of independent variables with quality of study as the covariate (see Table 19.7). These ANCOVA analyses were conducted in order to explore the potential impact of quality of study on effect sizes interacting with moderating variables.

The 15 independent variables in Table 19.7 are some important moderating variables that potentially may affect $\underline{d}$. The general pattern of these results, both in the ANOVA and ANCOVA analyses, is that the moderating variables have no effect on $\underline{d}$ in all four domains, with several exceptions. In the cognitive domain, none of the moderating variables indicated differences in the ANOVA analyses although year of study did show a significant difference $(F(1, 39) = 5.55, \underline{p} < .05)$ for the weighted $\underline{d}$ with lower unweighted $\underline{d}$s after 1985, and hours of care showed a significant difference $(F(1, 39) = 4.51, \underline{p} < .05)$ for the unweighted $\underline{d}$ for the ANCOVA analyses with higher number of hours resulting in higher $\underline{d}$s.

In the social-emotional domain, two variables moderated $\underline{d}$s. Year of study moderated the weighted $\underline{d}$ in the ANCOVA analysis where studies published after 1985 produced a significantly higher weighted $\underline{d}$ than did earlier studies $(F(1, 47) = 4.37, \underline{p} < .05)$. Ethnicity (white vs nonwhite) moderated effect size in the social-emotional domain where the negative effect of nonmaternal care was greater for nonwhite children than for white children in both the ANOVA and ANCOVA analyses $(F(1, 47) = 6.82, \underline{p} < .01)$.

In the behavioral domain, the number of children in the family moderated the unweighted $\underline{d}$ in the ANCOVA analysis $(F(1,5) = 11.72, \underline{p} < .05)$. Children with only child status fared worse in the nonmaternal care than did children with one or more siblings. Finally, in the attachment domain, the ratio of caregiver to children (1:4 or less vs 1:5 or greater) moderated both the weighted and unweighted $\underline{d}$s in both the ANOVA and ANCOVA analyses $(F(1,10) = 7.17, \underline{p} < .05)$. Children in higher ratio nonmaternal care fared worse compared to children in lower ratio nonmaternal care.

The significant outcomes from the ANOVA and ANCOVA analyses reported in Table 19.7 must be interpreted with extreme caution. The total number of ANOVAs (F tests) that were executed and are summarized in Table 19.7 are quite large (15 x 4 = 60). Accordingly, the risk of Type I errors is increased substantially (e.g., the Bonferroni Inequality, .05 x 60 = 3.00). In 60 statistical tests when alpha is set at .05, then, it is probable that three or four of the tests will emerge significant by chance alone. It may be prudent, therefore, to regard these "significant" results as potentially spurious (the same applies to the ANCOVA analyses). The most salient feature of the results summarized in Table 19.7 is that, generally, there are few, if any, significant effects of the 15 variables on $\underline{d}$ across all four domains even when quality of study is partialled out as a covariate.

Discussion

The major findings of the present study may be summarized as follows: 1) there were significant, nonzero effect sizes (both weighted and unweighted) in all four domains, 2) these indicate that there are negative sequela of nonmaternal care in the cognitive, social-emotional, behavioral, and maternal attachment domains, 3) boys tended to fare more poorly on cognitive and social-emotional outcomes than did girls, and 4) there was generally a lack of significant impact - with minor exceptions - of a number of potential moderating variables on the effect sizes (both weighted and unweighted) of maternal and nonmaternal care in all four domains assessed.

Previous conclusions on the impact of nonmaternal care on cognitive outcomes have been unclear and contradictory (Andersson, 1992; Chase-Lansdale, Mott, Brooks-Gunn & Phillips, 1991; Main, 1991; Vandell & Corasiniti, 1990). The results from the present study suggest that children in day care are probably at some risk for negative outcomes. The effect size in this domain was nonzero (unweighted $\underline{d}$ = .14; weighted $\underline{d}$ = .14) based on 40 studies involving 23,986 subjects. This suggest an increase of 7% over baseline for negative cognitive outcomes due to nonmaternal care. When male and female data were available separately, results indicated larger effect sizes than the aggregate data (Table 19.5) for both sexes, both for negative outcomes. Males show a larger negative outcome than do the females.

The results for the social-emotional domain show negative outcomes for nonmaternal care. Considerable confidence can be placed in these findings since they are based on a large number of studies (n = 48) involving many thousands of subjects (n = 7,795). The results from both the mixed sex samples (unweighted $\underline{d}$ = .26; weighted $\underline{d}$ = .16) and the single sex samples (male unweighted $\underline{d}$ = .28; male weighted $\underline{d}$ = .22; female unweighted $\underline{d}$ = .12; female weighted $\underline{d}$ = .11) are clear and consistent. As for the cognitive domain, it is the males that fare more poorly in comparison to the females. The increased risk for negative outcomes for boys compared to girls is consistent with many other findings (Eme, 1979; Emery, 1982; Stein, Newcomb & Bentler, 1993). Eme (1979), in a review of childhood psychopathology, concluded that boys are more vulnerable to family discord, instability and parental unavailability than are girls. These conclusions have been corroborated by others (Jouriles & LeCompte, 1991; Hetherington, 1989).

There are negative consequences for behavioral outcomes for children in nonmaternal care (unweighted $\underline{d}$ = .38; weighted $\underline{d}$ = .28). The pattern is consistent and there does not appear to be a significant difference between boys and girls in the behavioral domain (see Table 19.5).

The results for effect sizes on attachment show that children are at increased risk for insecure attachment due to full-time nonmaternal care. Indeed, for the overall sample (n of studies = 40; n of subjects = 2, 678) effect sizes, it is the largest of the four domains assessed (unweighted $\underline{d}$ = .39; weighted $\underline{d}$ = .38). According to the BESD results, nonmaternal care increases the risk for insecure attachment by 63% over the baseline prevalence rate. This is a notable effect that should be of concern. If this were an increase in the prevalence of an organic illness (e.g., lung cancer) due to environmental toxins (e.g., industrial air pollutants) this effect size and increased risk would be considered extremely serious (Lipsey & Wilson, 1993). Moreover, this effect on attachment is consistent with the direction of increase in social-emotional (8% from the weighted $\underline{d}$) and behavioral problems (14% from the weighted $\underline{d}$), suggesting at least correlated multivariate effects resulting in social maladjustment. While it does not necessarily follow that maladjustment is a causal outcome of insecure attachment, the pattern shows a clear relationship in the present results.

There is substantial evidence that attachment patterns formed in infancy and childhood are likely to remain stable into late childhood, adolescence and perhaps beyond (Harris & Bifulco, 1991; Sroufe, 1988). Moreover, there is also empirical evidence indicating that psychological adjustment in childhood and adolescence is related to early attachment patterns (Ainsworth & Bowlby, 1991; de Jong, 1992; Koback, Sudler & Gamble, 1991; Kwakman, Zuiker, Scheppers & Wuffel, 1988; Lyons-Ruth, Alpern, & Repacholi,1993; Parkes, 1991). The present results then, are in concordance with these findings and support the hypothesis that the increased rate of maladjustment of nonmaternal care children compared to maternal care children, may be due to the increased rate of insecure attachment among the nonmaternal care group. While this hypothesis requires direct testing in longitudinal, causal-comparative designs for confirmation, it is nevertheless plausible as an explanation for the present results.

While the overall d̲s can be considered robust, there is a noteworthy limitation in the present study. The large amounts of missing data on many of the moderating variables precluded multivariate analysis (e.g., regression analyses) of them on d̲. The univariate analyses undertaken in the present study suggest that moderating variables had little or no impact on d̲s. One theoretical interpretation is that it is the unavailability of the mother during periods of nonmaternal care that results in the negative outcomes in the cognitive, social-emotional, behavioral and attachment domains rather than the effect of any moderating variables. Moderating day care variables (e.g., licensed vs. nonlicensed) or family variables (e.g., maternal education) may be irrelevant to children's outcomes. To reiterate, it may be the unavailability of the mother during periods of nonmaternal care that results in the negative outcomes irrespective of other factors. Such an interpretation is consistent with attachment theory (Ainsworth & Bowlby, 1991).

This interpretation, however, can only be taken as suggestive rather than conclusive since there were so many gaps in the data. More research is needed to determine the effect of potentially important moderating variables such as quality of day care, family structure, parental education, etc. on children's cognitive, social-emotional, behavioral and attachment outcomes.

The effect of nonmaternal care, especially day care, on children's development continues to be an important scientific, social, political and economic issue. More Americans, Canadians and other people than ever before, are entrusting their preschool children to the care of others. In Canada and the United States there are currently debates about publicly as well as privately funded day care. The results from the present study indicate that children who experience substantial nonmaternal care during infancy and childhood are at risk for attachment, social-emotional, cognitive and behavioral problems. Accordingly, full-time nonmaternal care for infants and young children is contraindicated as this would put a substantial proportion of the population at risk for psychological maladaptation. The present findings do not conclusively rule out the possibility that various moderating variables such as quality of day care may have an effect on children's developmental outcomes. They do, however, indicate that conversely, there is no support for the belief that "high" quality day care (e.g., developmental curriculum, low ratio of children to caregiver, high quality physical environment) is an acceptable substitute for nurturing parental care. Further research may well clarify this matter further. Meanwhile, the present meta-analysis provides evidence for the negative impact of full-time nonmaternal care on the development of children.

Table 19.1   Study characteristics and effect size for the four domains and sex differences

Author	Yr	Size	M&F	Cogn M	F	M&F	S-E M	F	M&F	Bhvr M	F	M&F	Attch M	F
Ainslie et al.	84	35										1.04		
Altman et al.	90	72	0.70			0.80			0.77					
Andersson	89	119	0.00	0.00	0.00	0.00	0.00	0.00						
Bagley	88	512		0.16	0.23		0.31	0.22		0.20	0.28			
Banducci	67	3014	0.00	-0.02	0.00									
Barglow et al.	87	110										0.47	0.47	0.47
Bates et al.	94	589							0.26	0.26	0.26			
Baydar et al.	91	572	0.87	0.87	0.87									
*Belsky et al.	88	149										0.57	0.57	0.57
Belsky et al.	91	1248				0.21	0.21	0.21	0.22	0.22	0.22			
Benn	86	30											0.20	
Blehar	74	40				1.00						1.02		
Bronfenbrenner et al.	84	152				0.44	0.50	-0.46						
Brookhart et al.	76	33										0.00	0.00	0.00
Burchinal et al.	92	45										-0.67	-0.67	-0.67
Caldwell et al.	70	41	0.43	0.43	0.43							0.00		
*Chase-Lansd et al.	87	97										0.00	0.00	0.00
Cherry et al.	77	153	0.00											
Clarke-Stewart	81	150										0.57		
Cochran	77	120	0.00			0.29			0.00					
Cohen	77	44	0.81	0.81	0.81	0.82	0.82	0.82						
Cornelius et al.	75	63				0.00	0.00	0.00						
Crockenberg et al.	91	94							0.00	0.45	0.00			
Desai et al.	89	503	0.00	0.56	0.00									
Devall et al.	86	60				0.56	2.00	0.00	0.48					
Doyle et al.	78	39	0.00									0.00		
Doyle	75	24				1.35						0.00		
*Easterbrooks et al.	85	73				0.00	0.00	0.00				0.00	0.00	0.00
Egeland et al.	95	110				-0.02			0.46			0.40		
Everson et al.	84	224				0.11	0.11	0.11						
Faber et al.	82	110				0.43	0.65	0.62						
Farel	80	212	0.00	0.00	0.00	0.00								
Finkelstein	82	28							0.85					
Glueck et al.	57	539					0.16							
Gold et al.	80	379	0.00	0.00	0.00	0.00	0.00	0.00						
Gold et al.	78a	223	0.00	0.88	0.00	0.00	0.36	0.00	0.00	0.33	0.00			
Gold et al.	78b	110	0.37	0.75	0.00	-0.34	-0.34	-0.34						
Gold et al.	79	64	0.00	0.00	0.00	-0.10	-0.10	-0.10						
Gold et al.	78c	253	0.00	0.00	0.00	-0.33	-0.05	0.00						
Goossens	87	77										0.00	0.00	0.00
Gottfried et al.	88	130	0.05	0.05	0.05	0.00	0.00	0.00	0.00	0.00	0.00			
Haskins	85	59							0.55					
Hegland et al.	90	32							0.00	0.00	0.00			
Heyns et al.	86	3796	0.20	0.20	0.20									
Hock	80	97	0.00			-0.11								
Howes et al.	86	89							-0.08					
Howes et al.	92	106										0.20		
Howes et al.	88	42										0.37		
Hunter	72	1708	0.14											
Jacobson et al.	84	93										0.66		
*Jarvis et al.	91	32										0.00		
Kagan et al.	77	99	-0.06			0.30						0.02		

Table 19.1   (cont'd)

Author	Yr	Size	Cogn M&F	Cogn M	F	S-E M&F	S-E M	F	Bhvr M&F	Bhvr M	F	Attch M&F	Attch M	F
Lahikainen et al.	79	130										0.63		
Lamb et al.	88	140				0.00	0.00	0.00						
Lerner et al.	88	133	0.00	0.00	0.00	-0.03	-0.03	-0.03						
Levy-Shiff	83	86	0.55			0.45			0.00			0.00		
McCord et al.	63	149				0.76								
Melhuish et al.	90a	156	0.92	0.92	0.92	0.47	0.47	0.47	1.20	1.20	1.20			
Melhuish et al.	90b	193	0.11	0.11	0.11									
Melhuish	87	166				0.12	0.12	0.12				0.30		
Miller	75	34					0.00				0.84			
Milne, A.M. et al.	86	9450	0.15	0.15	0.15									
Moore, B.F. et al.	88	90				0.00	0.00	0.00						
Moore, T.W.	75	105		0.58	0.58		0.58	-0.58		0.58				
Moorehouse	91	112	0.45	0.45	0.45	0.31	0.31	0.31						
Moskowitz et al.	77	24				0.74	0.19					0.00	0.98	0.00
Nelson	71	312				0.00	0.00	0.22						
Nelson	69	312	0.00	0.00	0.00									
*Owen et al.	84	59	-									0.00	0.00	0.00
Owen et al.	88	38										1.07	1.07	1.07
Park et al.	91	105	-0.45			0.39			0.37					
Peterson et al.	86	66				0.30	0.30	0.30	0.45	0.45	0.45			
Pierrehumbert et al.	91	22										1.05		
Portnoy et al.	78	35										0.00	0.00	0.00
Poteat et al.	92	96				0.72	0.72	0.72						
Propper	72	229				0.35	0.56	0.36						
Quay	92	581				0.00								
Ragozin	80	34				1.66						2.35		
Roggman et al.	94	105										0.00	0.00	0.00
Roopnarine et al.	78	23				0.00						0.00		
Roy	61	303		0.87	0.00	0.00	0.00		0.00	0.00				
Rubenstein et al.	79	30				-0.13								
Rubenstein et al.	81	23	-0.85	-0.85	-0.85	0.47	0.47	0.47	1.27	1.27	1.27	0.00	0.00	0.00
*Sagi et al.	85	86										1.01	1.01	1.01
Sagi et al.	94	23										0.79	0.79	0.79
Schachter	81	70	0.26			-0.08	0.00	0.08						
Schubert et al.	80	30				0.27								
Schwartz	83	50										0.66		
Schwarz et al.	74	38	0.00	0.00	0.00	0.36	0.36	0.36	0.80	0.80	0.80			
Stifter et al.	93	73										0.20	0.20	0.20
Stith & Davis	84	30	0.00			0.40								
Thompson et al.	82	43										1.03		
Thornburg et al.	90	835	0.00	0.00	0.00	0.20	0.11	0.11	0.33	0.33	0.33			
Vandell et al.	90	236	0.11	0.00	0.35	0.23	0.47	0.00	0.39	0.39	0.39			
Vandell et al.	92	189	-0.28	-0.28	-0.28				0.00	0.00	0.00			
Vaughn et al.	80	104										0.80		
Weinraub et al.	91	65	0.00									0.63		
Wille	92	60										0.00		
Williams et al.	93	47	0.86	0.00	1.22									
Winett et al.	77	124	0.17			0.00								
Zaslow et al.	89	34	0.00	0.00	0.00							0.22	0.22	0.22

Notes to Table 19.1   1. Studies marked with an asterisk in the author column present data on attachment to father. 2. Abbreviations in column titles: Yr - year of publication of study, Size - number   of subjects in study,   Cogn - cognitive domain,   S-E - social-emotional domain, Bhvr -behavioral domain, Attch - maternal attachment domain, M&F - male and female, M - male, F - female

Table 19.2 Descriptive characteristics of the studies in the sample

Variable	N	Percent
1. Year of Publication		
1957 - 79	31	30.7
1980 - 85	23	22.8
1986 - 96	47	46.5
total	101	
2. Motive for the Research: Effects of		
daycare on child development	26	25.7
maternal employment on child	38	37.6
daycare on attachment	24	23.8
maternal employment on attachment	13	12.9
total	101	
3. Socioeconomic Status		
Upper-Middle class	63	62.3
Middle-Lower class	38	37.6
total	101	
4. Ethnicity		
White	77	76.2
Black	2	2.0
White/Black/Hispanic	17	16.8
Other	5	5.0
total	101	
5. Type of Sample		
High Risk	12	11.9
Low Risk	76	75.2
Mixed	13	12.9
total	101	
6. Country of the Study		
United States	78	77.2
United Kingdom	4	4.0
Canada	9	8.9
Sweden and Finland	6	5.9
Israel	3	3.0
Switzerland	1	1.0
total	101	

Table 19.2   (cont'd)

Variable	N	Percent
6. Family Structure		
Two Parent Intact	60	72.3
Various Family Configurations	23	27.7
total	83	
7. Age Categories of Children		
Infants (< 2 years)	47	46.5
Toddlers (2 to 3 years)	14	13.9
Preschool (4 to 5 years)	16	15.8
Middle Childhood (6 to 12 years)	14	13.9
Adolescents and older	10	9.9
total	101	
8. Hours of Nonmaternal Care		
20 to 30 per week	42	41.6
More than 30 per week	59	58.4
total	101	
9. Age of Child When Mother Began Working		
First year of life	48	77.4
Second and third year of life	4	6.5
Mixed Samples (first, second, third)	10	16.1
total	62	
10. Mothers Education		
High School or less	21	40.4
College and University	31	59.6
total	52	
11. Number of Children in the Family		
One only	15	60.0
Two or More	10	40.0
total	25	

Table 19.3   Descriptive characteristics of the day cares in the sample

Variable	N	Percent of Total (101)	Percent of Subt'l of Knowns
1. Sponsor of DayCare			
University	7	6.9	20.0
Public (State)	10	9.9	28.6
Private (Church, Employer)	16	15.8	45.7
Mixed Samples	2	2.0	5.7
subtotal of known values	35	34.7	
Unknown	66	65.3	
2. Education of Care Giver			
No training	4	4.0	20.0
Training	16	15.9	80.0
subtotal of known values	20	19.9	
Unknown	81	80.1	
3. Ratio of Caregiver to Children			
1:2 to 1:4	12	11.9	57.1
1:5 to 1:8	9	8.9	42.9
subtotal of known values	21	20.8	
Unknown	80	79.2	
4. Day Care Was Licensed			
Yes	16	15.8	55.2
No	13	12.9	44.8
subtotal of known values	29	28.7	
Unknown	72	71.3	
5. Quality of Care			
High	34	29.7	68.2
Low	10	13.9	31.8
subtotal of known values	44	43.6	
Unknown	57	56.4	

Table 19.4   Number and percentage of studies employing methods of assessing parents and children

Variable	N*	Percent
1. Interview	44	43.6
2. Questionnaire	51	50.5
3. Rating Scale	45	44.6
4. Standardized Tests	37	36.6
5. Observations	36	35.6
6. Observations (videotaped)	10	9.9
7. Strange Situation (not videotaped)	8	7.9
8. Strange-Situation (videotaped)	24	23.8
9. Mixed Methods (attachment assessments)	19	18.8

*Total N is more than 101 and total percent is more than 100 because many studies employed multiple methods.

Table 19.5 Unweighted and weighted effect size (d) in the four domains for total aggregate

	N Std	N Subj	Unweighted Effect Size (ES)				Weighted Effect Size (ES)			
			Mean d	95% C.I. lower	upper	% Increase BESD*	Mean d	95% C.I. lower	upper	% Increase BESD*
Cognitive	40	23986	0.14	0.03	0.25	7%	0.14	0.14	0.14	7%
Male	30	10123	0.22	0.08	0.37	11%	0.19	0.19	0.19	10%
Female	30	10261	0.18	0.03	0.32	9%	0.16	0.15	0.16	8%
Social-Emotional	48	7795	0.26	0.15	0.37	13%	0.16	0.15	0.16	8%
Male	36	4026	0.28	0.15	0.41	14%	0.22	0.21	0.23	11%
Female	34	3499	0.12	0.02	0.22	6%	0.11	0.11	0.12	6%
Behavioral	22	4588	0.38	0.21	0.54	19%	0.28	0.27	0.29	14%
Male	16	2330	0.41	0.21	0.59	20%	0.28	0.27	0.29	14%
Female	16	2327	0.38	0.17	0.59	19%	0.27	0.26	0.28	13%
Attachment	40	2678	0.39	0.22	0.55	19%	0.38	0.36	0.40	19%
Male	18	616	0.27	0.06	0.48	13%	0.28	0.25	0.31	14%
Female	17	518	0.22	0.01	0.42	11%	0.25	0.22	0.28	13%

*% Increase negative outcome for nonmaternal care computed with the binomial effect size display (BESD) from Rosenthal & Rubin (1982); 95% C.I. = 95% confidence interval; N Std = number of studies; N Subj = # of subjects

Table 19.6   Unweighted and weighted effect size (d) in the four domains for day care and maternal employment research aggregates

	N Std	N Subj	Unweighted Effect Size (ES)				Weighted Effect Size (ES)			
			Mean d	95% C.I. lower	upper	% Increase BESD*	Mean d	95% C.I. lower	upper	% Increase BESD*
Daycare										
Cognitive	15	2190	0.10	-0.10	0.30	5%	0.12	.0.10	0.13	6%
Male	9	1008	0.09	-0.22	0.39	4%	0.12	0.10	0.13	6%
Female	9	1050	0.13	-0.18	0.44	7%	0.18	0.17	0.20	9%
Social-Emotional	26	3092	0.38	0.21	0.55	19%	0.25	0.24	0.26	12%
Male	16	1382	0.27	0.15	0.38	13%	0.23	0.22	0.24	12%
Female	15	1406	0.23	0.10	0.36	12%	0.17	0.16	0.18	9%
Behavioral	13	2364	0.56	0.35	0.78	27%	0.41	0.39	0.42	20%
Male	9	1175	0.54	0.25	0.84	26%	0.36	0.35	0.38	18%
Female	9	1217	0.55	0.26	0.84	27%	0.38	0.37	0.39	19%
Attachment	27	1643	0.41	0.20	0.63	20%	0.41	0.39	0.43	20%
Male	7	156	0.16	-0.26	0.57	8%	0.06	-0.01	0.14	3%
Female	7	157	0.02	-0.30	0.33	1%	0.04	-0.02	0.09	2%
Maternal Employment										
Cognitive	25	21796	0.16	0.03	0.29	8%	0.14	0.14	0.14	7%
Male	21	9115	0.28	0.12	0.44	14%	0.20	0.19	0.20	10%
Female	21	9211	0.19	0.03	0.35	10%	0.15	0.15	0.16	8%
Social-Emotional	22	4703	0.13	0.01	0.25	6%	0.10	0.05	0.10	5%
Male	20	2644	0.29	0.06	0.51	14%	0.21	0.20	0.23	11%
Female	19	2093	0.03	-0.11	0.16	1%	0.08	0.07	0.09	4%
Behavioral	9	2224	0.11	-0.02	0.24	6%	0.15	0.15	0.16	8%
Male	7	1155	0.23	0.05	0.40	11%	0.20	0.19	0.21	10%
Female	7	1110	0.15	-0.08	0.38	8%	0.15	0.14	0.16	7%
Attachment	13	1035	0.32	0.11	0.54	16%	0.34	0.32	0.36	17%
Male	11	460	0.34	0.11	0.57	17%	0.36	0.32	0.39	18%
Female	10	361	0.35	0.10	0.61	17%	0.34	0.31	0.38	17%

*% Increase negative outcome for nonmaternal care computed with the binomial effect size display (BESD) from Rosenthal & Rubin (1982); 95% C.I. = 95% confidence interval; N Std = number of studies; N Subj = number of subjects

Table 19.7 Analysis of variance and covariance of variables potentially affecting effect sizes in four domains with quality of study as the covariate

Independent Variable	Unweighted				Weighted			
	Cognitive	Social-Emotional	Behavioral	Attachment	Cognitive	Social-Emotional	Behavioral	Attachment
1. Year of Study Publication	1.22a/2.72b	0.12 / 0.18	0.89 / 0.96	0.63 / 1.96	3.07 /5.55*	5.29*/4.37*	2.73 / 2.22	0.31 / 2.61
2. Age of Child in Care	0.50 / 1.33	0.06 / 0.04	0.79 / 0.93	0.05 / 0.61	1.15 / 0.55	0.38 / 0.72	0.53 / 0.26	0.02 / 0.50
3. Social Economic Status	0.30 / 0.76	0.28 / 0.30	0.32 / 0.34	1.31 / 1.69	2.24 / 1.60	0.60 / 0.48	0.03 / 0.07	0.04 / 0.08
4. Ethnicity	0.14 / 0.08	0.18 / 0.15	0.01 / 0.03	0.00 / 0.14	1.25 / 1.13	7.4**/6.8**	1.67 / 2.43	0.08 / 0.86
5. Country of Research	0.19 / 0.09	1.29 / 1.22	0.18 / 0.16	0.00 / 0.05	0.79 / 1.14	1.66 / 1.43	0.19 / 0.13	0.02 / 0.42
6. Hours of Care	1.20 / 4.51*	0.11 / 0.08	0.12 / 0.15	0.00 / 0.04	0.13 / 1.39	0.84 / 1.30	0.22 / 0.43	1.26 / 1.69
7. Beginning Age of Care	0.12 / 0.34	0.33 / 0.18	2.54 / 2.81	0.00 / 1.14	1.95 / 1.65	1.19 / 0.77	2.68 / 1.65	0.35 / 0.39
8. Sponsor of Day Care	0.85 / 1.19	0.49 / 0.45	0.12 / 0.08	0.25 / 0.04	2.09 / 1.97	0.00 / 0.00	2.67 / 2.27	2.12 / 0.86
9. Ratio Caregiver to Child	0.27 / 0.17	0.69 / 0.59	0.14 / 0.05	6.11* / 4.92	0.20 / 0.25	0.00 / 0.02	0.47 / 0.20	8.21*/7.17*
10. Caregiver's Education	1.22 / 1.30	0.36 / 0.28	c / c	0.49 / 2.95	0.78 / 0.99	0.27 / 0.24	c / c	0.00 / 2.82
11. Licensing of Day Care	0.72 / 0.25	0.01 / 0.00	0.33 / 0.20	1.71 / 0.47	0.55 / 0.34	0.16 / 0.06	0.05 / 0.00	3.02 / 0.18
12. Quality of Care	0.56 / 0.09	0.00 / 0.00	0.69 / 0.64	1.21 / 1.00	0.13 / 0.01	0.00 / 0.02	0.07 / 0.07	0.93 / 1.05
13. Mother's Education	0.14 / 0.11	0.30 / 0.31	0.02 / 0.05	1.04 / 1.09	1.08 / 0.64	0.04 / 0.04	0.40 / 0.39	0.09 / 0.10
14. Number of Children	2.39 / 1.92	0.15 / 0.53	14.3*/11.7*	0.84 / 0.27	0.60 / 1.26	0.09 / 0.28	5.75 / 4.31	1.11 / 0.50
15. Family Structure	0.25 / 0.83	0.45 / 0.27	0.45 / 0.63	1.43 / 1.67	0.17 / 0.00	2.78 / 1.59	0.53 / 0.41	0.19 / 0.34

*p < .05
**p < .01
a = F Ratio for Anova
b = F Ratio for Ancova with quality of study as the covariate
c = no value in this category

References

Ainslie, R. C., & Anderson, C. W. (1984). Day care childrens' relationships to their mothers and caregivers: An inquiry into the conditions for the development of attachment. In R. C. Ainslie (Ed.), *The child and the day care setting* (pp. 98-132). New York: Praeger Publishers.

Ainsworth, M. D. S., Blehar, M., Waters, E., & Wall, S. (1978). *Patterns of attachment*. Hillsdale, NJ: Erlbaum.

Ainsworth, M. D. S., & Bowlby, J. (1991). An ethological approach to personality development. *American Psychologist, 46*(4), 333-341.

Ainsworth, M. D. S., & Wittig, B. A. (1969). Attachment and exploratory behavior of one-year-olds in a strange situation. In B. M. Foss (Ed.), (Vol. 4, pp. 111-136). London: Methuen.

Altman, J. S., & Mills, B. C. (1990). Caregiver behaviors and adaptive behavior development of very young children in home care and day care. *Early Child Development and Care, 62*, 87-96.

Andersson, B.E. (1992). Effects of daycare on cognitive and socio-emotional competence of thirteen-year-old Swedish school children. *Child Development, 63,* 20-36.

Andersson, B.E. (1989). Effects of public day care: A longitudinal study. *Child Development, 60*, 857-866.

Bagley, C. (1988). Day care, maternal mental health and child development: Evidence from a longitudinal study. *Early Child Development and Care, 39*, 139-161.

Banducci, R. (1967). The effect of mother's employment on the achievement, aspirations, and expectations of the child. *Personnel and Guidance Journal*, 263-267.

Barglow, P., Vaughn, B. E., & Molitor, N. (1987). Effects of maternal absence due to employment on the quality of infant-mother attachment in a low-risk sample. *Child Development, 58*, 945-954.

Bates, J. E., Marvinney, D., Kelly, T., Dodge, K. A., Bennett, D. S., & Pettit, G. S. (1994). Child-care history and kindergarten adjustment. *Developmental Psychology, 30*, 690-700.

Baydar, N., & Brooks-Gunn, J. (1991). Effect of maternal employment and child-care arrangements on preschoolers' cognitive and behavioral outcomes: evidence from the children of the National Longitudinal Survey of Youth. *Developmental Psychology, 27*(6), 932-945.

Belsky, J. (1986). Infant day care: A cause for concern? *Zero to Three, 6*(5), 1-7.

Belsky, J. (1987). Risk remains. *Zero to Three, 7*(3), 22-24.

Belsky, J. (1988). The "effects" of infant day care reconsidered. *Early Childhood Research Quarterly, 3*, 235-272.

Belsky, J., & Braungart, J.M. (1991). Are insecure-avoidant infants with extensive day-care experience less stressed by and more independent in the Strange Situation? *Child Development, 62*, 567-571.

Belsky, J., & Eggebeen, D. (1991). Early and extensive maternal employment and young children's socioemotional development: Children of the National Longitudinal Survey of Youth. *Journal of Marriage and Family, 53*, 1083-1110.

Belsky, J., & Rovine, M. J. (1988). Nonmaternal care in the first year of life and the security of infant-parent attachment. *Child Development, 59*, 157-167.

Belsky, J., & Steinberg, L. D. (1978). The effects of day care: A critical review. *Child Development, 49*, 929-949.

Benn, R. K. (1986). Factors promoting secure attachment relationships between employed mothers and their sons. *Child Development, 57*, 1224-1231.

Blehar, M. C. (1974). Anxious attachment and defensive reactions associated with day care. *Child Development, 45*, 683-692.

Bretherton, I. & Waters, E. (Eds.). (1985). Growing points of attachment theory and research, *Monographs of the Society for Research in Child Development, 50* (1-2), Serial no. 209.

Broberg, A., Wessels, H., Lamb, M., & Hwang, P. (1997). Effects of day care on the cognitive abilities in 8-year-olds. *Developmental Psychology, 33*, 62-69.

Bronfenbrenner, U., Alvarez, W.F. & Henderson, Jr., C. R. (1984). Working and watching: Maternal employment status and parents' perceptions of their three-year-old children. *Child Development, 55*, 1362-1378.

Brookhart, J., & Hock, E. (1976). The effects of experimental context and experiential background on infants' behavior toward their mothers and a stranger. *Child Development, 47*, 333-340.

Burchinal, M. R., Bryant, D. M., Lee, M. W., & Ramey, C. T. (1992). Early day care, infant-mother attachment, and maternal responsiveness in the infant's first year. *Early Childhood Research Quarterly, 7*, 383-396.

Caldwell, B. M., Wright, M. A., Honig, M. A., & Tannenbaum, B. S. (1970). Infant day care and attachment. *American Journal of Orthopsychiatry, 40*(3), 397-412.

Carlson, E. A., Jacobvitz, D., & Sroufe, A. L. (1995). A developmental investigation of inattentiveness and hyperactivity. *Child Development, 66*, 37-54.

Chase-Lansdale, P. L., Mott, F. L., Brooks-Gunn, J., & Phillips, D. A. (1991). Children of the National Longitudinal Survey of Youth: A unique research opportunity. *Developmental Psychology, 27*(6), 918-931.

Chase-Lansdale, L. P., & Owen, M. T. (1987). Maternal employment in a family context: Effects on infant-mother and infant-father attachments. *Child Development, 58*, 1505-1512.

Chess, S. (1987). Comments: "Infant day care: A cause for concern?" *Zero to Three, 7*(3), 24-25.

Cherry, F. F., & Eaton, E. L. (1977). Physical and cognitive development in children of low-income mothers working in the child's early years. *Child Development, 48*, 158-166.

Clarke-Stewart, A. K. (1981). Observation and experiment complementary strategies for studying day care and social development. *Advances in Early Education and Day Care, 2*, 227-250.

Clarke-Stewart, K. A. (1988). "The 'effects' of infant day care reconsidered": Risks for parents, children, and researchers. *Early Childhood Research Quarterly, 3,* 293-318.

Clarke-Stewart, K. A. (1989). Infant day care, maligned or malignant? *American Psychologist, 44,* 266-273.

Cochran, M. M. (1977). A comparison of group day and family child-rearing patterns in Sweden. *Child Development, 48,* 702-707.

Cochran, M. M., & Gunnarsson, L. (1985). A follow-up study of group day care and family-based childrearing patterns. *Journal of Marriage and the Family, 47,* 297-309.

Cohen, S. E. (1977). Maternal employment and mother-child interaction. *Merrill-Palmer Quarterly, 24*(3), 189-197.

Cornelius, S. W., & Denney, N. W. (1975). Dependency in day care and home care children. *Developmental Psychology, 11*(5), 575-582.

Crockenberg, S., & Litman, C. (1991). Effects of maternal employment on maternal and two-year-old child behavior. *Child Development, 62,* 930-953.

de Jong, M.L. (1992). Attachment, individuation, and risk of suicide in late adolescence. *Journal of Youth and Adolescence, 21,* 357-371.

Desai, S., Chase-Lansdale, P. L., & Michael, R. T. (1989). Mother or market? Effects of maternal employment on the intellectual ability of 4-year-old children. *Demography, 26*(4), 545-561.

Devall, E., Stoneman, Z., & Brody, G. (1986). The impact of divorce and maternal employment on pre-adolescent children. *Family Relations, 35,* 153-159.

Doyle, A. (1975). Infant development in day care. *Developmental Psychology, 11*(5), 655-656.

Doyle, A., & Somers, K. (1978). The effects of group and family day care on infant attachment behaviors. *Canadian Journal of Behavioural Science, 10*(1), 38-45.

Easterbrooks, M. A., & Goldberg, W. A. (1985). Effects of early maternal employment on toddlers, mothers, and fathers. *Developmental Psychology, 21*(5), 774-783.

Egeland, B., & Hiester, M. (1995). The long-term consequences of infant day-care and mother-infant attachment. *Child Development, 66,* 474-485.

Eme, R.F. (1979). Sex differences in childhood psychopathology: A review. *Psychological Bulletin, 86,* 574-595.

Emery, R.E. (1982). Interparental conflict and the children of discord and divorce. *Psychological Bulletin, 92,* 310-330.

Etaugh, C. (1980). Effects of nonmaternal care in children: Research evidence and popular views. *American Psychologist, 35,* 309-319.

Everson, M. D., Sarnat, L., & Ambron, S. R. (1984). Day care and early socialization: The role of maternal attitude. In R. C. Ainslie (Ed.), *The child and the day care setting* (pp. 63-97). New York: Praeger Publishers.

Faber, E. A., & Egeland, B. (1982). Developmental consequences of out-of-home care for infants in a low-income population. In G. Zigler & E. W. Gordon (Eds.), *Day care scientific and social policy issues* (pp. 102-125).

Farel, A. M. (1980). Effects of preferred maternal roles, maternal employment, and sociodemographic status on school adjustment and competence. *Child Development, 51*, 1179-1186.

Fein, G.G. & Fox, N. (1990). Infant day care: A special issue. In G.G. Fein and N. Fox (Eds.), *Infant day care: The current debate*. Norwood, NJ: Ablex.

Finkelstein, N W. (1982). Aggression: Is it stimulated by day care? *Young Children, 37*(6), 3-9.

Frye, N.A. (1982). The problem of infant day care. In E.F. Zigler and E.W. Gordon (Eds.), *Day care: Scientific and social policy issues*. Boston: Auburn House.

Gallagher, M. (1998). Day careless. *National Review*, January, 26, 37-43.

Gamble, T.J., Zigler, E. (1986). Effects of infant day care: Another look at the evidence. *American Journal of Orthopsychiatry, 56*, 26-42.

Glueck, E., & Glueck, S. (1957). Working mothers and delinquency. *Mental Hygiene, 41*, 327-341.

Glass, G. V. (1976). Primary, secondary and meta-analysis of research. *Educational Researcher, 10*, 3-8.

Glass, G., McGaw, B., & Smith, M. (1981). *Meta-analysis in social research*. Beverly Hills: Sage.

Gold, D., & Andres, D. (1978a). Comparisons of adolescent children with employed and non employed mothers. *Merrill-Palmer Quarterly, 24*(4), 243-254.

Gold, D., & Andres, D. (1978b). Developmental comparisons between ten-year-old children with employed and non employed mothers. *Child Development, 49*, 75-84.

Gold, D., & Andres, D. (1978c). Relations between maternal employment and development of nursery school children. *Canadian Journal of Behavioral Science, 11*(2), 169-173.

Gold, D., & Andres, D. (1979). The development of Francophone nursery-school children with employed and nonemployed mothers. *Canadian Journal of Behavioral Science, 11*(2), 169-173.

Gold, D., & Andres, D. (1980). Maternal employment and development of ten-year-old Canadian Francophone children. *Canadian Journal of Behavioral Science, 12*(3), 233-240.

Goossens, F. A. (1987). Maternal employment and day care: Effects on attachment. In L. W. C. Tavecchio & M. H. van IJzendoorn (Eds.), *Attachment in social networks* (pp. 135-224). New York: North-Holland.

Gottfried, A. E., Gottfried, A. W., & Bathurst, K. (1988). Maternal employment, family environment, and children's development. In A. E. Gottfried & A. W. Gottfried (Eds.), *Maternal employment and children's development* (pp. 11-57). New York: Plenum Press.

Gray, E.B. (1983). Child care and family functioning: A review. *Journal of Child Care, 1* 15-16.

Harms, T., & Clifford, R.M. (1980). *Early childhood environment rating scale*. New York: Teachers College Press.

Harris, T., & Bifulco, (1991). Loss of parent in childhood, attachment style, and depression in adulthood. In C.M. Parkes, J. Stevenson-Hinde, & P. Marris (Eds.), *Attachment across the life cycle*. London: Routledge.

Haskins, R. (1985). Public school aggression among children with varying day care experience. *Child Development, 56*, 689-703.

Hegland, S., & Rix, M. K. (1990). Aggression and assertiveness in kindergarten children differing in day care experiences. *Early Childhood Research Quarterly, 5*, 105-116.

Hennessy, E., & Melhuish, E.C. (1991). Early day care and the development of school-age children: A review. *Journal of Reproductive and Infant Psychology, 9*, 117-136.

Hetherington, E.M. (1989). Coping with family transitions: Winners, losers and survivors. *Child Development, 60*, 1-14.

Heyns, B., & Catsambis, S. (1986). Mother's employment and children's achievement: A critique. *Sociology of Education, 59*, 140-151.

Hock, E. (1980). Working and non working mothers and their infants: A comparative study of maternal caregiving characteristics and infant social behavior. *Merrill-Palmer Quarterly, 26*(2), 79-101.

Hock, E., & DeMeis, D. (1990). Depression in mothers of infants: The role of maternal employment. *Developmental Psychology, 10*, 204-228.

Hoffman, L. W. (1984). Maternal employment and the young child. In M. Perlmutter (Ed.), *The Minnesota Symposia on Child Psychology* (Vol. 17, pp. 101-127), Hillsdale, NJ: Erlbaum.

Hoffman, L. W. (1989). Effects of maternal employment in the two-parent family. *American Psychologist, 44*, 283-292.

Howes, C. (1990). Can age of entry into child care and the quality of child care predict adjustment in kindergarten? *Developmental Psychology, 26*, 292-303.

Howes, C. (1983). Caregiver behavior in center and family day care. *Journal of Applied Developmental Psychology, 4*, 99-107.

Howes, C., & Hamilton, C. E. (1992). Children's relationships with child care teachers: Stability and concordance with parental attachments. *Child Development, 63*, 867-878.

Howes, C., & Olenick, M. (1986). Family and child care influences on toddler's compliance. *Child Development, 57*, 202-216.

Howes, C., & Rubenstein, J. (1985). Determinants of toddler's experience in day care: Age of entry and quality of setting. *Child Care Quarterly, 14*, 140-151.

Hunter, F. C. (1972). Mother's education and working: Effect on the school child. *The Journal of Psychology, 82*, 27-37.

Jacobson, J. L., & Wille, D. E. (1984). Influence of attachment and separation experience on separation distress at 18 months. *Developmental Psychology, 3*, 477-484.

Jarvis, P. A., & Creasey, G. L. (1991). Parental stress, coping, and attachment in families with an 18-month-old infant. *Infant Behavior and Development, 14*, 383-395.

Jouriles, E.N., & LeCompte, S.H. (1991). Husbands' aggression toward wives and mothers' and fathers' aggression toward children: Moderating effects of child gender. *Journal of Consulting and Clinical Psychology, 59*, 190-192.

Kagan, J., Kearsley, R. B., & Zelazo, P. R. (1977). The effects of infant day care on psychological development, *Evaluation Quarterly, 1*(1), 109-142.

Koback, R.R., Sudler, N., & Gamble, W. (1991). Attachment and depressive symptoms during adolescence: A developmental pathways analysis. *Developmental Psychopathology, 3*, 461-474.

Kontos, S., & Fiene, R. (1987). *Child care quality: What does research tell us?* Washington: National Association for the Education of Young children.

Kwakman, A.M., Zuiker, F.A., Scheppers, G.M., & Wuffel, F.J. (1988). Drinking behavior, drinking attitudes, and attachment relationships of adolescents. *Journal of Youth and Adolescence, 17*, 247-253.

Lahikainen, A. R., & Sundquist, S. (1979). The reactions of children under four years to day nursery. *Psychiatria Fennica*, 73-86.

Lamb, M. E., Hwang, C. P., Bookstein, F. L., Broberg, A., Hult, G., & Frodi, M, (1988). Determinants of social competence in Swedish preschoolers. *Developmental Psychology, 24*(1), 58-70.

Lamb, M. E., Thompson, R. A., Gardner, W. P., Charnou, E. L., & Estes, D. (1984). Security of infantile attachment as assessed in the "strange situation": Its study and biological interpretation. *The Behavioral and Brain Sciences, 7*, 127-171.

Lerner, J. V., & Galambas, N. L. (1988). The influences of maternal employment across life. In A. E. Gottfried & A. W. Gottfried (Eds.), *Maternal employment and children's development* (pp. 59-83). New York: Plenum Press.

Levy-Shift, R. (1983). Adaptation and competence in early childhood: Communally raised Kibbutz children versus family raised children in the city. *Child Development, 54*, 1606-1614.

Lipsey, W.W., & Wilson, D.B. (1993). The efficacy of psychological, educational, and behavioral treatment: Confirmation from meta-analysis. *American Psychologist, 48*, 1181-1209.

Lyons-Ruth, K., Alpern, L., & Repacholi, B. (1993). Disorganized infant attachment classification and maternal psychosocial problems as predictors of hostile-aggressive behavior in the preschool classroom. *Child Development, 64*, 572-585.

Main, M. (1991). Metacognitive knowledge, metacognitive monitoring, and singular (coherent) vs. multiple (incoherent) model of attachment: Findings and directions for future research. In M. C. Parkes, J. Stevenson-Hinde, P. Marris (Eds.), *Attachment across the life cycle*. New York: Routledge.

McCartney, K., Scarr, S., Rocheleau, A., Phillips, D., Eisenberg, M., Keefe, N., Rosenthal, S., & Abbot-Smith, M. (1997). Social development in the context of typical center-based child care. *Merrill-Palmer Quarterly, 43*, 426-450.

McCartney, K., Scarr, S., Phillips, D., Grajek, S., & Schwartz, J.C. (1982). Environmental differences among care centers and their effects on children's development. In E.F. Zigler & E.W. Gordon (Eds.), *Day care: Scientific and Social Policy Issues*. Boston: Auburn House.

McCord, J., McCord, W., & Thurber, E. (1963). Effects of maternal employment on lower-class boys. *Journal of Abnormal and Social Psychology, 67*(2), 177-182.

McGurk, H., Caplan, M., Hennessy, E., & Moss, P. (1993). Controversy, theory and social context in contemporary day care research. *Journal of Child Psychology and Psychiatry, 34*, 3-23.

Melhuish, E. C. (1987). Socio-emotional behavior at 18 months as a function of day care experience, temperament, and gender. *Infant Mental Health Journal, 8*(4), 364-373.

Melhuish, E. C., Lloyd, E., & Mooney, S. M. (1990a). Type of childcare at 18 months - II. Relations with cognitive and language development. *Journal of Child Psychology and Psychiatry, 31*(6), 861-870.

Melhuish, E. C., Mooney, A., Martin, S., & Lloyd, E. (1990b). Type of childcare at 18 months - I. Differences in interactional experience. *Journal of Child Psychology and Psychiatry, 31*(6), 849-859.

Melhuish, E.C., & Moss, P. (Eds.). (1991). *Day care for young children.* London: Tavistock/Routledge.

Miller, S. M. (1975). Effects of maternal employment on sex role perceptions, interests, and self-esteem in kindergarten girls. *Developmental Psychology, 11*, 405-406.

Milne, A. M., Myers, D. E., Rosenthal, A. S., & Ginsburg, A. (1986). Single parents, working mothers, and the educational achievement of school children. *Sociology of Education, 59*, 125-139.

Moore, B. F., Snow, C. W., & Poteat, M. G. (1988). Effects of variant types of child care experience on the adaptive behavior of kindergarten children. *American Journal of Orthopsychiatry, 58*(2), 297-303.

Moore, T. W. (1975). Exclusive early mothering and its alternatives. *Scandinavian Journal of Psychology, 16*, 255-272.

Moorehouse, M. J. (1991). Linking maternal employment patterns to mother-child activities and children's school competence. *Developmental Psychology, 27*(2), 295-303.

Moskowitz, D. S., Schwarz, C. J., & Corsini, D. A. (1977). Initiating day care at three years of age: Effects on attachment. *Child Development, 48*, 1271-1276.

NICHD Early Child Care Research Network (1998). Early child care and self control, compliance, and problem behavior at twenty-four and thirty-six months. *Child Development, 69*, 1145-1170.

NICHD Early Child Care Research Network (1997). The effects of infant child care on infant-mother attachment security: Results of the NICHD Study of Early Child Care. *Child Development, 68*, 860-879.

Nelson, D. (1969). A study of school achievement among adolescent children with working and nonworking mothers. *The Journal of Educational Research, 62*, 456-458.

Nelson, D. (1971). A study of personality adjustment among adolescent children with working and nonworking mothers. *The Journal of Educational Research, 64*, 328-330.

Owen, M. T., & Cox, M. J., (1988). Maternal employment and the transition to parenthood. In A. E. Gottfried & A. W. Gottfried (Eds.), *Maternal employment and children's development* (pp. 85-119). New York: Plenum Press.

Owen, M. T., Easterbrooks, M. A., Chase-Lansdale, L., & Goldberg, W. A. (1984). The relation between maternal employment status and the stability of attachments to mother and to father. *Child Development, 55,* 1894-1901.

Park, K. J.A., & Honig. A. S. (1991). Infant child care patterns and later teacher ratings of preschool behaviors. *Early Child Development and Care, 68,* 89-96.

Parkes, C.M. (1991). Attachment, bonding, and psychiatric problems after bereavement in adult life. In C.M. Parkes, J. Stevenson-Hinde, & P. Marris (Eds.), *Attachment across the life cycle.* London: Routledge.

Peterson, C., & Peterson, R. (1986). Parent-child interaction and day care: Does quality of day care matter? *Journal of Applied Developmental Psychology, 7,* 1-15.

Phillips, D., McCartney, K., & Scarr, S. (1987). Child-care quality and children's social development. *Developmental Psychology, 23*(4), 537-543.

Pierrehumbert, B., Frascarolo, F., Bettschart, W., & Melhuish, E. C. (1991). A longitudinal study of infant's social-emotional development and the implications of extra-parental care. *Journal of Reproductive and Infant Psychology, 9,* 91-103.

Portnoy, F. C., & Simmons, C. H. (1978). Day care and attachment. *Child Development, 49,* 239-242.

Poteat, M. G., Snow, C. W., Ironsmith, M., & Bjorkman, M. A. (1992). Influence of day care experiences and demographic variables on social behavior in kindergarten. *American Journal of Orthopsychiatry, 62*(1), 137-141.

Propper, A. M. (1972). The relationship of maternal employment to adolescent roles, activities, and parental relationships. *Journal of Marriage and Family,* 417-421.

Quay, L. C. (1992). Personal and family effects on loneliness. *Journal of Applied Developmental Psychology, 13,* 97-110.

Ragozin, A. S. (1980). Attachment behavior of day care children: Naturalistic and laboratory observations. *Child Development, 51,* 409-415.

Raikes, H. (1993). Relationship duration in infant day care: Time with a high-ability teacher and infant-teacher attachment. *Early Childhood Research Quarterly, 8,* 309-325.

Richters, J.E., & Zahn-Waxler, C. (1988). The infant day care controversy: Current status and future directions. *Early Childhood Research Quarterly, 8,* 309-325.

Roggman, L. A., Langlois, J. H., Hubbs-Tait, L., & Rieser-Danner, L. A. (1994). Infant day-care, attachment, and the "file drawer problem". *Child Development, 65,* 1421-1435.

Roopnarine, J. L., & Lamb, M. E. (1978). The effects of day care on attachment and exploratory behavior in a strange situation. *Merrill-Palmer Quarterly, 24,* 85-95.

Roy, P. (1961). Maternal employment and adolescent roles: Rural-urban differentials. *Marriage and Family Living,* 340-349.

Rosenthal, R., & Rubin, D. B. (1982). A simple, general purpose display of magnitude of experimental effect. *Journal of Educational Psychology, 74,* 166-169.

Rubenstein, J. (1985). The effects of maternal employment of young children. *Applied Developmental Psychology, 2,* 99-120.

Rubenstein, J. L., & Howes, C. (1979). Caregiving and infant behavior in day care and in homes. *Developmental Psychology, 15*(1), 1-24.

Rubenstein, J. L., Howes, C., & Boyle, P. (1981). A two-year follow-up of infants in community-based day care. *Journal of Child Psychiatry, 22*(3), 209-218.

Rutter, M. (1987). Psychosocial resilience and protective mechanisms. *American Journal of Orthopsychiatry, 57*(3), 316-331.

Sagi, A., Lewkowicz, K. S., Lamb, M. E., Shoham, R., Dvir, R., & Estes, D. (1985). Security of infant-mother, -father, and -metapelet attachments among kibbutz-reared Israeli children. *Monographs of the Society for Research in Child Development, 50* (1-2, Serial No. 209).

Sagi, A., van IJzendoorn, M. H., Aviezer, O., Donnell, F., & Mayseless, O. (1994). Sleeping out of home in a Kibbutz communal arrangement: It makes a difference for infant-mother attachment. *Child Development, 65,* 992-1004.

Scarr, S. (1998). American child care today. *American Psychologist, 53,* 95-108.

Scarr, S., Phillips, D. & McCartney, K. (1990). Facts, fantasies and the future of child care in the United States. *Psychological Sciences, 1,* 26-35.

Schachter, F. (1981). Toddlers with employed mothers. *Child Development, 52,* 958-964.

Schubert, J. B., Bradley-Johnson, S., & Nuttal, J. (1980). Mother-infant communication and maternal employment. *Child Development, 51,* 246-249.

Schwartz, P. (1983). Length of day-care attendance and attachment behavior in eighteen-month-old infants. *Child Development, 54,* 1073-1078.

Schwartz, C. J., Strickland, R. G., & Krolick, G. (1974). Infant day care: Behavioral effects at preschool age. *Developmental Psychology, 10*(4), 502-506.

Sroufe, L. A. (1988). A developmental perspective on day care. *Early Childhood Research Quarterly, 3,* 283-291.

Stein, J.A., Newcomb, M.D., & Bentler, P.M. (1993). Differential effects of parent and grandparent drug use on behavior problems of male and female children. *Developmental Psychology, 29,* 31-43.

Stifter, C. A., Coulehan, C. M., & Fish, M. (1993). Linking employment to attachment: The mediating effects of maternal separation anxiety and interactive behavior. *Child Development, 64,* 1451-1460.

Stith, S. M., & Davis, A. J. (1984). Employed mothers and family day-care substitute caregivers: A comparative analysis of infant care. *Child Development, 55,* 1340-1348.

Thompson, R. A., Lamb, M. E., & Estes, D. (1982). Stability of infant-mother attachment and its relationship to changing life circumstances in an unselected middle-class sample. *Child Development, 53,* 144-148.

Thornburg, K. R., Pearl, P., Crompton, D., & Ispa, J. M. (1990). Development of kindergarten children based on child care arrangements. *Early Childhood Research Quarterly, 5,* 27-42.

Tsiantis, J., Caldwell, B., Dragonas, T., Jegede, R.O., Lambidi, A., Banaag, C., & Orley, J. (1991). Development of a WHO child care facility schedule (CCFS): A pilot collaborative study. *Bulletin of the World Health Organization, 69*, (1).

Vandell, D. L., & Corasaniti, M. (1990). Variations in early child care: Do they predict subsequent social, emotional, and cognitive differences? *Early Childhood Research Quarterly, 5*, 555-572.

Vandell, D. L., & Ramanan, J. (1992). Effects of early and recent maternal employment on children from low-income families. *Child Development, 63*, 938-949.

Vandell, D.L., Henderson, V.K., & Wilson, K.S. (1988). A longitudinal study of children with varying quality day care experiences. *Child Development, 59*, 1286-1292.

Vaughn, B. E., Gove, F. L., & Egeland, B. (1980). The relationship between out-of-home care and the quality of infant-mother attachment in an economically disadvantaged population. *Child Development, 51*, 1203-1214.

Vaughn, B. E., Deane, K.E., & Waters, E. (1985). The impact of daycare on child-mother attachment quality: Another look at some enduring questions. In I. Bretherton & E. Waters (Eds.), Growing points in attachment theory and research (pp. 110-123). *Monographs of the Society for Research in Child Development, 50* (1-2, Serial No. 209).

Weinraub, M., & Jaeger, E. (1991). Timing the return to the workplace: Effects on the mother-infant relationship. In J. S. Hyde & M. J. Essex (Eds.), *Parental leave and childcare* (pp. 307-322). Philadelphia: Temple University Press.

Willie, D. E. (1992). Maternal employment: Impact on maternal behavior. *Family Relations, 41*, 273-277.

Williams, E., & Radin, N. (1993). Paternal involvement, maternal employment, and adolescents' academic achievement: An 11-year follow-up. *American Journal of Orthopsychiatric, 63*, 306-312.

Winett, R. A., Fuchs, W. L., Moffatt, S. A., & Nerviano, V. J. (1977). A cross-sectional study of children and their families in different child care environments: Some data and conclusions. *Journal of Community Psychology, 5*, 149-159.

Zaslow, M. J., Pedersen, F. A., Suwalsky, J. T. D., & Rabinovich, B. A. (1989). Maternal employment and parent-infant interaction at one year. *Early Childhood Research Quarterly, 4*, 459-478.